threshing machines and the widespread adoption of steam engines. Farmers initiated informal threshing groups, typically called "threshing rings," to provide the twelve to twenty men needed to complete the grain harvest at each member's farm. The development of some of these groups into formally organized threshing cooperatives is interpreted as an important transition to agricultural styles and structures resembling contemporary agribusiness patterns. The introduction and adoption of the combine ended neighborhood participation in threshing by enabling farmers to harvest and thresh their own grain.

Rikoon places particular emphasis throughout this study on the question of cultural change and the impact of agricultural mechanization on traditional rural patterns and values. Farm families are not viewed as passive respondents to new technologies; rather, they are seen in periodic debate over the retention, abandonment, or alteration of existing practices. Threshing patterns, including the local significance of the itinerant thresherman and the social functions of cooperative work sessions, reveal dominant rural traits and give meaning to the notion of "agriculture as a way of life." The book's subject spans that crucial period of agricultural mechanization in which important social and occupational changes took place. In providing an intimate and detailed look at a dynamic phase of rural development, *Threshing in the Midwest, 1820–1940* broadens our understanding of the region's overall historical and cultural change.

THRESHING IN THE
MIDWEST, 1820–1940

Midwestern History and Culture
GENERAL EDITORS
James H. Madison and Thomas J. Schlereth

THRESHING IN THE MIDWEST, 1820–1940

A Study of
Traditional Culture and
Technological Change

J. SANFORD RIKOON

INDIANA UNIVERSITY PRESS
Bloomington and Indianapolis

©1988 by J. Sanford Rikoon
All rights reserved

No part of this book may be reproduced or utilized in any form or by any means, electronic or mechanical, including photocopying and recording, or by any information storage and retrieval system, without permission in writing from the publisher. The Association of American University Presses' Resolution on Permissions constitutes the only exception to this prohibition.

Manufactured in the United States of America

Library of Congress Cataloging-in-Publication Data

Rikoon, J. Sanford.
Threshing in the Midwest, 1820–1940.

(Midwestern history and culture)
Bibliography: p.
Includes index.
1. Threshing—Middle West—History. 2. Agricultural innovations—Middle West—History.   I. Title.
II. Series.

SB189.74.R55   1988   633.1'046   87-45407
ISBN 0-253-36047-1

92 91 90 89 88 1 2 3 4 5

In memory of Ira Edger, a former thresherman who taught me about threshing in the community; and of Leola Edger, a former schoolteacher who recognized the community in threshing.

For the Fitches are not threshed
with a threshing Instrument, neither is a
Cartwheel turned about upon the
Cummin: but the Fitches are beaten out
with a Staff, and the Cummin with a Rod.

—Isa. 28:27

Traditional Riddle:
Up on the hill stands an old red bull;
He eats and he eats, but he never gets full.

(Answer: threshing machine)

CONTENTS

PREFACE	ix
ACKNOWLEDGMENTS	xiv
I. Flailing and Treading	1
II. The Mechanization of Threshing: Initial Adoption and Accommodation	20
III. Nineteenth-Century Stack Threshing	39
IV. Twentieth-Century Shock Threshing and Threshing Rings	58
V. Threshing Ring Organization and Formalization	89
VI. "Threshing Was Something Social, Too": Food and Practical-Joking Traditions of the Threshing Ring	113
VII. The Continuity and Decline of Threshing Rings	135
Conclusion	154
APPENDIXES	165
NOTES	170
BIBLIOGRAPHY	190
INDEX	208

FIGURES

1. Flail Designs and Couplings — 7
2. Work Relationships (Shock Threshing) — 71
3. Straw Shed Constructions — 76
4. Farms Included in White Plains Threshing Ring during 1921, 1925, 1932, and 1940 Harvests — 91
5. Core Farm Memberships, Rock Creek Threshing Ring, Lincoln Township, Harrison County, Missouri — 138
6. Labor Crew Sizes, from Flail to Combine — 145

TABLES

1. Small Grain Production in the Midwest, 1840–1900 — 26
2. Labor Requirements of Threshing Systems — 84
3. Yield Statistics of Sample Threshing Runs — 93
4. Sample Difference System Page (Illinois) — 104
5. Other Associations between Members of the Stateline Threshing Ring (Butler County, Ohio) — 136
6a. Threshing Statistics, 1928–1940, White Plains Threshing Ring — 149
6b. Error Computations Using Labor Rates — 149

PREFACE

My fieldwork in the Midwest over the past ten years has been done from behind a tape recorder rather than a tractor's engine or a horse's hindquarters. And instead of producing crops or caring for stock, my interest has been raising the opinions and recollections of older rural residents and retired farmers. Open-ended discussions with farm people about their occupations, traditions, and neighborhood life turn inevitably to talk about the consequences of new ideas and practices. From the osage orange hedge to minimum-till farming, and from government grants to federal foreclosures, the one constant in midwestern rural and agricultural patterns since the settlement period is the confrontation with change.

Farmers in the region do not simply spend their lives responding to the influences of a world changing around them. The notion of "farmers in a changing world," the title of the 1940 United States Department of Agriculture Yearbook, implies passivity, stasis, and lack of control on the part of rural families. The external world does indeed evolve, and, often enough, in directions wildly beyond one's plans or expectations. Importantly, farmers enact change also. They consciously form their own agricultural styles and their views of farming as an occupation, as a way of interacting with community, family, and the past. Rural residents construct their own local worlds. They build private realities based on how they work the land and the cultural practices and social relations they choose to pursue. The outside world does not dictate change in this sequence, but it exists as a stage with an amazing series of props. Each act occurs within the stage and with the props available, yet each performance ultimately reflects the choices and preferences of the regional actors.

Farmers tend to talk about change in a series of scenes like the brief glimpses of the countryside seen under safety lights during a drive down a dark rural road. Each scene is a marker kept illuminated in memory because it indicates an important personal experience or turning point from the past. Older farmers asked generally to compare how they used to farm against how people farm today typically respond with a catalogue of incidents or a set of neighborhood events rather than an inventory of devices or an accounting of crops and chemicals. And one of the most common subjects conjured up by discussions of rural evolutions is grain threshing. Without any prompting, a question about farm changes is more likely than not to initiate a discussion about how people used to "thrash."

Why do older rural residents like to talk about threshing? Why do they flock to old threshermen's reunions and brave the summer heat at old-machinery exhibitions? Anyone who has talked with midwestern men or women who lived on farms in the 1920s and 1930s knows that threshing is not a simple agricultural task recalled today with complete objectivity. To an agricultural historian or economist, grain threshing denotes the separation of the seeds from straw, chaff, weed seeds, and other debris. It is the final component of the grain harvest. To "talk threshing" with an older farmer, however, is not to engage solely in conversation about agricultural tools, machinery, or techniques, although many men can comment intelligently on threshing machines and their eventual replacement—the combined harvester-thresher (or "combine"). To discuss threshing changes also goes beyond remarks about agricultural tasks, although evolutions in occupational responsibilities are part of the topic. Threshing implies an agricultural process *and* a social experience in the midwestern rural worldview. The adoption of the combine is a threshold in community life separating two styles of agriculture. Precombine threshing represents a past, older way of agriculture involving families and neighborhoods. The use of tractor-pulled combines marks a different regional style, one that stresses individual enterprise and high capital expense. "People don't farm like they used to," remarked former Jackson County, Ohio, farmer Dan Jones. "They don't thresh together anymore."

Some of the most alluring yet elusive questions about American Midwest culture center around changes in rural life motivated by the introduction and adoption of new agricultural technologies.[1] The mechanization of agriculture, in particular, marks for many people the important transition of the region's rural lifestyle from a supposed traditional past with reliance on group custom and folk culture to an agribusiness present replete with constant innovation and high capital requirements. Popular conceptions of rural evolutions are often founded, of course, on a number of emotional and nostalgic attitudes that lead too easily to a regret for something lost from bygone "good old days." How "good" those days were is not a question with an easy or obvious answer. Older patterns are complex, and they are difficult to document because of both the patina of experiences and attitudes following any change and the problems of sifting through the written and oral sources that can inform us of the experiences and values characterizing everyday life.

This study describes and interprets midwestern social and cultural responses to changing technologies for grain threshing, beginning with the earliest hand techniques and ending with the adoption of the combine. The emphasis is on patterns associated with the region's major small cereal crops of wheat and oats, although some attention is given to threshing barley, rye, buckwheat, and grass seeds. The experiences described in the following chapters are drawn largely from the lives of farmers working in the three-state heart of the Old Northwest—Ohio, Indiana, and Illinois—and Iowa. The cultural and geographic traits of this regional core are shared, certainly, by contiguous areas, including southern Minnesota, Michigan, and Wisconsin, and northern Missouri. Therefore, the "region" named in this work includes most of the "trans-Appalachian frontier": the land mass north of the Missouri and Ohio rivers, west of Pennsylvania, and east of Kansas, Nebraska, and the Dakotas.

While the evolution of threshing technologies provided occupational alternatives, the machinery is not described in detail in this book. Mechanical threshing designs and devices are popular industrial products rather than the artifacts of local cultural processes, and the designs and styles of available devices are satisfactorily treated in other publications. F. B. Mumford, the "father" of agricultural research in Missouri, wrote in 1920 that "agriculture is not only an industry, it is a type of life and discussion of the industry minus a consideration of the human values is entirely inadequate and withal uninteresting."[2] Technical descriptions are provided here only if they have a direct impact on the creation and preservation of a given social or cultural trait. Actual on-farm practices are emphasized over mechanical details and technological designs because of an assumption that the evolution of any new technology, whether hand-tool or machine, is not necessarily synonymous with either its use or its method of employment. Questions of origin and diffusion serve to establish the existence and adoption sequences of certain technologies. But people adapt as well as adopt. They alter their lifestyles before, during, and after adoption of a new device.[3] They also may modify their use of the nonindigenous technologies and the item itself to fit local conditions. Investigations in Sweden and Germany, for example, have documented the subregional "improvements" made on mass-produced plows by area blacksmiths and the employment of the new devices according to preexisting agricultural customs.[4] Midwestern agricultural periodicals, from their origins to the most recent issues, typically include stories of farmers who modify tools and machinery, sometimes even combining two or more items to accomplish a particular task.

Another reason for avoiding a treatment of various technologies without reference to how they were used is that the tools of agriculture do not in themselves denote any particular thought process, social practice, or approach to farming. Many appraisers of the rural scene are fond of equating a complexity of technology with a complexity of culture. According to this formula, farmers driving tractors are more "progressive" agriculturalists than those men still walking or riding behind horses. And an operator who has recently purchased a new John Deere 4240 tractor is more "advanced" than his neighbor coaxing a few more years out of a Ford 8N. It is erroneous to assume, however, that the mere presence of a particular tool reveals everything about social and cultural evolutions. If the equation were true, interpreters of midwestern social history and culture could rest their eyes, pens, and tape recorders. Without a doubt, the tools of farmers become more exact and more efficient with each passing decade. Can we say the same is true of social relations or perceptions of a quality of life? A simple hammer in the hands of a skilled carpenter becomes a tool applied with scientific acumen and precision. An air hammer in the hands of a novice is a dangerous weapon. Tools are the intermediary between a builder, his plans, and the final product. Threshing techniques are no different. Questions of reasoning, logic, aesthetics, and ethics are resolved by the people who handle the technology and are not carried, *sui generis*, in the artifacts themselves.

The information on midwestern threshing patterns presented in this book was culled from three types of sources: diaries, journals, autobiographies, reminiscences, and other forms of first-hand written accounts; agricultural periodicals; and oral interviews with more than 110 midwestern farmers, families, and threshermen. Oral sources become most useful as the narrative winds its way to the twentieth century. However hard one might wish for those occasions of cultural lag or isolation that allow contact with people familiar with the oldest folk patterns, the experiences characteristic of mid-nineteenth-century farming are beyond the knowledge of current Midwest residents. It is simply not possible at this late date to utilize the kinds of questionnaires and fieldwork that still prove successful in Europe and the British Isles for documenting premechanical agriculture. Except for the survival of some traits in usually unconnected contexts, the sweep of change in the Midwest is so great as to make the life of 100 or more years ago a sort of Dark Ages to current oral tradition and knowledge.

While enough data are available to delimit the practices and organization of threshing activities, the region cannot be studied via a rigorous sampling technique. The short historical depth of most oral traditions and contemporary practices requires a reliance on written sources. Yet nineteenth-century publications, especially newspapers, handbooks, and settlement guides, are surprisingly bare of descriptions of traditional threshing and harvesting practices. This gap is probably due to the fact that older techniques such as flailing and treading grain were so common and widespread as not to require (in a correspondent or editor's opinion) any description. Contributors to the agricultural press were also busy promoting and discussing other new ideas and practices being utilized before mechanical threshing devices became widely available. Descriptions of innovations occupied printed space in place of documentation of techniques already tried and true.

Diaries, journals, recollections, and personal reports in the agricultural press provide valuable veins of information, though they must be mined carefully in the search for information on everyday life and attitudes. The representativeness of any account is a crucial variable, although it is foolish to believe there exists any such person as "*the* typical farmer" in the Midwest. Information on the writer's occupational undertakings and socioeconomic status are usually apparent in descriptions of farm activities, acres cultivated, and patterns of hired labor. The diaries and first-hand accounts used in this study were chosen with an eye to providing a cross-section of practices, attitudes, and geographic areas. The focus on everyday life "in the mainstream" cannot exclude the writings of wealthy or "progressive" farmers, especially during the first decades of midwestern life, because these men were important as local innovators. Richer farmers hiring threshing labor provided contexts for the exchange of practices and ideas between community innovators and other residents. In general, the diffusion of threshing technologies and systems for organizing threshing tasks follow sociocultural lines as much as economic axes. Social stratification has always existed in the Midwest, yet many facets of the harvest and threshing entailed cooperative practices across simple economic lines.

Only signed correspondence and specific reports of actual farm practices in the agricultural press are used as evidence of particular local traditions. Editorials on innovations and advertisements illustrating threshing equipment are cited to point to the different options available at a specific time. Personal reports of agricultural techniques offer a more reliable account of real farm experiences, although the men who would write up their activities *and* send them for publication are most often from the group of larger commercial farmers. Historian Paul Gates estimates that one of every ten farmers in 1860 subscribed to an agricultural journal.[5] The percentage increases greatly over time, however, and varies between journals. Reading the correspondence to a variety of publications reveals that some papers became more widely circulated among a broad spectrum of farm operations and attempted to appeal to varied sensibilities. These trends are most pronounced in the "state" agricultural journals early in this century.[6] Notable among this group are the Prairie Farmer, Ohio Farmer, Indiana Farmer's Guide, and Wallace's Farmer and the Iowa Homestead, which combined in 1929. All of these journals published many accounts of threshing ring activities throughout the 1910s and 1920s. Circulation figures for the five publications increased from approximately 88,000 in 1898 to over 500,000 by 1923.[7] These statistics do not reveal the limits of the audience, however, as newspapers and journals were often circulated among friends and neighbors.

ACKNOWLEDGMENTS

This study of midwestern threshing from the flail to the combine would not have been possible without the help of many people. Former threshermen and their families introduced me to the life of the itinerant operators who served neighborhoods throughout the region. Specifically, I would like to note the assistance of Ira and Leola Edger of Greenville, Ohio, who introduced me into many communities in the western part of the state. My work would not have been possible without their encouragement and insights. Thanks are also due to about twenty other former threshermen, from eastern Ohio to western Iowa, who patiently explained their work, showed their records, and shared their memories. Equally valuable sources of information for this research were the farmers and rural families who consented to tell of their own experiences as members of cooperative threshing rings. Threshing was a family and community affair, and the men and women who recounted their experiences taught me about threshing as an agricultural process and a social experience. Each person cited in this book is in part a coauthor, but any of its shortcomings are mine alone.

Other people and institutions have helped with the preparation of this book by providing intellectual and research assistance. Warren Roberts, Elaine Lawless, Christoph Lohmann, and Mary Ellen Brown read and reread portions of the manuscript with little complaint and the offering of sound advice. Assistance in the location of diaries, journals, photographs, and other source materials was given by indefatigable staffs at the National Agricultural Library, Ohio Historical Society, Indiana State Historical Society, Illinois Historical Society, State Historical Society of Iowa, Iowa State Historical Department, Joint Collection of the University of Missouri Western Historical Manuscripts Collection and State Historical Society of Missouri, Wisconsin State Historical Library, Midwest Old Threshers Museum, and may community libraries and county historical societies throughout the Midwest. Indiana University and the National Endowment for the Humanities provided financial help when it was most needed and appreciated. The most special patience came from those individuals forced to share in the everyday process of research and writing. I want to express my heartfelt gratitude to Elaine Lawless for inspiring intellectual exchanges and continuing personal support. And our daughter, Jesse, although too young to contribute to this work, bravely faced noisy steam engine shows and countless miles down the region's country roads.

THRESHING IN THE
MIDWEST, 1820–1940

I.

FLAILING AND TREADING

The initial wave of families arriving in the Midwest to test the region's virgin soil raised wheat as their first important cash crop. The grain's market value provided the funds or barter to purchase essential supplies and equipment and to pay off accumulated debts. Farmers sold wheat to newcomers who had not yet worked their own fields and hauled it into nearby towns whose residents depended on the the foods raised by local producers. Grain preserved well and was certainly more easily handled in bulk than corn, the other principal crop of this period. The general popularity of wheat also lay in its usually dependable growth (for a few years at least) on newly cleared land and the inexpensive tools required for planting, cultivating, harvesting, and threshing. Farmers also raised oats, buckwheat, barley, and rye, but typically in limited subregional areas defined by special ethnic or ecological traits. Oats did not become a major crop until later in the nineteenth century, with the settlement of prairie regions in Illinois and Iowa.

Prior to the adoption of mechanical devices, midwestern farmers chose between two traditional threshing techniques with roots predating the writing of the Old Testament. Some men beat out their crops using a flail—a two-piece, jointed wooden tool swung with the hands such that one section crashed down on grain bundles laid on a wooden floor or hard packed ground. In the other process, called "treading," "tramping," or "tromping," the hooves of horses and oxen made to walk or trot on the sheaves replaced the striking action of the flails. The final task was winnowing or "fanning" the good grain away from the remaining chaff, weed seeds, and other debris. Occasionally, a farmer used a unique threshing practice representing an extension of one of the basic processes. O. K. Ormson recalls how his Norwegian immigrant father threshed grain near Kendall, Wisconsin, in the 1850s: "He loaded his wagon with stone and drove his oxen and wagon in a circle" on the threshing floor.[1] Weighted sleds and other novel methods, however, never gained any widespread acceptance.

Geographic distributions of the two major threshing techniques in the Midwest do not fall into the neat patterns characterizing regional practices along the East Coast during the Colonial period. In general, farmers in New England swung flails, mid-Atlantic operators used both techniques, and landholders along the coast south of Pennsylvania led their animals onto the treading ground.² Eastern regional differences reflect the general ethnic origins of early settlers, the economic importance of grain crops grown on average farms in each area, and the diffusion of cultural practices. New England farmers hailed mainly from England and Scotland and brought with them the strong preference for flailing that dominated premechanical threshing systems throughout the British Isles.³ Most settlers in the Northeast farmed small acreages, raising enough grain to meet the needs of the home family and stock and, perhaps, to provide a small surplus for bartering with local merchants. The slower and more individualistic flailing technique suited regional needs and became a common task carried out during the long New England winters.

New York and Pennsylvania traditions reveal the region's mixed cultural and settlement heritage. Anglo-American settlers in the region generally flailed their crops, but the area attracted an influx of Central and South-Central European immigrants undoubtedly familiar with both threshing processes from their native countries. Many mid-Atlantic farmers raised market grain crops to feed residents in nearby coastal cities. Treading provided cereal producers with the best method of threshing a large harvest in the shortest period of time. The faster treading methods were also favored on large estates in eastern Virginia, in Maryland, and along the Chesapeake Bay, where farmers raised vast amounts of wheat and oats for commercial markets. Although wealthier men could afford to hire laborers or purchase slaves to flail a large crop, landholders more commonly preferred to thresh with horses and oxen. Treading methods were learned from European immigrants in the area and via the diffusion of threshing practices south from the mid-Atlantic region.

The Midwest scene is more complicated, because emigrants from all of these regions settled in the Old Northwest. Variations in farm sizes and agricultural styles in each locale supported the persistence of both flailing and treading techniques. Moreover, farmers often changed from manual to animal threshing as they brought more land under cultivation and established grain as their primary market crop. Pioneer descriptions of Midwest threshing typically mention the simultaneous use of both processes in the same neighborhood or county, with some intervening occupational or ethnic variable providing the basis for use of either technique. When John Reynolds moved from Tennessee to begin farming near Kaskaskia, Illinois, in the 1820s, he found established French families cultivating small acreages, storing the grain in vertical post barns, and threshing with flails. The recent Anglo-American arrivals from the mid-Atlantic and Upland South areas raised more extensive market crops, stacked their grain, and tramped with horses.⁴ Generally, small-acreage farmers in the Midwest, particularly newcomers with New England and mid-Atlantic origins, flailed their grain, while men raising large acreages favored the use of animals on the threshing ground.

Nineteenth-century immigrants to the United States constituted a significant portion of settlers breaking ground in the newly surveyed Midwest. These newcomers added their Old World harvest technologies to an already diverse situation. Swiss-German immigrants claiming land around Tiffin, Ohio, and Decorah, Iowa, and Scandinavians settling in the Upper Midwest brought the use of flails into areas in which treading techniques were the still-practiced norm of the first wave of families arriving from mid-Atlantic regions. The Swiss-German homesteaders continued to use hand techniques after most of their neighbors switched to mechanical separation.[5] Simultaneous support for treading traditions came from German and other Central European immigrants arriving in the 1840s and establishing farms in southern Indiana and Ohio and in eastern Missouri and Iowa. Although threshing machines became widely available around this time, these newcomers did not grow enough grain to justify the purchase price of a mechanical device.

A man choosing between flailing and treading techniques had to consider his future plans for use of the straw, the major by-product of threshing. Threshers swinging flails retained more control over the direction of the strikes against the sheaves and could separate the grain head from the straw without much damage to the stems. Farmers threshed exclusively with a flail if they required long, unbroken straw for thatching, ropemaking, filling horse collars, or domestic products. There are no midwestern reports of stick threshing, rubbing, lashing, or other techniques practiced contemporaneously in the British Isles to produce the finest and longest straw. Control over horses and oxen during treading could never be as precise as the aim of a thresher's flail. Tramped straw always suffered some bruising and breaking, even though workers led the animals over the grain and gave special attention to keeping the floor clean. Desiring a compromise between the speed of treading and the need for good straw, some Missouri families initially tramped their grain with horses and then finished up the threshing with flails.[6]

The decision to flail or tread also depended on the specific crop and the intended use of the grain. May farmers flailed wheat and rye and brought out their animals for threshing oats and barley.[7] Farm diarists provide little explanation of occupational practices, but their choices likely depended in part on the ease of threshing a particular cereal and the potential quality of the straw. Wheat and rye straw is longer than oat stems and thus better suited for such farm and domestic functions as animal bedding and filling mattress ticks. Further, wheat and rye grain heads adhere more closely to the straw and require the careful eye-hand coordination of the flailer for sure threshing. Oats, particularly when ripe, are more easily knocked loose and thus are more appropriately threshed via the imperfect control of animal hooves. Some farmers also flailed those portions of the grain crop or grasses set aside for use as seed for the next year's planting. John Miller, homesteader of eighty acres in Miami County, Ohio, in the 1830s, flailed clover seed and wheat and tramped oats (see Appendix A).[8] Hancock

County, Illinois, settler Willis Berry also tramped the bulk of his oats during the same decade, but he flailed a small portion each fall for use as seed for the next annual planting.[9] Again, these threshing patterns reflect specific qualitative differences between flailing and treading, as the direct impact of a hoof could easily bruise, crack, or split the kernels. Damaged seeds were unlikely to germinate if planted the following season.

Flailing

The flail is a wooden tool consisting of two lengths of unequal size fastened together with a universal coupling. The hand-held longer pole is typically called the "handle," "staff," or "handstaff." This piece is generally three to four feet in length, although handles up to six feet long were fashioned, and is commonly shaped from ash, hickory, or oak. The form is long, narrow, and generally rounded like a broom handle to fit comfortably in the flailer's clenched hand. The shorter length is usually called the "beater," although such British terms as *souple, swingel,* or *swingle* or the German *schlegel* are sometimes recorded in regional diaries and journals. The beater is generally twenty to forty inches long. It may also be rounded, but in most cases at least two sides are slightly flattened to provide a broader striking surface. Beaters on flails used in Clay County, Missouri, and Darke County, Ohio, were shaved in a hexagonal design to provide a multi-angle striking surface. This section bears the brunt of the pounding and is consequently formed of oak, hickory, or other strong hardwood.

The coupling between the two pieces is the most important structural item. The joint had to be fashioned in such a way that the beater could pivot in all directions around the handle without the two pieces becoming entangled. Proper flailing is carried on almost entirely through actions of the flailer's hands, forearms, and wrists.[10] The thresher positions himself in a standing position about three feet in front of the grain he intends to strike. The legs and lower body are turned between fifty and ninety degrees away from the grain, and the right foot is placed forward (for a right-handed flailer). The flailer grasps the handle tightly near the bottom with the left hand and loosely wraps his other hand around the middle of the piece. The lower hand remains tucked in near the body for most of the process. A stroke begins with the beater resting on the grain. The flailer lifts the beater from the ground by pressing down on the handle's end and pulling up at the middle. The left hand remains almost stationary as the right hand pulls up the handle until it is at least perpendicular to the body and approximately three to four feet off the ground (photo, p. 5). The thresher then turns the handle sharply with his left hand, relaxing the right to allow the handle to pivot. The rapid motion flicks the beater into the air at head level or above. The source of power now shifts between hands, with the left relaxing its grip while the right hand, palm facing upwards,

Herbert Kleinman demonstrating his method of holding a flail prior to swinging it above wheat laid on the ground. Parke County, Indiana, 1981.

firmly grasps the turned handle. The flailer turns his right hand and wrist to the side and immediately down towards the ground in a snapping motion that slants the handle towards the targeted grain. The beater follows the angling of the handle and strikes flat against the grain if the motion ends with the tip of the handle close to the ground.

Flail couplings consist of a flexible tie directly between the beater and handle or a connecting component, often called the "cap" or "hood," fixed to the handle and then attached to the beater. Flails with caps on the ends of both pieces are also known. Threshers commonly used leather to fashion simple joints, although they preferred eelskin, when available, because of its longer-lasting quality. A basic construction includes holes in the top end of the handle and lower end of the beater and a thong passing through the openings (see Fig. 1).[11] A more elaborate formation that allowed the beater to swivel easily on a tightly held handle required wrapping a coupling material in a small groove incised an inch or two from the handle top. A buttonlike knob above the hollowed-out area kept the leather wrapping firmly in place. The coupling cord passed through a hole in the beater and connected to the handstaff.

Cap coupling designs are pictured in the flails used in eastern Missouri (pp. 8–9) and Parke County, Indiana (Fig. 1). The modified Missouri flail contains a coupling piece composed of an oaken arch about eight inches long on each side. It is fitted around the handle's end and tied to it by two leather binds lashed through small square notches cut into the arch. The wood cap is connected to the beater via a leather thong passing through a hole in the beater and tied loosely to the arch to allow free movement. The oaken flail used in Indiana in the early 1900s contains a hybrid form of coupling. A thin piece of leather is looped through a hole in the beater and in turn passes through a strip of one-inch leather formed into a loop cap with overlapping ends fitted over the handle. A bolt extends through each end of the cap and the handle and is held in place with pinhole fasteners. The thicker loop moves freely around the bolt head to provide universal movement. This design is typical of one style of machine-formed coupling available at the end of the nineteenth century.[12] The last flail pictured in Figure 1 is a double-capped example reportedly last used in Butler County, Ohio. Both caps are machine-formed from metal and riveted to the oaken handle and beater.

Midwest farmers' diaries report average daily outputs of 7 bushels of wheat or rye and about twice that amount of oats. Actual threshing numbers vary considerably, though, according to the ability of the threshers, the type and quality of the grain, the care taken with the straw, and whether or not the flailer also winnowed the chaff away from the grain. In Mercer County, Illinois, Albert Drury homesteaded an eighty-acre farm in the late 1830s. From August through December, 1838, he devoted between 3 and 7 days each month to flailing his spring wheat. In August, Drury flailed on the

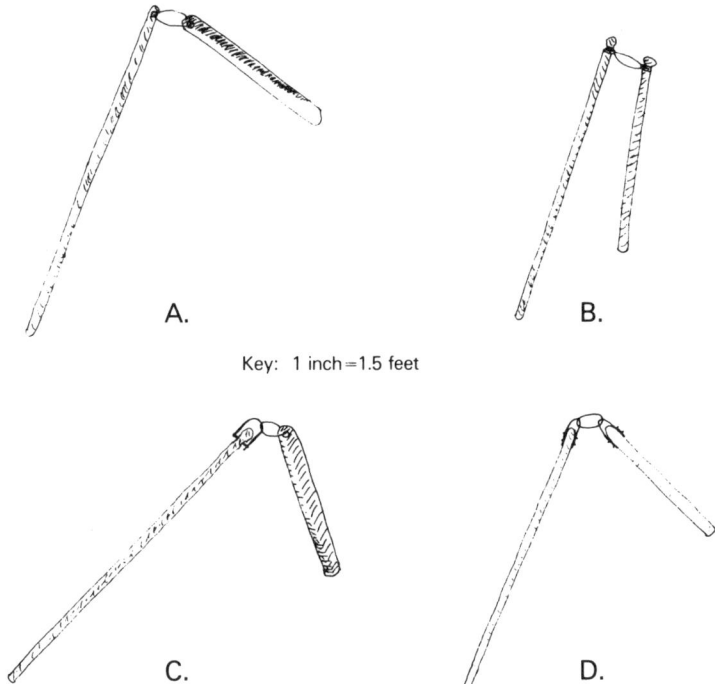

Key: 1 inch = 1.5 feet

A. Central Illinois; coupling of braided leather through holes in handle and beater
B. Miami County, Ohio; leather coupling attached to ties wrapped around handle and beater
C. Parke County, Indiana; bolt and loop cap on handle connected with leather tie to beater
D. Butler County, Ohio; coupling composed of metal caps riveted to handle and beater and connected with leather thong

Figure 1: Flail Designs and Couplings

17th, 18th, and 20th. On the 21st, he cleaned this wheat and reported a total of 21 bushels, or an average of 5¼ bushels per day.[13] To the west in Lee County, Illinois, William Hubbard recorded his threshing in September, 1844. He flailed 109 dozen sheaves in 5½ days; on the seventh day Hubbard borrowed a neighbor's fanning mill to clean the grain. He claimed a yield of 37 bushels, or about 6 bushels flailed, but not winnowed, per day.[14] In the same year, Lake County farmer James Page flailed and cleaned out 8 bushels of wheat and 16 bushels of buckwheat in 2 days' work with a neighbor.[15]

Interestingly, day-by-day farmers' documentations tend to be twenty-five to forty percent lower than the figures claimed in government reports and

Central Indiana flail (left) with a leather coupling wrapped around a groove cut into the handle and Eastern Missouri flail (right) showing an arched, oak cap strapped to the handle with leather ties.

reminiscences published long after the adoption of mechanical threshing devices. An 1898 study by the United States Commission of Labor, for example, concluded that one man could thresh and stack the straw from one bushel of grain at the following rates: one bushel of barley in eighteen minutes, or approximately thirty-three bushels in one ten-hour work day; one bushel of oats in thirty minutes, or twenty bushels a day; and one bushel of wheat every forty minutes, or fifteen bushels per day.[16] The differences reflect in part an "ideal" system versus the everyday practicalities of diversified farming on most Midwest homesteads. Agricultural press reports and the reminiscences of farmers in their later years suggest an output based on a long day's devotion to flailing by hired workers; thus, they reveal more accurately the style followed only by more wealthy farmers. Most families flailed their own grain and, while perhaps devoting the

greater part of the day to the job, spent part of their working hours caring for stock, milking, and other chores.

Midwestern farmers flailed in sequences of two to five days between early autumn and late summer. Jacob Stewart, owner of sixty-five acres in Fairfield County, Ohio, threshed his wheat crop over twelve days dispersed through August, September, and December, 1820, and April and July, 1821, with an average monthly total of 8¾ bushels. He flailed the year's rye in August, October, December, March, April, and July at a monthly clip of 7½ bushels.[17] Intermittent threshing of 10 to 20 bushels netted a new supply of straw for stock use. Farmers preferred freshly threshed straw because the nutritional quality of loosely stored straw and its attractiveness to animals as food decreased considerably after only a few weeks.

Descriptions of the work often distinguish between "short" and "long" straw removed during flailing. Capable threshers could "thresh out" most of the grain after a few well-placed strikes near the heads. The unbroken straw remaining on the ground constituted the "long" straw. Farmers collected it by hand or fork and carefully stacked the material for use in animal bedding, ropemaking, and straw ticks. The "short" straw was the mixed broken straw and chaff removed by the threshers with a rake at the end of the flailing and then fed to cattle over the next few days. The poor quality of most granaries in use during the settlement period also supported periodic flailing. Early provisions for grain storage included hollowed logs stood on end and small rail pens chinked with straw and mud and lined with slough hay or straw.[18] Farmers throughout the southern areas of the Midwest fashioned sycamore wood grain containers made through a process outlined in the following Missouri description:

> [We went] to the creek bottoms and cut down a hollow sycamore tree from four to six feet through. The tree was then sawed into cuts eight feet long. The hollow logs were hauled home and there burned and scraped out till those cuts were reduced to a shell with walls from three to four inches thick. These hollow logs were then placed on end in a row on the granary floor and covered with clapboards. All holes and cracks were filled with clay.[19]

When families needed fresh grain for flour or feed, threshing from the stack usually produced a higher-quality product than the cereals previously threshed and stored in granaries.

A farmer possessing a good wooden or earthen threshing floor built into his barn needed only to sweep it clean to prepare for flailing. In the common double-crib or English three-bay barn, the space reserved for flailing was the passage between the two cribs or bays.[20] Threshing floors in the bank barns built by German settlers and Anglo-American imitators were typically on the second level. In both cases, farmers used the mows on either side of the threshing area to store the grain bundles. Low permanent walls, sometimes called the "mowsteads," or removable board walls provided easy access to these storage areas. Tightly laid plank surfaces on the threshing floor prevented the passage of any threshed grain between the boards. Most barn builders laid single-layer floors with two-inch-thick planks that could withstand the constant pounding. Other farmers constructed special threshing surfaces of two board layers running perpendicular to one another or with their joints overlapped. Cross beams laid under the floor supported and strengthened the boards in the central work area.[21]

Only farmers owning large-capacity barns able to hold harvested grain in storage mows had access to permanent wooden threshing floors for annual use. The typical outbuilding in the region, however, was a multipurpose structure in which livestock, horses, crops, and tools competed for available space. This pattern differs markedly from European styles, where larger farms contained a variety of buildings constructed for specific purposes. English farmers used the "barn" solely for storage of grain bundles, threshing, and the granary. They kept horses in a stable, housed cows in the byre, and put their pigs in a sty. The corresponding structures in France

Flailing and Treading

and Germany were, respectively, the *écurie*, *étable*, and *porcherie* and the *pferdestall*, *kuhnstall*, and *schweinestall*. Mid-nineteenth-century midwestern barns often contain a central area either called or corresponding to the "threshing floor" of European counterparts, but many farmers eschewed the use of wooden threshing floors inside the barn for flailing and instead carried their grain bundles to a specially prepared floor or cleared piece of ground near the barn.

Open-air flailing typically occurred directly on the ground, although in his travels through Ohio in 1818, the Englishman James Flint observed "people [flail] threshing buckwheat; they had dug a hollow in the field, about twenty feet in diameter and six feet in depth."[22] A few farmers built outdoor platforms or laid temporary plank surfaces resembling in-barn threshing floor constructions. The majority, though, preferred a piece of ground with a dry, level, and hard surface. Outdoor threshing areas were one of the few agricultural contexts in which clay soil proved particularly appropriate. Some men added clay to their black dirt to form a more solid mixture. In Wayne County, Indiana, in the 1820s, Isaiah Harris "would take his hoe and scalp off a spot of earth" before flailing. Then he would "pack it with his maul and make it as smooth and level as a brickyard."[23] A few men finished their preparations by encircling the threshing ground with a pole or rail fence. Farmers performed most of their outdoor flailing during cold and dry periods in December, January, and February, as moisture and heat caused the grain heads to adhere more solidly to one another and the straw and allowed the ground to become muddy or pocket-marked.

A major difference between midwestern flailing and treading was the number of workers and animals generally employed. Use of a flail required no work animals, and first-hand accounts reveal that most flailing was done with the labor of only one or two men. There are a few references to the availability of "threshing gangs" to flail during the winter in Ohio in the 1820s and 1830s. Martin Welker, for example, recalls a group of itinerant threshers traveling throughout central Ohio in search of flailing work during the mid-1830s.[24] There is no evidence, however, for the common hiring of itinerant labor gangs on the levels associated with premechanical harvests on large farms in England and Scandinavia.

Two or more men flailing together set up a rhythmic striking of the grain heads and a patterned movement across the threshing floor. As one Ohio farmer remembers: "These regular strokes of the thrashers, keeping musical time, enlivened the work and kept them warm in the cold weather; and he who failed to keep the stroke properly would often suffer from his carelessness by a blow from one of the conflicting and rebounding flails."[25] The men alternated their strokes to set a consistent flailing rhythm. While one man's flail struck down on the floor, the other worker raised and poised his flail for the next blow. According to Herbert Kleinman of Parke County, Indiana, a thresher liked to maintain a striking rate of about one beat per

Artist's rendering of flailing in *The Growth of Industrial Art* (1892), p. 18. The depiction is erroneous as flailers working together in close quarters would alternate strokes rather than risk entangling their flails in near-simultaneous strikes.

second. Two men flailing together set up a rhythm of one beat every two seconds, proportionally spaced like quarter notes in a four-beat musical measure.[26]

Cooperative flailers generally employed two different styles of setting out the sheaves. The workers first laid the sheaves on the ground, cut the ties binding the bundles together, and removed the larger weeds. A simpler arrangement called for each man to take responsibility for flailing and turning his own sheaves. Farmers preferring a more patterned method set the sheaves in a "flooring" of a double row of bundles with their heads crossed in the middle or laid to the outside of each row. Flailers began usually at one end of the flooring and worked to the opposite edge. If the sheaves overlapped in the center, the workers flailed down the middle of the row in alternating strikes, with each succeeding blow hitting a little farther along the line. With the heads laid to the outside, the men still worked parallel to one another, but each worker struck only the heads on his side. When they completed a "line," the laborers turned the sheaves over and began flailing in the opposite direction. The process continued

Flailing and Treading 13

until all the grain was threshed out. Then the flailers removed the straw to a pile at one side of the floor and raked the grain to another location. Reports of flooring sizes range from 36 to 120 sheaves.

Wealthier farmers hiring men to flail paid the workers either a percentage of the threshed crop or a straight rate per day worked. Payment in grain is a traditional form of wages with European roots and was the common practice employed by landowners in Colonial New England.[27] Continuity of the in-kind system remained appropriate in early midwestern contexts because the grain could be used directly by the laborer's family, exchanged for flour at the nearest mill, or tendered as barter in trade with town merchants. Flailers customarily received between one-eighth and one-tenth of the total amount threshed, or about one bushel per day devoted to threshing wheat.[28]

Monetary payment eventually became the favored system in the Midwest, a result of the growth of a cash-oriented economy and the efforts of young men to accumulate funds to begin their own farming operations. In Fairfield County, Ohio, farmer and weaver Jacob Stewart paid his flailers by the bushel in 1817. His ledgers note rates of 6¼ cents for a bushel of rye and 7 cents per bushel of wheat. On December 3, 1817, "Negro George Johnson" earned 50 cents "to threshing 8 bushels of rye"; and on December 5, Thomas Edwards received 53 cents for completing 8½ bushels.[29] William Gardner employed men to flail on his farm near Freedom, Ohio, for 60 cents per day in 1831–33.[30] He sold his own wheat for 70 and 75 cents per bushel; thus, payment in kind or by wages in this case resulted in similar expenses and earnings per day. The ratio of in-kind versus cash payments varied according to labor rates and the market price for wheat. In April, 1840, another Ohio farmer, Enoch Jones, paid Banabus Knowles and Jacob Cook $1.50 each for, respectively, "two days work at threshing of wheat and one fence making," and "two days threshing of wheat and one cutting of rail timber." In July, however, the West Liberty, Ohio, settler managed to sell his wheat for $1.00 a bushel, or twice the daily wage.[31]

Rates paid for flailing were either below the norm or, at best, similar to wages paid for reaping and shocking grain or performing general farm labor. The level of compensation never reflected a local perception of flailing as a specialized skill deserving of the higher wages given to men known for their expertise in stacking or cradling grain. Available threshers had few other employment opportunities during the winter months, and the task required more physical endurance than complex technique. On the Stewart farm just cited, monthly laborers received $9.00 per month, and daily harvest hands earned 45 and 50 cents per day, or about the same amount given to a flailer who threshed out about seven bushels per day.[32] Yet over in western Ohio near Carlisle, day laborers on the Andrew Lesher farm in 1846 and 1848 received $1.00 for stacking or shocking, $1.25 for cradling, 60–70 cents for reaping or hauling grain, and only 40 to 50 cents for flailing. The thresher's rate exceeded only the 40 cents a day paid to cornhuskers; women raking after the reapers received a higher wage of 62½ cents.[33]

Treading

Treading grain provided a quicker means of threshing but required at least two laborers and a team of horses or oxen. The work began with the "driver" leading the horses in a walk over the bundles for a few passes. The other worker(s) then "drew off" the "long straw" and stacked it for other farm uses. The animals and driver returned to the grain and increased the pace of the circling passes until the threshing was completed. Crews usually added an extra driver for each additional span unless the animals were roped together and controlled by a single lead. Multiple independent teams followed each other across the threshing area at equidistant intervals. Some farmers treading with eight or ten animals employed a laborer to "catch the droppings,"[34] but normally workers charged with turning the sheaves also handled this task. Treading participants preferred to use horses, and some operators used the controlled pace as a task to help break colts. Reports of harnessing oxen for the treading ground are less common and are typically associated with farmers of English or Norwegian backgrounds.[35]

Treading required a larger work space than that normally used for flailing, because animals could thresh a larger number of bundles in each session. Some farmers simply piled opened sheaves to a height of one or two feet in a loosely laid "bed."[36] Most men placed bundles in a consistent form within the treading area. Patterned designs were either circular or, less frequently, in the shape of long and narrow rectangles. Workers cut and removed the bundle ties as they laid the sheaves on the ground. Straight-line sheaf arrangements were particularly appropriate inside large three-bay structures with sufficient area between the wing cribs to allow the passage of two or three horses. The long side of the "flooring" design followed the length of the threshing corridor.[37] Farmers opting for circular placements laid the sheaves in paired rings with the head overlapping. Round treading floors were typically located outdoors, as barns did not normally have enough open space. A Norwegian immigrant in Dane County, Wisconsin, described the method used on his 1857 crop:

> A circular piece of ground was cleared and well cleaned and then allowed to freeze very hard. The buckwheat was scattered about ten inches deep; then the grain was trodden out by the horses, which by dint of shouting and the frequent cracking of Ole Olson's long whip were kept going round and round as he ran along beside them. The straw was lifted off, the grain scooped up and later run through a fanning mill.[38]

Flailing and Treading

In 1938, eighty-seven-year-old Margaret Archer Murray wrote a more detailed account of her participation in treading in Jones County, Iowa, in the late 1850s.

> When all was in shock it was hauled to the slacking [stacking] ground near the stable & the threshing floor was made ready for thrashing a big round ring was scraped with hoes till the ground was clean and hard then the wheat was laid around that with the heads laping and the buttes of the sheaves out 2 such rings side by side was laid then tramped out with horses going round & round till all the wheat was tramped out I cant discribe a thrashing floor so you will understand but some day I can show you just how it was done but the horse on the inside had a bridle & the other one a halter with lead strap well I couldn't of been more than 6 or 7 years old when I was elected for the job of riding on the thrashing floor rode the inside horse and led the other one poor little me I rode and cryed & cryed & rode but to no avale had to do my share of what I was able to do that was supposed to be an easy job well I some times droped a sleep & slid off or the boys to hurry the horses would punch a horse with the fork handle he would jump & off I would flap and they would take me by one arm and leg up I would go again we all did our share of work big & little they used a pitch fork to turn the wheat over as it thrashed out and take the straw away and then gathered up the grain.[39]

The diameters of the treading circles ranged from 40 to over 100 feet, although the grain bundles occupied only a swath of 10 to 16 feet along the outer edge. Farmers often fenced outdoor treading grounds to the inside and outside as a means to contain and control the stock.[40]

Reports of the amounts of grain threshed in one day's work vary according to the number of teams and men available and the quality of the crop. Treading crews could not work one team of horses all day long without risking injury to the animals from the constant pounding on a hard surface. Farmers who possessed or borrowed additional teams rotated the stock and kept the treading going without interruption.[41] A single team generally "trod out" about 25 bushels of wheat per day; four "platoons" of horses "with a considerable labor force to turn the sheaves over" threshed between 150 and 200 bushels in a full day's work.[42] The typical midwestern treading included two or three men, perhaps one child to help with the animals, and four or six horses alternated in teams of two at a time. This arrangement yielded between 50 and 90 bushels a day.[43] A minority of farmers tramped out their grain at intervals throughout the fall, winter, and spring, with a single team threshing only 15 to 20 bushels at a time. Frederick Loehr, a German immigrant farmer living near Paris, Ohio, used two horses to thresh wheat and oat "beds" in five of the first six months of 1838. His periodic efforts never contributed more than 16 bushels of grain to the granary. Diary references to "feeding the straw" after each treading

Artist's illustration of barn treading a circular grain "bed" with two horses and four men; in *The Growth of Industrial Art* (1892), p. 18.

sequence suggest Loehr's desire to provide fresh bedding and straw to his stock.[44]

The labor requirements of treading supported a slightly higher level of cooperative aid than the social organization of flailing, although neither process required more than minimal help or organization. Families without enough workers or stock to fill a treading crew often exchanged work and a team with one or two neighbors. There is only sparse evidence of itinerant "treading gangs" and only scattered reports of wider neighborhood participation in tread threshing.[45] In comparison to the larger gatherings of families for corn shucking and butchering, farmers followed plans emphasizing small-group threshing in flexible schedules in the fall and winter. Rural residents did not attach any special social importance to threshing in general, because it neither involved a large labor collective nor occupied any regular calendrical position. Only those large-acreage farmers who wanted to get their crops to market as soon as possible after harvest viewed treading as a fixed task in occupational cycles. For example, Revolutionary War veteran General Chauncey Eggleston established a major farming operation in northeast Ohio in the first decade of the nineteenth century. In addition to his interest in purebred stock, Eggleston had one of the larger commercial grain operations in the region. He annually hired a crew of twenty to thirty men to reap, bind, and shock his wheat. About half of the labor force stayed on for threshing the grain on the treading ground and then transported the grain to Cleveland markets.[46]

Winnowing

Grain threshed from the straw still had to be separated from the chaff, pieces of debris, weed seed, and other remaining waste. Winnowing took

place directly after threshing and before carrying the final product to granary, mill, or market. Farmers typically cleaned seed grain again within a few days of sowing. The primary winnowinig techniques made use of a current of air to blow off the lighter waste and weed materials.[47] The standard work context was inside a barn where a natural wind passed through two open doors, or a door and window, on opposite sides of the winnowing area. Most barns with a threshing area contained the appropriate openings along the short sides of the rectangular work space. Alternatively, the work took place outside on a platform or packed piece of ground, on which winnowers placed a cloth or other material to protect the cleaned grain.

An individual winnowing alone used a simple sequence of baskets, sieves or riddles, and a fork sometimes called the "chaff fork." Winnowing baskets were typically of shallow depth and constructed with a close weave to prevent grain from falling through the bottom. The worker gathered threshed grain into the basket and raised the receptacle high off the ground. He then slowly poured the contents over the edge "through the wind." The heaviest good kernels dropped to the ground near the pourer, while the lighter waste materials blew away with the wind.[48] The winnower repeated the process a number of times until satisfactory results were obtained. This ancient technique has contributed some important additions to our dialect, including "the head of the heap," referring to the plump grain falling near the winnower, and "tailings," denoting the lighter, shriveled grain or "seconds" blowing away from the good grain.

Winnowers used sieves or riddles with a wire or wood mesh bottom of appropriate apertures to separate out larger waste particles and weed seeds remaining with the grain. The worker placed the grain in the sieve, held it off the ground, and shook the sieve in back-and-forth or up-and-down motions. Larger weed seeds, broken pieces of straw, and other oversized foreign materials remained in the sieve, as only the grain and small waste materials passed through the sized mesh. The winnower then took a chaff or winnowing fork to clean the crop of any remaining debris by tossing the grain in the air and allowing the wind to carry off the lighter chaff.[49]

Midwestern farmers usually made their own forks by carefully splitting a piece of oak or hickory wood at one end to form three or four closely spaced tines.

An alternative system for cleaning grain involved a group of three workers using a sheet or large piece of linen sometimes called the "winnowing sheet" or "fanning blanket." In Wayne County, Indiana, Isiah Harris called on his neighbors to help winnow wheat in the 1820s:

> At that time there were no [mechanical winnowing] fans. Then the two men would use a bed sheet, or a piece of woven flax or tow linen, a man at each end of the sheet; then by a quick revolving motion they would create wind enough to separate the chaff from the wheat. The third man, with a half bushel or basket filled with wheat in the chaff, would stand in front of the two men holding the sheet, pouring it out very slowly, while the other two men by the quick revolving motion of the sheet would raise wind enough to separate the chaff from the grain.[50]

The "revolving" motion of the sheet is perhaps more familiarly described as an up-and-down or side-to-side flapping action. William Howells's reminiscences of central Ohio farm life in the 1830s include his recollection of winnowing the family's grain:

> Then two persons would take a sheet, which they doubled in to an oblong shape, and each standing opposite to the other, they took hold, one with the right hand uppermost and the other with the left up, and with the other hands they clutched the edge of the sheet about two-thirds of the width from the top as it hung from the upper hands. They would then give it a motion a little like the blade of an oar in rowing. This produced a good blast, before which the grain and chaff was shaken down from a coarse sieve.... This winnowing with the sheet was hard work, and if there was much to be done, hands were changed.[51]

A last winnowing method, used by a small minority of farmers, combined the natural culling action of a breeze and the large surface capacity of the winnowing sheet. Workers placed the grains directly on the sheet and then tossed the whole mass into the air. The grain and other heavier materials fell back onto the sheet, while the wind carried away the lighter materials.[52]

Grain producers enlisted their families to form multi-worker crews and only infrequently exchanged winnowing work with one or two neighbors.[53] Interestingly, these sessions often included the participation of younger or female family members, who normally had little or no role in flailing and treading tasks. The different occupational patterns derive from socially demarked labor divisions and the lessened physical demands of pouring and gathering the grain. Midwestern cultural patterns were consistent with practices in the British Isles, where women participating in threshing generally carried sheaves and handled the threshed grain.[54]

Flailing and Treading

Finally, many midwestern settlers used mechanical means to speed the separating process before the adoption of threshing machinery. Boxlike mills, typically called "fanning mills," "cleaners," or "winnowing machines," created an internal artificial wind with a series of wooden "paddles" or blades connected to a hand-cranked shaft. The common labor crew for mechanical cleaning included three persons: one each to feed the device from the top, turn the crank, and gather the clean grain from the bottom or side of the machine. These devices cost between ten and twenty dollars around 1830. There is insufficient information to state accurately the diffusion of fanning mills during the settlement period, but farmers not owning machines often carried their grain to other farms or borrowed a device from a neighbor. Cooperative use generally centered on cleaning weed seeds from the grain set aside for fall or spring planting.

II.

THE MECHANIZATION OF THRESHING
INITIAL ADOPTION AND ACCOMMODATION

The adoption of mechanical devices for grain threshing occurred generally between 1825 and 1860 in the older settled areas of the Midwest and between 1860 and 1880 throughout the remainder of the region. Unfortunately, the pace of change from hand to mechanical technologies is difficult to establish with any greater certainty because of inadequate records of first uses and the lack of reliable nineteenth-century surveys. As historian Earle Ross notes about tracing agricultural mechanization in general: "With the inadequacy of farm statistics, the great variations between regions and communities, and the tendency towards neighborhood use of the more expensive implements, it is difficult to track the spread of agricultural mechanization . . . with an approximation to accuracy."[1] The impact of cooperative use particularly complicates efforts to trace Midwest threshing mechanization because, from the earliest periods, itinerant operators owned the majority of machines and offered their services to farmers throughout their community.

Threshing machine use remained limited and sporadic until the early 1840s. The first farmers to abandon flailing and treading were Ohio landowners living near the region's major population centers. Hamilton County, in southwest Ohio, boasted ten machines by 1828, and at least six farmers adopted mechanical devices in northeast Ohio by 1831.[2] The earliest claim for a threshing machine in Indiana is historian John Conner's contention that one newly arrived settler brought a device into the southeastern part of the state in 1837. By the early 1840s, machines were reported inland in Boone and Parke counties.[3] Chroniclers of Illinois agriculture place initial adoption between 1835 and 1840, although farmers' diaries reveal regular use of mechanical threshers by 1837.[4] These initial dates might seem late considering the pace of settlement in the region prior to 1830 and the importance of grain to the agricultural economy. Settlement and crop statistics must be tempered, however, with the realities of early Midwest farming.

Although over 200 different threshing machines were advertised in agricultural periodicals by 1835, Midwest adoption progressed slowly because of inadequate transportation and access to commercial grain markets and the subsistence level of most agricultural operations. Until the mid-1840s, eastern companies manufactured almost all of the threshing machines used in the United States. The dominant producers were Pitt Brothers of Winthrop, Maine, A. B. Allen of New York, Joseph Pope in Boston, and the Emery and Wheeler companies of Albany.[5] The devices had to be shipped via railroad, steamboat, or canal boat, with the purchaser responsible for all freighting costs. The long distances between factory and field also left prospective Midwest owners without any trained help for setting up the machine, making repairs, or fabricating spare parts.

The first adopters of threshing machines hailed from two main subgroups of the rural population. Some men were the so-called progressive farmers, who owned larger acreages and generally purchased a variety of the most recent agricultural innovations for their own use. Progressive farmers were not necessarily the wealthiest men in the region. In many cases, rich farmers remained conservative agriculturalists who continued to hire laborers to flail and tread their crops. Middle-class men with a desire to increase their profits and participate in the growing push for "scientific" farming during the 1830s were more likely to purchase labor-saving devices and act as agents for threshing manufacturers seeking midwestern markets.[6] The thrust for measured application of the latest mechanical designs to farming resulted in the creation of the region's first agricultural societies and farmers' clubs. At least some early organizations conducted experiments with the latest implement innovations. Local innovators in formal groups also attempted to influence their more conservative neighbors through public exhibition of mechanical threshers and via advertised field trials complete with awards to the most efficient demonstrators.[7]

Another innovator group in the Midwest included community blacksmiths, wagon makers, and general mechanics. Early threshing devices were not terribly complicated machines, although the variety of early designs suggests that a successful prototype of widespread appropriateness was not initially available. Some independent blacksmiths simply copied the design of a device that appeared to solve local needs or purchased the area sales or manufacturing rights of a particular company. Other enterprising men developed their own models. Iron and wood were the only major necessary materials, and community establishments could easily produce a few prototypes. A few shops developed successful models and eventually produced a number of machines for regional consumption. James Moffit, a local mechanic and inventor in Piqua, Ohio, sold several devices made in his shop in Miami County in the mid-1850s. Moffit's design was more notable than most others because he included a set of reciprocating knives at the mouth of the thresher to automatically sever the bundle ties. Although he received one of the first patents for a modification that would fifty years later be a standard item on all threshing machines, Moffit appears to have abandoned the manufacturing field by 1856.[8]

Local craftsmen not only built machines, but in many cases they also became the first entrepreneurs to transport their devices to thresh for local farmers. The journals of South Lebanon, Ohio, farmer Frank Lytle reveal that he regularly paid a blacksmith for itinerant threshing work in the 1840s and 1850s.[9] His local smiths constructed and operated two machines. They initially offered their services only to farmers willing to haul their grain bundles into town. By 1850, the blacksmiths had mobilized at least one machine by mounting it on a wagon pulled by two horses. Parallel developments occurred throughout the region, at least as far west as Henry County, Iowa, where a millwright named James Arnold supplemented his income by purchasing a threshing machine and contracting its use to farmers throughout the fall and winter.[10]

Sporadic adoption before 1850 can be attributed in part to the inadequate performance of many early machines. Innovative designs appeared on the market for a few years, only to be withdrawn when they proved ineffective. An Indiana farmer wrote to his brother in New York in 1842: "I have had some experiences with [threshing] machines, but I never saw one at my barn, or my neighbors, that did not leave grain enough in the straw to make the stacks green with sprouted grain as soon as the rains wet them."[11] The level of experimentation on the part of inventor-innovators is suggested by the 267 patents granted by the United States Patent Office for "machines for threshing" between 1790 and 1835, a pace that only increased throughout the nineteenth century.[12]

The most popular machine around 1845 was commonly called the "groundhog" thresher because of its posture and, according to some early innovators, the growling noises made as the grain worked its way through the threshing mechanism. Other ephemeral names for the first generation of threshing devices included "bull-roarer," "chaff-piler," and "bob-tail." These machines only threshed the grain from the straw; farmers still had to fan or winnow the grain to prepare it for market, mill, or next year's seeding. The mechanical threshing took place near the "feeding mouth" of the machine, where a cylinder revolved within a larger concave. Teeth or, less frequently, bars attached to the rapidly turning drum rubbed out the seeds in the small space between the cylinder and concave.[13] Grain dislodged from the straw fell into a chute that directed it out of the machine's bottom. Internal baffles pushed the straw over (overshot design) or under (undershot design) the cylinder towards the rear. Although farmers in the East used other experimental designs during the same period, midwestern farmers generally avoided alternatives to the toothed-cylinder machines. Among the more popular innovative devices rejected in the Old Northwest were spiked rollers dragged across the grain and rotary flailing machines consisting of a number of flaillike assemblages connected to a fast-turning drum.[14]

Threshing mechanization in the late 1830s centered in the expanding grain-raising areas of eastern and central Ohio. By 1840, farmers had increased cultivated acreage to the point that Ohio families raised almost twenty percent of the nation's crop and ranked number one among wheat producing states. Over the next decade, northern Ohio, Indiana, and Illinois farmers increasingly employed threshing machines as a replacement for hand techniques. The transition signified general subregional shifts to commercial agriculture. The completion of the Wabash and Erie Canal in 1841, as well as other transportation improvements and the growth of metropolitan areas in the region itself, supported a movement to market cropping systems.[15] Wherever cash grains were raised by a number of families in the same locale, one enterprising individual often purchased a machine and contracted his services to other area farmers. As more people in a neighborhood opted for mechanical threshing, farmers started to view threshing as a viable context for cooperative work exchanges. An early sequence of local planning and mutual effort began near Paris, Ohio. By 1837, at least five families were exchanging labor for mechanical threshing with the rig of a local custom thresherman by the name of Ben Ames.[16]

During the middle period of threshing machine adoption, roughly 1845 to 1860, the change from hand to mechanical technologies occurred more rapidly and on a wider geographic scale. Although some historians of Ohio agriculture state that "the flail had given way to the threshing machine previous to 1850," the generalization is premature for such newly settled or isolated parts of the state as the northwestern corner near Toledo.[17] By the outbreak of the Civil War, most reports provided by county organizations to state agricultural boards in Ohio, Indiana, and Illinois claimed the prevalent use of mechanical devices. These summaries were certainly not comprehensive for entire counties or all classes of farmers. Two knowledgeable commentators on Illinois farming practices of the mid-1850s noted that a large quantity of grain in the state was still tramped out by horses.[18] In truth, the shift to mechanical techniques was by no means complete in any section of the region by 1860.

The adoption of the first threshing machine in Wayne Township in Darke County, Ohio, illustrates a common sequence near mid-century. The first settlers arrived in the area in 1815, or twelve years after statehood. Emigrants from other parts of Ohio trickled in through the 1820s, and French and German immigrants followed during the next two decades. Township residents established the first churches and platted small towns in the 1830s. Land changed hands frequently, but by 1840 there were a number of firmly established family operations.[19] Among the early settlers was William English, a Scotch-Irish Presbyterian who purchased 160 acres of a government claim. English became a successful farmer and a member of the "progressive" agricultural movement. A chronicler of the township's early history notes that his "residence was one of the finest in the settlement," and his farm included a large orchard and "the great cider press of that time."[20] English purchased the first threshing machine in the area in 1847 or 1848. After operating it on his own farm for four years, he gave the machine to his sons, Samuel and James, who transported the device to other nearby farms for custom threshing jobs.

The direct impact of English's purchase on his neighbors' threshing practices cannot be reconstructed. His successful use of the device likely prompted other farmers to request the itinerant services offered by his sons.[21] The initial purchase of the machine in the late 1840s, though, parallels significant changes in threshing technology and manufacturing between 1845 and 1860. More efficient machinery, coupled with further improvements in transportation, supported a rapid increase in the speed of adoption. The major change in machine design was the combination of threshing and separation capabilities, an innovation patented by John and Hiram Pitts in 1837 and included in most new machines built after 1845 (see below). The complete thresher negated the need for fanning mills, except perhaps to clean grain a final time for market or mill or for use as next year's seed.[22]

In 1848, the "Racine (Wisconsin) Threshing Machine Works, J. I. Case, Proprietor," announced its opening for the sale of machines manufactured in a new, three-story brick building. Case had been selling agricultural implements in the area for three years, but his new facility and first advertisements to a wider audience symbolize a geographic shift in the thresh-

Hiram A. Pitts's 1847 "groundhog" machine that pioneered the combination of threshing machine and fanning mill into a single device.

ing machine industry from the East to the Midwest. Around the same time, Hiram Pitts split off from his brother and began building threshing machines in Alton, Illinois. He moved to Chicago in 1852 and again entered the market. Other important Midwest manufacturers beginning operations at this time included C. M. Russel and Company of Massillon, Ohio, Gaar-Scott of Richmond, Indiana, and the C. Aultman Company of Canton, Ohio. The location of threshing machine companies in America's top grain-growing region gave farmers a chance to see new products at the factory and at local, regional, and statewide events. Threshing machine trials and competitions at agricultural exhibitions became increasingly popular during the second half of the nineteenth century.[23] From their midwestern facilities, manufacturers sent salesmen into areas where grain threshing proceeded still via the flailing or treading techniques and commissioned community implement dealers to act as company agents.

The threshing machine industry's move followed a more general national pattern of developing regional agricultural prominence. Mid-nineteenth-century improvements providing greater access to eastern and international markets motivated midwestern farmers to increase their grain acreages and to adopt mechanical devices to speed occupational processes. New canals and railroad networks opened the possibilities of transporting grain to consumers at less cost and increased speeds. The ability to market crops supported the quickest acceptance of new technologies, because the amount of grain that a farmer could harvest and thresh certainly influenced the number of acres sown in the spring or fall.[24] By 1860, the top four wheat-producing states in the country were, respectively, Illinois, Indiana, Wisconsin, and Ohio (see Table 1).[25] Widespread change occurred initially in the northern sections, where Chicago and other grain centers routed cereals through the Erie and, later, Illinois and Michigan canals. Solon Robinson, the well-traveled agricultural writer, noted on a trip through Illinois in 1848 that "in that whole distance [between Vandalia and St. Louis] I saw but one threshing machine. How curiously that contrasts with a trip through the northern counties where a traveller will often see twenty in a single day's ride."[26] The southern sections did not tarry for long. Towns such as Cincinnati, Evansville, and St. Louis soon passed from occasional river trading in grains to full-fledged market centers.[27] Secondary grain centers developed to supply larger ones, and all were eventually connected by rail. Of course, the canals, highways, and railroads were two-way travel routes. They gave farmers access to eastern markets and also carried immigrant waves to midwestern cities. Higher demands for grain products by urban populations were compounded by the needs of new regional manufacturers, particularly breweries and distilleries, for rye, barley, and wheat.[28] Oats remained costly to haul over long distances because of their bulk, but farmers could generally sell their surplus crops in nearby population centers.

Threshing machines became almost universal in the region during the final period of adoption from 1865 to 1880. Mechanization occurred in

TABLE 1 **Small Grain Production in the Midwest, 1840–1900**

	Ohio	Indiana	Illinois	Iowa
1840—oats	14,393,103(3)*	5,981,605(5)	4,988,008(6)	216,385(17)
wheat	16,571,661(1)	4,049,375(6)	3,335,393(8)	154,693(20)
rye	814,205	129,621	88,197	3,792
barley	212,440	28,015	82,251	728
buckwheat	633,139	49,019	57,884	6,212
1850—oats	13,472,742(3)	5,655,014(8)	10,087,241(5)	1,524,345(20)
wheat	14,487,351(2)	6,214,458(6)	9,414,575(5)	1,530,581(15)
rye	425,918(7)	78,792(18)	83,364(16)	19,916(23)
barley	354,358(2)	45,483(11)	110,795(7)	25,093(14)
buckwheat	638,060(4)	149,740(10)	184,504(9)	52,516(16)
1860—oats	15,409,234(3)	5,317,831(8)	15,220,029(4)	5,887,645(7)
wheat	15,119,047(4)	16,848,267(2)	23,837,023(1)	8,449,403(8)
rye	683,686(8)	463,495(12)	951,281(5)	183,022(17)
barley	1,663,868(3)	382,245(9)	1,036,338(4)	467,103(8)
buckwheat	2,370,650(3)	396,989(7)	324,117(8)	215,705(12)
1870—oats	25,347,549(4)	8,590,409(10)	42,780,851(1)	21,005,142(5)
wheat	27,882,159(3)	27,747,222(4)	30,128,405(1)	29,435,692(2)
rye	846,890(6)	457,468(11)	2,456,578(3)	505,807(10)
barley	1,715,221(5)	356,262(11)	2,480,490(3)	1,960,779(4)
buckwheat	180,341(8)	80,231(14)	168,862(9)	109,432(11)
1880—oats	28,664,505(6)	15,599,518(10)	63,189,200(1)	50,610,591(2)
wheat	46,014,869(3)	47,284,853(2)	51,110,502(1)	31,154,205(6)
rye	389,221(11)	303,105(14)	3,121,785(2)	1,518,605(5)
barley	1,707,129(7)	382,835(15)	1,229,523(8)	4,022,588(4)
buckwheat	280,229(9)	89,707(16)	178,859(10)	166,895(11)
1890—oats	40,136,732(7)	31,491,661(12)	137,624,828(2)	146,679,289(1)
wheat	35,559,208(5)	37,318,798(4)	37,389,444(3)	8,249,786(19)
rye	1,007,156(10)	877,532(11)	2,628,046(5)	1,445,283(7)
barley	1,059,915(11)	250,200(19)	1,197,206(10)	13,406,122(3)
buckwheat	162,833(9)	99,959(14)	107,080(13)	286,746(6)
1900—oats	42,050,910(6)	34,565,070(10)	180,305,630(1)	168,364,170(2)
wheat	50,376,800(3)	34,986,280(7)	19,795,500(14)	22,769,440(10)
rye	257,120(16)	564,300(11)	1,104,670(8)	1,179,970(7)
barley	1,053,240(13)	260,550(21)	686,580(8)	18,059,060(4)
buckwheat	164,305(10)	102,340(13)	65,050(15)	151,120(11)

Sources: United States Census Returns 1840, 1850, 1860, 1870, 1880, 1890, and 1900; and Louis B. Schmidt, "The Westward Movement of the Wheat Growing Industry in the United States," *Iowa Journal of History and Politics* 18 (1920): 396–412.

*Figures represent total production in bushels; the number in parentheses represents the state's rank within the country.

some areas as a late replacement for flailing and treading. Traditional practices persisted longest in locales not yet serviced by transportation links, market centers, and the growing horde of implement salesmen and agents.[29] Most reports of hand techniques beyond 1880 generally suggest a crop too small to justify the cost of mechanical separation or drought-stricken grain shriveled in the heads. There is no evidence of "cultural fixations" in the sense of farmers consciously maintaining manual techniques because of their association with a particular agricultural style identified with a "better" way of life.[30]

Annual reports of hand or animal threshing in areas where machines were already the norm typically involve the continuity of ethnic and subsistence agricultural practices. Flailing persisted longer because farmers planting larger acreages appropriate to treading were more likely to find economic justification for the expense of adopting mechanical processes. There are no one-to-one correlations of flailing continuity as a cross-regional practice of particular ethnic groups. Most situations of late use occur within unconnected subregional settlements that attracted immigrants familiar with a specific hand process and choosing to raise small crops for family or farm use. The choice of threshing technique thus reflected both ethnic origins and speed of acculturation into more commercial agricultural styles. Nineteenth-century immigrants from Europe generally hailed from areas in which flailing remained a common cultural practice for small landholders. The continuity of Old World patterns depended on such additional factors as geographic isolation, crop patterns, and cultural settlement. German immigrants to Darke County, Ohio, in the 1830s and 1840s adopted mechanical threshing by 1860. Yet settlers with roughly the same Old World origins arriving in Parke County, Indiana, and Gasconade County, Missouri, in the 1860s flail threshed grain crops well into the later stages of the nineteenth century.[31] In Parke County, Indiana, German-American families raised small amounts of rye and barley for domestic and brewing purposes, in addition to fairly normal amounts of wheat and oats. While these farmers used mechanical threshers for their major crops, they flailed the rye and barley because the amounts were too small to pay machine charges, and farmers did not want the risk of rye and barley seeds remaining in the machine, where they could mix with the next crop.[32]

Sweep and Tread Powers

Threshing machine owners in the mid-nineteenth century operated their devices with two different styles of power: the "sweep power" that transferred the motion of circling horses to gears and shafts leading to the threshing cylinder, and the "treadmill," "tread power," or "railway power" that utilized a simple belt system to transmit the energy expended by one or two horses made to walk an endless incline. Internal improvements in each style resulted in "better" machines as the nineteenth century progressed, yet the two types remained consistent in their general design and function throughout their period of use. Although efficient tread powers were not perfected until 1810, both styles were widely available from threshing machine manufacturers by the middle period of threshing mechanization.[33]

The horse-sweep was the overwhelming choice of threshing machine owners prior to the widespread adoption of steam engines for threshing in the last decades of the nineteenth century. Farmers could harness up to twelve animals on a sweep and thus provide more power to the separator.[34] Two-horse mills had a top capacity of around 200 bushels per day; an eight-horse sweep easily threshed double that amount in the same period.[35] Owners of small sweep powers made for two to four horses staked the device to the ground for threshing and then hoisted it into wagons for transport to other locations. The larger units favored by traveling threshermen rode on their own wheeled carriages and contained, over the central gear, a small stationary platform for the "driver" or "power boss." With careful use of his whip and constant verbal encouragement, the driver's task was to keep eight to fourteen circling horses moving at the correct steady pace during the threshing. The pull of the horses determined the speed of the threshing cylinder's rotations. Bundles fed into the threshing mechanism required increased power to compensate for the friction of the grain against the cylinder teeth. Former driver LeRoy Shutes of Iowa recalls that the "hum of the cylinder was the real tip if feeding was to [sic] slow or to [sic] fast"; the proper pitch was "tenor," with "baritone" or "bass" indicating an insufficient speed for threshing the incoming grain.[36]

The process of transmitting the energy of circling horses to the threshing drum started at a central revolving gear mechanism. Wooden beams, usually called the "sweeps" or "arms," to turn the gears extended fifteen to twenty feet from the gear housing. The driver hitched one or, more commonly, two horses to the outside end of each sweep. The power transfer began as the horses' forward movement turned the gears located in the central housing. A rod between two and four inches in diameter extended downwards from the gears. Where it reached the ground, always short of the path of the circling horses, there was a universal joint, the "knuckle," and a bearing block staked to the ground. The universal joint transferred the energy to another rod length extending along the ground, through the horses' area, and ending at a second bearing and universal joint located outside the animal path. A final rod length extended upwards from this junction to the threshing machine, where the upper end was connected to a large cog wheel between twelve and sixteen inches in diameter. This gear activated a small drive pinion on the end of the cylinder's shaft. While the horses moved slowly in circles, the sized gears increased the turning pace

The Mechanization of Threshing

J. I. Case 12-horse sweep being demonstrated at the Wisconsin Centennial Exposition. The "driver" is standing on the raised platform above the central gears and the "tumbling rods" to the threshing machine can be seen to the left. Courtesy of Ohio Historical Society.

of the tumbling rods, and the cog at the separator end quickened the speed of the cylinder's revolutions.

The sweep power design required the circling teams to walk over the tumbling rods during each circuit. A horse stepping on a rod could easily mangle the iron shaft and, too often, bruise its hoof or break its leg. Serious accidents usually occurred to inexperienced animals borrowed from a farmer's general work stock, as sweep power owners carefully trained their teams to avoid the turning rods. After 1870, most sweep power manufacturers provided wooden housings to enclose the rod sections standing in the path of the circling teams, and an 1874 Iowa law stipulated that the revolving mechanism had to be boxed.[37] Horses continued to occasionally stumble over the obstacle, but at least the iron shaft received better protection.

The adoption of sweep powers brought an end to the use of oxen in threshing. These beasts were simply not able to drive the power fast enough to raise the cylinder's revolutions to the required speed. Norwegian-American Andrew Estrem learned that oxen also rebelled against attempts to place them on the threshing sweeps:

> One year, in the threshing season, a horse disease broke out, and it was impossible to find in the neighborhood a sufficient number of well horses

to finish the threshing. The oxen were tried, but this turned out to be trying all around. The oxen refused to speed up sufficiently; they simply couldn't see why they should walk faster in a circle than in a straight line. So the threshing had to wait until the horses recovered.[38]

Neighborhood farmers initiated their own local systems to provide the necessary number of animals for eight or ten horse sweeps. As a rule, the thresherman provided two or three teams, as this many were normally needed to transport the separator and power between farms. The host farmer contributed a team of his own stock or, if available, enough horses to complete the required number. Neighbors furnished the remainder needed to complete the power team, and the exchanges of animals for threshing became additional factors in the reciprocity networks established during the threshing season.[39]

While most farmers threshed with the services of traveling threshermen using sweep powers, those larger-acreage men who desired to own their own machinery favored tread powers.[40] One-horse machines cost between $100 and $150 in the 1840s, with another $100 for a two-horse device. Treadmills provided energy to turn the threshing cylinder by utilizing the power of horses walking steadily on an endless floor constructed of slatted boards. Movement of the floor rotated a drum or shaft cylinder with a large wheel located outside the treadmill's frame. A belt connected this wheel to a smaller one fastened to the threshing cylinder on the separator. A series of straps and traces held the horses in place on the mill. The whole moving apparatus was slanted; once the horses began to walk, their momentum caused the floor to turn, with the result that the animals had to continue their uphill climb in an (ideally) endless cycle.

Manufacturers of treadmills and sweeps promoted their machines as useful powers to drive threshing machines, fanning mills, grindstones, buzz saws, corn shellers, cob crushers, lathes, and straw cutters. Treadmills were more easily stored in the barn, though, where they could be quickly harnessed to other devices.[41] Farmers with larger operations were more likely to use a variety of the latest mechanical innovations, and thus were more inclined to purchase a treadmill for year-round use. They threshed in the fall or winter with the labor of their family, hired hands, and perhaps one or two neighbors. Diaries and correspondence note typical outputs of between 75 and 150 bushels per day for two-horse mill threshing. Andrew Lesher, a farmer living near New Carlisle, Ohio, first purchased a treadmill and threshing machine to complete his 1848 harvest. He worked his crop on September 27, October 14, January 25, February 11, and February 18, with a total yield of 422 bushels, or about 84 bushels per day.[42] While a treadmill owner could thresh his crop in one continuous period, farmers keeping stock believed, in the words of one Illinois man, that "cattle are apt to fare better where newly threshed and sweet straw is daily flung out

The Mechanization of Threshing 31

J. I. Case two-horse treadmill and separator, with a capacity of 200 bushels per day, advertised in *Prairie Farmer* in 1853.

to them."[43] Periodic threshing also lessened the strain on horses prone to back and leg injuries because of the constant uphill pounding on the mill's wooden floor.

The adoption of horse-powers for threshing machines had minimal impact on other rural patterns, including the design of midwestern farm buildings. In contrast, for example, English farmers in the Lake Counties, Eden Valley, West Cumberland, and Northumberland added structural appendages to their barns for the permanent setting of horse-sweep powers.[44] Scottish examples are known as far north as Orkney.[45] These sheds were known locally by a variety of names, including "horse engine house," "gin case house" (Lake Counties), and "wheelhouse" (Northumberland). Builders placed the circular or octagonal shelters along either of the outside bays of the common three-bay English barn. Drive shafts and tumbling rods, including the popular overhead gearing design produced in English factories, led to the main barn area.

Midwestern farmers used their horse-powers in a subdivided portion of the barn's interior area.[46] In 1883, a Grand Blanc, Michigan, farmer owning a two-horse Emery Railroad treadmill described a typical plan:

> After harvest, when I get my barn filled with wheat and grain of other kinds, I set the [threshing] machine right on the floor, and let it remain there until all the grain is threshed, which may not be till spring. My barn floor is of such size that it does not inconvenience me in the least. When the thrashing is all done, I take it down, and put it away under the swing beam, where it is entirely out of the way. I thrash my grain as I want to feed the straw, and it is all done within my own family.[47]

Midwest practices reflect the designs of adopted powers and the early widespread adoption of itinerant threshing rig systems. The more popular permanent power, the treadmill, occupied less space than the sweep power. Owners of the device sacrificed only an area equal to that needed for a "common wagon," according to one report.[48] The minority of farmers who purchased sweep powers for their own use normally acquired the machinery during the main period of threshing mechanization. By this time, the bulk of the mechanical components were manufactured from metal and iron and could easily withstand the weather if used outside the barn with little or no protection. Whereas the earlier overhead designs favored in the British Isles included many wooden pieces, American sweep power owners were concerned only with protection of the detachable wooden sweeps and ground-level shafts.

Obstacles to Mechanization

Although threshing speed obviously increased with machine use, not all Midwest farmers immediately adopted mechanical innovations to replace existing practices. A man's decision to change his threshing technology was based on more than simple formulas of bushels threshed per hour or labor hours saved. The choice to employ threshing devices, through either purchase or the employment of an itinerant thresherman, implied consideration of other traditional agricultural practices and existing sociocultural norms. For most men, mechanized threshing created new harvest expenses, stimulated different cooperative relations with neighbors, and entailed dependence on itinerant contractors to see the harvest through to its completion.

The desire to contract the services of an area thresherman did not mean necessarily that one would be available or able to mesh his schedule with each farmer's occupational cycle. There were usually some years during the early period of adoption when farmers encountered difficulty finding a machine for hire. Some threshermen simply left the business after one or two seasons. Other machine operators made fall runs but were not willing to return periodically to farmers who wanted small threshing jobs done every six or eight weeks throughout the winter. In the mid-1840s, Thomas Page farmed seventy acres in Lee County, Illinois, raising a variety of grains and keeping small herds of beef and dairy cattle. Each summer he threshed a portion of his crop with itinerant operators but then tramped wheat with horses in the late fall and winter. In 1845–46, for example, Page threshed oats with a neighbor's machine on September 20, 1845, but used his own horses to tread wheat on October 22, February 2, March 2, and April 1. On April 27, he procured the services of another machine to thresh the remainder of his crop.[49] These threshing dates yielded approximately 118 bushels of wheat and 128 bushels of oats.

Farmers who wanted to plow or otherwise utilize their ground soon after shocking required predictable threshing and labor schedules. Elisha King, owner of a quarter-section near Milroy, Indiana, wrote in his diary on August 21, 1855: "I started out to hunt a thresher but did not engage any because they could not do it in time for me to seed [wheat]. I do not know when I can get it done."[50] King ended up hauling the wheat sheaves to his barnyard for stacking; threshing that season waited until mid-October. The following year he began his search for hands a month later, but with no better results: "trying to get hands to help thresh tomorro [sic] got the promises of none."[51] Farmers who kept stock and wanted fresh feed and straw throughout the winter faced more difficulties arranging periodic threshing sessions than those men concerned solely with a market grain crop.

The opportunity to employ itinerant operators required landowners to consider the financial cost of machinery use in the context of personal agricultural styles. As noted previously, each family, with perhaps the aid of one or two neighbors, provided most of the labor needed to complete manual threshing. Farmers giving their time to one another typically were not paid in cash; rather, they exchanged labor in threshing or other chores. Importantly, producers stored and threshed their crops as needed, because no immediate market sales were necessary to pay for the threshing. Hiring the services of a professional thresherman, who generally brought two or three additional men as part of his crew, stimulated creation of a new pattern based on a commercial market economy, fixed threshing expenses, and specialization of labor.

Some threshermen continued the more traditional practice of harvest compensation of a percentage of the threshed crop, generally one of every ten bushels, during the earliest periods of the technological transition.[52] The use of in-kind payments for machine threshing rarely lasted, though, for more than a few years. Occasionally, farmers and the machinery operators disagreed over the amount of the threshed crop. (Automatic weighers on the threshing machine that alleviated, though did not entirely solve, this problem were not widely adopted until the 1890s.) In 1847, a Mercer County, Illinois, landowner, John Drury, paid his thresherman one-tenth of the threshed crop. Threshing took place in April, and on the 24th Drury wrote that "Mr. Doke [the thresherman] got on this day and before this 22 bushels of wheat for thrashing and wants 5 more." On June 18 appears the following entry: "Friend Doke called on me for the balance of his wheat that I promised him—but not having the wheat and finding that he had only threshed 192 bushels and having paid him for thrashing 220, the case was turned over for future consideration."[53] While few disagreements over charges required legal solutions, in-kind payments by crop percentage were not compatible with mechanical threshing systems. Sometimes there were differences in agreeing on the weight of a bushel of grain. On September 22, 1882, Benjamin Linvill documented the results of threshing on his

Cabel, Ohio, farm: "had 455 [bushels] machine measure or about 425 bu. by weight."[54] Most farmers did not immediately weigh the grain and place it in bushel sacks but stored the threshed crop in a granary. Total crop yields were not finally determined until producers delivered the grain to market or mill. The interval between threshing and use of the crop explains why John Drury did not know the total of his April threshing until June. Threshermen did not condone the lengthy lapse before weighing grain because it forced them to wait for payment.[55] Further, grain could be lost in transport from the machine to the granary and then to market, or suffer from poor storage facilities and the depredations of barn vermin.

Machine owners needed cash as a return for their services in order to meet notes on their equipment, provide wages for their crew, and pay for new items or repairs. Few merchants or agents of implement companies accepted grain as barter or payments on machine purchases after 1860. Thus, from the beginning of itinerant threshing practices or soon after the system began, threshermen expected cash payment for their work. They customarily charged by the bushel threshed, a rate system maintained until the adoption of the combine. Payment scales varied between threshermen and changed yearly according to current market prices. Threshing charges between 1830 and 1860 averaged three to five cents per bushel of wheat, buckwheat, and barley, two to four cents for oats, and three to six cents for rye.[56]

A new and popular system initiated by itinerant threshermen during the middle portions of the nineteenth century was the charge by the "setting." The term is derived from the common method of positioning the machinery prior to threshing from grain stored in open-air stacks. Farmers arranged their stacks in adjacent pairs, with enough space within each pair or between each row to "set" the threshing machine and power in the middle. Four stacks threshed typically required two settings, the number of times the threshing machine and power had to be moved and set; six stacks connoted three sets, and so on.[57] Pulling the machine and power to a farm and placing it in position to thresh involved a good deal of time and effort on the part of the machinery crew. Operators therefore established a minimum rate for any setting and a base charge of one full setting fee per farm. Rates varied from $4.00 to $7.00 during the middle decades of the nineteenth century. The "setting" system remained in use well into the twentieth century in areas where farmers continued to request small stack jobs. In Jackson County, Indiana, Kenneth Tracey threshed from the stack with minimum "setting" prices until farmers began using combines. In 1938, his fee was $3.00; by 1947, his last year in the business, Tracey charged $7.50 for a "set job" of wheat, rye, or oats.[58]

Under a formula charge of four cents per bushel of wheat, a farmer needed to thresh 125 bushels of wheat to approximate a five-dollar setting fee. Settlers with self-sufficient operations sometimes found the minimum charge prohibitive in light of a small acreage or a poor yield. In Rock

County, Minnesota, where Norwegian immigrants established small farms in the 1850s, landowners raised grain only for home and farm use. Threshermen working in the area charged a five-dollar minimum per setting. The first-generation immigrants felt that this charge did not suit their agricultural style, and they continued to flail "as done in the old country" until they increased their grain acreages in the mid-1860s.[59] Other farmers continued to flail and tread their crops after a local thresherman offered his services because they were reluctant to have their crop threshed at one time and did not want to pay the thresherman the minimum charges for each return visit to their grain stacks. In essence, the minimum yield required to warrant use of threshing machines was higher than the amount of grain needed to support average self-sufficient operations. The expense of periodic settings in relation to farming practice supported a delay in technological innovation until appropriate changes occurred in general agricultural patterns. Threshing machines became more universally used throughout the Midwest when the majority of families raised grain as a commercial venture or increased their stock numbers to levels requiring a larger feed crop.[60]

Farmers also complained about the poor quality of the straw and grain after it passed through the threshing machine cylinder. Rural residents found mechanically threshed straw difficult to preserve and inferior to the by-product produced by flailing or treading. Farmers who threshed their entire crop at one time and required straw for bedding and feed had to find some means of preserving large piles for use throughout the winter. Many farmsteads did not include barns with enough mow room for straw storage. Competition for available space increased as threshing became a fall chore and thus coincided with the time of year when farmers required available mows to lay away hay for winter use. No matter how families preserved machine-threshed straw, it lost nutritional value over time. An Indiana farmer wrote in 1843 that machines were appropriate for larger-acreage farmers who wanted access to early markets, but "such [farms] as have stock in winter, I fancy will see little profit in [the machines]. . . . *Cattle like horse threshed straw better than any other*, and where it can be done through the winter, and fed out from the floor, a snug tidy job is made of it."[61]

Most nineteenth-century farmers reserved a portion of their crop as seed for the next year's planting and hesitated to use machines to thresh their entire crop as long as they feared that the mechanical process damaged the seed. Early comparisons of machine- versus hand- or horse-threshed grain used to sow the next year's crop concluded often that the manual techniques produced a superior seed. In an 1850 discussion of how much seed to sow per acre, a correspondent to the *Valley Farmer* (St. Louis, Mo.) called for "a bushel and a half, if threshed with a flail, or trodden out by horses. . . . If the seed was threshed with a machine, two bushels per acre was necessary."[62] Most experimenters attributed problems with machine-threshed seeds to the cracking and breaking of the grain as it passed through the cylinder and concave teeth. A northern Indiana operator warned in 1843 that the "new machines, before the edges of the teeth are worn smooth, will destroy the vital principle of many kernels, but that old machines will not injure grain seed more than the flail."[63] Other farmers observed poor seed performance but could not so easily explain the damage. One grain producer in Jefferson County, Ohio, described an 1845 experiment using seed from both machine and tramping methods. He reported to readers of the *Ohio Cultivator* that "that tramped out came up first, and covered the ground soonest, looked best, until harvest, and ripened about three days first." At harvest he found about one-fifth more wheat on the ground sown with tramped wheat seed. He added:

> Some persons, perhaps, say there were the most broken grains in that thrashed by the machine. I took the pains to clean it all through a Cockle sieve as long as a small grain or broken one would pass through, so that I believe the seed was alike pure and sound. I am unable to account for the result, unless the friction in passing through the machine injures the germ of the grain.[64]

Some farmers in Ohio and Indiana responded to this problem by flailing or treading the portion of the crop marked for seed, and machine threshing the remainder.[65]

Farmers' objections against the immediate adoption of threshing devices centered around the quality of the work, availability and expense of a thresherman, and notions of the proper time for grain threshing within annual agricultural cycles. These concerns were based on individual comparisons with existing practices and concepts of an ideal farming system. The contemporary traditions reconsidered in light of mechanical alternatives included techniques and attitudes developed in other parts of the country or, even, regions of the world. The lack of long, continuous traditions in the Midwest likely eased the evolution and adoption of new practices and ideas, because minimal conflicts occurred between mechanical technologies and existing local patterns.[66] The period of farm establishment and solidification in the middle decades of the nineteenth century coincided with the widespread availability of mechanical innovations in almost every agricultural process. Apart from members of isolated utopian and religious communities, the families settling the Midwest were generally eager to establish economically successful farms on the basis of a commercial market economy. Emigrants left older settled areas in other parts of the United States because of limited or deficient land; immigrants fled Europe in many cases because of the lack of economic freedom. The available lands attracted people who "were not fleeing the machine; they were opening the areas in which it could operate."[67]

There is scant evidence that the introduction of the threshing machine

The Mechanization of Threshing 37

ever stimulated any grassroots antiindustrial verbiage or symbolic debate over the social or cultural consequences of mechanization. Moreover, any antitechnological ideals circulating in the nineteenth century, such as those first described by Leo Marx in *The Machine in the Garden*, had no identifiable impact on midwestern threshing complexes.[68] It was only by the middle decades of the present century, generations after the initial commitment to mechanized farming, that there was any overt expression of dissatisfaction on the part of regional farmers participating in technological revolutions. Interestingly, twentieth-century writers attempting to portray oppositions or conflicts within early threshing mechanization situations usually emphasize a conservative minority interest standing in stark (and typically feeble) contrast to the majority's infatuation with agricultural machines. The principal actors holding forth against change in this schema are preachers, women, and an occasional Old World immigrant dissatisfied with the new American trends.[69] These spokespersons do not argue against the pragmatic aspects of mechanical innovations; thus, their stance reveals a lack of understanding of the technological variables that are the central concerns of the adopters themselves. Instead, their stance rests on social or religious grounds, such as placing winnowing machines in opposition to "God's wind" or threshing machines in contrast to the few descriptions of Biblical threshing.[70] For a number of reasons, including the general push towards rationalization and industrial enlightenment in the nineteenth century, such arguments had little impact on the general progress of midwestern agricultural mechanization.

Threshing machinery stimulated overt change in a major agricultural task, but it did not impose upon the rural landscape. The complete separator remained relatively small, innocuous, and relatively danger-free. Nestled on its own carriage and pulled by horses, it did not require new transport routes or vehicles or pollute the environment with dirt or noise beyond the immediate workplace. The device was also a specialized tool designed to be applicable in only a limited context, and the techniques required for machine use were neither radically discontinuous with already familiar rural skills nor necessary acquisitions for each farmer desiring to change his threshing process. Therefore, while creating a potential for change in the threshing complex, mechanization did not directly encroach on other spheres of agricultural or rural activity during the early adoption period. The specialty of threshing innovation is balanced, of course, by the fact that speeding the threshing process stimulated farmers to use increasingly complex machinery in other components of the grain cycle. The ability to process so much grain inevitably promoted the discovery and adoption of new ways to more quickly sow and reap.[71]

The ease of adapting to threshing innovations can also be attributed in part to the basic mechanical properties of the devices and the rapid growth of a group of itinerant custom operators. Farmers lacked the ability to construct threshing devices or make major repairs, but many men understood how the machine and power worked. The treadmills and sweep powers harnessed to threshing machines during the early adoption period utilized sources and systems familiar to traditional sensibilities. And the early separators were not the great technological mysteries or potential threats to customary habits and knowledge that such later farm innovations as steam engines or tractors were. The adoption of any new device occurs only after the necessary spread of knowledge to utilize it. In the Midwest, the growth of a class of itinerant threshermen eased the shift from hand to mechanical threshing. The abilities of a minority of men allowed the majority to take advantage of the innovation without becoming mechanical experts. Many early itinerant threshermen were local farmers who chose to purchase machines to increase their incomes. Not all operators possessed the technical or business expertise to become successful, yet adoption of the devices did not require a special class of experts from outside rural communities.

III.

NINETEENTH-CENTURY STACK THRESHING

Farmers' oral and written accounts of threshing days in the nineteenth century typically distinguish between "barn threshing" with mowed grain, "stack threshing," and "shock threshing." The modifiers designate alternative processes for storing reaped grain prior to carrying the cured bundles to the threshing machine. Stacking and mowing are Old World harvest patterns originally characteristic of, respectively, the British Isles and Central Europe. The ability to continue these traditional techniques in the Midwest inhibited wider cultural disruptions due to threshing mechanization because use of machines did not wholly disturb existing harvest procedures or require farmers to learn new harvest skills. "Mowing" involved the orderly laying of grain bundles in storage areas above or beside the threshing floor.[1] The practice required farmers to have ample mow room and thus was favored only on farms with the larger banked, three-bay, or tripartite barns large enough for crop storage. Farmers "barn threshed" in intervals through the winter with the aid of small tread powers placed on the floor between the grain mow and another area set aside for housing straw. "Stack threshing" refers to the crop-storage system dominating the region until at least 1880 and practiced in some areas well into the twentieth century. Farmers loaded tied grain bundles onto wagons in the field and brought them to an area in or near the barnyard where the stack builders carefully laid the sheaves in patterned piles of circular or rectangular design (see photo, p. 40).[2]

Stack threshing with the aid of an itinerant threshing rig including a sweep power became popular in the mid-1850s and remained the regional norm until 1890. Typical labor crews consisted of eight to fourteen workers, including the two to four men who accompanied the traveling rig. The "host farmer"[3] filled the rest of the labor force with members of his family, hired men, or other neighborhood residents. Two to four men worked on the grain stacks, one or two band-cutters cut the sheaves at the machine, one worker fed the bundles into the threshing cylinder, two to four people worked on the straw pile, one or two participants cleared the threshed grain away from the machine, and one person "drove" the horses on the power.

The "stackmen" or "stack pitchers" moved the bundles from the stacks to the "feeding tables" or "bundle shelves" of the separator. The shelves extended like small wings away from the threshing cylinder opening at the front of the machine. "Taking down" a new stack required two men to pitch bundles from each pile. One worker climbed to the peak and pitched the sheaves down one at a time to the other man positioned at the base near the machine. Pitchers attempted to remove bundles in the reverse order of stack construction in order to prevent the pile from toppling and to help preserve its rain-shedding abilities in case of a sudden storm. The second man, sometimes called the "table man," picked up each sheaf with his hand or fork and laid the bundle, with the grain heads pointed towards the cylinder, on the feeding shelves.[4]

A band-cutter stood on a small platform or stool in front of each feeding table. He maneuvered each sheaf forward to the cylinder side of the table, making sure that the heads were properly laid towards the cylinder. At the same time, the cutter severed the bundle tie with one quick slash of a hand-held knife. The "feeder" working in front of the separator opening grabbed the sheaves and manually placed them into the threshing concave. The band-cutters and feeder needed to establish a close work harmony because

Building a grain stack in central Ohio, ca. 1900.

Nineteenth-Century Stack Threshing

Stack threshing with three stackmen, two band-cutters, and a feeder in central Ohio, ca. 1900.

bundles started to open as soon as the knife blade cut through the sheaf tie. Two or three extra gathering motions would be necessary if the feeder failed to grasp the whole bundle on his first reach towards the spreading grain.[5] The band-cutter had to be especially careful that his motion to slash the tie did not coincide with his partner's grab for the bundle, as poor synchronization resulted in knife cuts to the feeder's hand or arm. Men who worked with these crews recall that threshing groups preferred to have one left-handed and one right-handed band-cutter, so that the slashing knife always fell to the outside of the feeder's position.[6]

The sharp-edged blades favored by band-cutters ranged from common jackknives to homemade tools that over time might earn a special local reputation. A piece of twine or leather attached to the handle and wrapped around the cutter's hand prevented the knife from slipping into the machinery or flying towards the feeder. The handles were generally rounded and between four and eight inches long. Some workers fashioned the blades of their knives from a tooth of a mower sickle bar because the piece's serrated edge provided a strong cutting surface. They embedded the blade in a slot cut into a short wooden handle and lashed it in place with a leather thong or length of treated rawhide (photo, p. 42).[7] Other band-cutters favored a hooked blade that caught the binding on the downward thrust and then cut through as they pulled the knife back towards their bodies.[8]

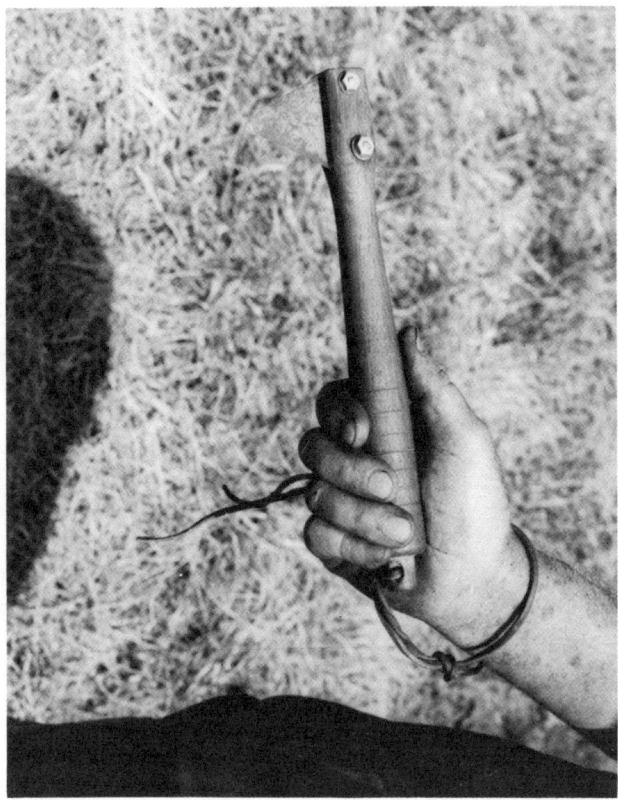

A threshing crew member in eastern Indiana fashioned this eight-inch band-cutter's knife made from a discarded mower bar tooth

All cutting instruments were sure to be dulled by slicing through an endless succession of straw or twine bands. Each man carried his own whetstone or other sharpening surface and made frequent use of it, as the need to make two or three strokes to sever a band increased the chances of cutting the feeder's hand.

Band-cutting required precise movement and continuous action, but it did not demand the physical stamina of taking down grain stacks or handling the threshed straw. Farmers often placed younger participants as band-cutters, and experienced men viewed the task as the most appropriate position for indoctrinating novices into the threshing crew. Crews viewed the job as a good learning context because a band-cutter worked between the stackmen and feeder, and thus he was not a major influence on the threshing speed. As long as the cutter did his job correctly, and the feeder working near him provided constant and instant corrections for improper actions, the new threshing member could soon feel part of the crew. Joe

Meachem remembers his grandfather's boast that in his first year with a Montgomery County, Ohio, crew he "never drew a drop of blood off of the feeder all season."[9] Dan Jones cut bands as a teenager in Jackson County, Ohio. He recalls both the initial thrill of being "almost a man working alongside other men" and the trying circumstances under which he labored:

> When the machine was running well there was no time for a shift in position, or even a glance away from the stream of bundles from the load. Butts raked across my face, sweat trickled in my eyes, my legs ached from the unvarying strain. My skin itched from the chaff that sifted inside my shirt. Still there was no relief.... The rule was one band, one slash.[10]

Threshing crews considered the feeder's position as the most significant job in the work hierarchy. He generally held ultimate authority over the entire operation and often owned the threshing rig. The feeder regulated the machine's action and took responsibility for its maintenance and repair. And he alone received the title of "thresherman" during the age of horse-power threshing.[11] The threshing machine was a nexus between the growing industrial complex and rural society. Few other agricultural devices of the period contained the technological complexity of the complete separator, and the man controlling the feeding and care of the machine earned a reputation as a mechanic, an increasingly prestigious social recognition in rural areas during the nineteenth century. Horse-power threshing groups reserved the second position in their crew hierarchy for the driver, whose main duty involved keeping the power running at a steady pace. As Iowan LeRoy Shutes stated it: "The 'Power Boss' was important, but the 'Thrasher Boss' was the one who ran the show, he was the boss."[12] The ability to handle eight to twelve horses on the sweeps was certainly deserving of respect in a society where animals were the primary source of power for most farm tasks. The sweep driver garnered acclaim for mastering a significant, albeit familiar, rural trade, yet his distance from the thresher and its activity was greater than the slender connections of tumbling rods.

The feeder worked at a table centered in front of the cylinder (see Photo 9). From this position he reached across or back to the band-cutters for the opening bundle, fanned out the grain heads in a semicircular pattern, and pushed them heads first down a feedboard slanting towards the toothed threshing cylinder. Feeders spread the bundle across the face of the separator opening because even distribution of the threshing action around the cylinder required less power to force the sheaves through the threshing drum. Efficient threshermen paid special attention to the particular qualities of each farmer's crop. They spread damp bundles more loosely and shook them as they entered the machine. Very rank bundles were held by the stems while the grain was threshed and were then pulled back, and the straw was thrown aside. Feeders exercised extreme caution in this motion because the spinning cylinder with its curved teeth could easily mutilate hands placed haphazardly around a bundle.[13]

The feeder's pace provided the final determination of the speed and quality of threshing. By listening closely to the sounds of the grain passing through the machine, threshermen determined how quickly new bundles could be pushed into the threshing cavity. Careless men who crammed in the sheaves stalled or choked the device, a cardinal offense requiring a slow hand-clearing of the cylinder. Crowded bushels were also more likely to pass through the initial mechanical steps without complete threshing of the grains.[14] If for any reason a sudden stop was required, though, the feeder purposely choked the cylinder. Steady movements kept the cylinder humming smoothly and constantly. As one former Ohio feeder remarked: "It was one of them jobs when you always had to be on the job"[15] Because of the difficulty of the feeder's task, two or three members of the machine crew sometimes alternated in the position.

The "straw crew" took responsibility for clearing away the ever-growing pile from the back of the machine and building it into stacks near the barn. Although farmers recognized "straw work" as among the most difficult of all threshing tasks, they took special care in building their winter straw stacks. An axiom for determining farm worth and agricultural expertise in the nineteenth-century Midwest was the quality and form of the straw pile. Neighbors regarded haphazard stacks as "wasteful and the sign of a poor farmer."[16] Threshermen or host farmers hiring master straw stackers paid them higher wages than the rates given for general threshing labor. Few grain raisers hired a man solely for this task, however, as most crews allowed the host farmer to direct the formation of his own straw stacks. This custom continued into the twentieth century and suggests the importance of the straw pile and the recognition that each farmer had his own concept of proper stack construction.

It took two or three men to handle the steady stream of straw produced with an eight-horse power. The earliest threshing devices, appropriately nicknamed "chaff pilers" in some areas, simply dumped the straw and chaff out of the back of the machine. The straw crew labored under hot and dirty conditions because threshermen set their machines with "the tail downwind to prevent the chaff from blowing back on the other workers."[17] Moving and dragging the discharge to the specified stack locations entailed continuous labor with pitchfork. A smoothly running machine provided no respite, as straw accumulating at the back of the separator could quickly dam the discharge and interfere with the threshing quality. Some early threshing crews, including one formed in Bureau County, Illinois, in the 1870s, used a "bucking" system to drag away the straw.

> I was kept out of school in order to ride the bucking rail, a pole ten feet long, to the ends of which was attached a rope with plenty of belly room. A horse was hitched to this rope. Driving around to the rear of the machine,

and standing on that pole, I gathered up a large pile of straw and bucked it to the pile.[18]

The straw from the machine fell into the "belly" space between the "bucking rail" and the horse.

Most threshing machines produced after 1860 included a chain-driven straw carrier equipped with an endless webbed belt to drop the straw a short distance away. Men pulling the straw from the machine now had to take care that the tines of their forks did not get caught in the chain driving the carriers. Accidents resulted in the chain being flipped off its sprockets or, worse, the fork tines becoming enmeshed in the chain and bending the links enough to require "downtime" repairs.[19] Straw carriers eased the crew's task by elevating the discharge to a height of six to twelve feet. Yet even with improved carriers, two or three men kept busy moving the straw around the stack or to the top of the expanding pile. Various innovations patented over the last decades of the nineteenth century improved the reach of the carriers (illus. below). By 1875, the Gaar Company of Richmond, Indiana, and other manufacturers sold machines equipped with an extended carrier that folded in half during transportation. J. I. Case later introduced a swiveling folding elevator that rode on its own carriage behind the separator.[20] Longer web carriers deposited the discharge far enough away from the machine to negate the need for horses, bucking poles, or other systems to move the straw. Most devices still dumped their contents in one spot, and stackers continued to labor directly behind the machine.

Swiveling stacker-elevator advertised in an Aultman-Taylor Company (Masillon, Ohio) catalogue in 1895.

They formed the center base of the stack by allowing the straw to fall in a loose pile and then tramping it down. The most popular stack design included a low profile built perpendicular to the threshing machine setting. Stackers worked largely at the pile's middle, constantly tramping the straw and packing the center more solidly than the edges to build a stack that shed water to the outside. Farmers topped off straw piles with rounded caps resembling the peak constructions on common grain stacks or ricks.[21]

Straw crew members can often be identified in photographs of early threshing crews by a layer of chaff and straw pieces on their clothes and, more noticeably, the presence of bandanas tied around their necks. The handkerchiefs were lifted over their faces as protection from the swirling dust and chaff. The danger of contracting respiratory illnesses, often called "dust chills," was most prevalent when men worked close to machines not equipped with any straw carrier. Threshing participants tried several kinds of local remedies. Albert Merkle's grandfather, an early settler in Dubois County, Indiana, made light cotton face masks with holes cut for vision.[22] A Butler County, Ohio, man described another solution in 1847:

> To protect the lungs in thrashing, H. N. Lowry, in the *Ohio Cultivator*, gives the following mode, which is perfectly effectual. A piece of the finest sponge, large enough to cover the mouth and nostril, is hollowed out so as to fit closely; a tape is fastened round and tied over the top of the head. Soak it in soft water, and then squeeze it well. When ready for work, tie it over nose and mouth, and you can breathe and talk through it almost as well as without; and in a perfect fog of dust, the air will be as clear as in a cornfield. He states that it will, however, prove troublesome to those who use the "filthy weed."[23]

Careful attention by farmers to their stacks reflects the continuing importance of straw to nineteenth-century midwestern agricultural operations. Only a minority of farmers, generally men in western prairie regions who kept little stock, typically burned their threshing by-product or returned it to the field without first putting it to some other use. The majority favored newly threshed straw as an inexpensive, nutritious feed. Rush County, Indiana, farmer John Arnold documented his use of neighbors' stacks in the spring of 1860:

> January 7—Took six yearlings and one heifer from W. Logan's strawstack. Paid him $4 for the strawstack. Turned 15 head of cattle to Jerry Stark's strawstack at 60c per month.
>
> 19—Took seven head of cattle and turned them to the strawstack I bought from Loyd for $5.
>
> February 7—Took eight head from Stark's, turned the five steers to Loyd's and brought three cows home.

March 14— Brought cattle home from Loyd's and began feeding them hay; most of them in good condition. Loyd's stack had 18¾ months feed, and as I gave him $5 for it, it cost me only 27c per month so that I made a good bargain.[24]

Families fed fresh straw, particularly from oat threshing, to stock during the weeks following threshing. Later, they added bran, grain, or other supplements to improve the nutritional content. Most of the wheat straw went into the stables and barns for bedding. Farmers then gathered up the used bedding, now enriched with important manure fertilizer, and either returned it directly to the fields or placed it in a stack to await springtime spreading.

Rural residents used machine-threshed straw for other traditional domestic and commercial uses. Families took the material to fill ticks (mattresses) and solidify the cores of horse collars. Women in the Ashton area of Lee County, Illinois, established a cottage industry based on the use of threshed straw for the fabrication of straw hats.[25] Rural residents rarely thatched the roofs of houses or outbuildings in the Midwest, but for this purpose thatchers required unblemished rye or oat straw. Finally, farmers increasingly found markets for their straw among townspeople requiring feed and bedding for their horses and through company agents collecting raw materials for paper and bag manufacturing. The sale of straw for papermaking did not have any sizeable impact on the region's economy until the later portions of the nineteenth century. By the early 1900s, most companies wanted baled straw, particularly rye for the brown paper bag industry, for which they paid farmers four to six cents per bale.[26]

As most threshing machine owners expected to be paid by the number of bushels threshed, crews gave one man the task of collecting and measuring the exiting grain with half-bushel or one-bushel basket measures. Generally an older farmer with a reputation for honesty filled the position; he was rarely an employee of either the machine owner or host farmer.[27] Midwestern farmers stored their threshed grain in granaries or in sacks. The measurer kept a running tally of the crop as he dumped it into a wagon box or two-bushel bag. One popular accounting system involved the use of a board with rows of holes and pegs for keeping track by the half-bushel, single bushels, tens of bushels, and hundreds of bushels. As he filled and dumped his measures, the man kept tally by moving his pegs. This system became so well-known that some threshing machine companies later provided a pegboard with their separators.[28] Bagging the crop required at least two more additional workers to hold the sacks for the measurer, tie or stitch the filled bags, load the sacks on wagons, and deliver them to the granary.

Each farmer did not have to master the whole range of skills in order to participate in the adoption of mechanical separators, because itinerant machines were always accompanied by a two- to four-person crew. A two-man "machine crew" took responsibility for the feeder and driver's positions. The more common three- or four-man unit took care of the band-cutting, feeding, and operation of the power. Farmers preferred larger machine crews because of the need for the band-cutter and feeder to act in practiced harmony. The labor group assembled by each farmer handled the bound sheaves, threshed grain, and straw. Each responsibility demanded certain skills, yet none of the general threshing crew tasks required either direct contact with machinery or prior understanding of mechanical processes. Indeed, pitching sheaves from a stack and building straw piles were familiar agricultural tasks, albeit in association with different harvest procedures. The role of band-cutter had no rural precedent, but it demanded no special technological responsibility or knowledge. In summary, the use of itinerant machines in combination with the labor requirements of stack threshing enabled farmers to participate in early mechanization without becoming "machine literate" and without the need to learn a whole new set of occupational skills.

Organizing the Threshing Crew

The change in labor requirements from flailing or treading to machine threshing stimulated major changes in the social organization of the threshing season. The usual two to four workers used to flail or tread generally quadrupled under threshing with the itinerant machines becoming popular by the 1860s. As the nuclear or extended family rarely contained the necessary number of laborers, threshing styles became dependent for the first time on wider community reciprocal participation or hiring a large crew of temporary workers. Further, machine owners did not like to bring their rigs into the same neighborhood at intermittent times. Itinerant operators encouraged the farmers in each neighborhood to arrange their threshing in one continuous period. As most men exchanged labor with at least some of their neighbors, each farmer began to set aside a block of days to thresh his own crop and return reciprocal labor obligations while the machine was in the area. The threshing season thus became increasingly compressed into a shared designated time sequence with an annual, relatively fixed position within local agricultural cycles.

The cohesive cooperative groups that older rural residents today normally associate with precombine threshing in the twentieth century did not develop concomitantly with the initial adoption of the separator. The early decades of mechanization are characterized instead by the existence of heterogeneous threshing styles reflecting subregional social and cultural differences. One important cause of local variation was the diversity of systems that farmers used to assemble the necessary number of laborers. During the transitionary period to horse-powered threshing devices, hand

Nineteenth-Century Stack Threshing

Twelve workers posed for this photograph of stack threshing with a 14-horse sweep in Buffalo County, Nebraska. Courtesy of Nebraska Historical Society.

and mechanical processes were often carried on in the same neighborhood. With most farmers developing diversified operations that stressed self-sufficiency in daily work tasks, the first men to hire threshing machines were often those landowners who opted to hire the necessary crew and provide boarding. When farmers added the thresherman's cost and responsibilities of organization to the fees for hired labor, they sometimes discovered that the new pattern compared inferiorly to older manual methods. An Ohio farmer complained to readers of the *American Agriculturalist* in 1858 that "with a machine, if the rate is 6 cents a bushel, the farmer has to supply three or four hands and perhaps a horse or two. This could double or treble the price per bushel (also meals must be provided)."[29] Two years earlier, northeast Missouri farmer George King made some interesting comparisons between the costs of machine and flail threshing:

> The ordinary price for threshing wheat with the traveling machines here is five cents per bushel, the owner of the machine having with it two men and four horses that the farmer must feed. The farmer must provide six more horses, and from five to eight men—say an average of seven. All the expenses will bring the cost of threshing to ten cents a bushel. . . . Wheat makes so good a comparison for the machine, for ten cents is just a fair price for

flailing out wheat in the winter, the thrasher binding up the long straw, and feeding short straw during the day to the cattle. . . . Barley can be thrashed with a flail for three cents less than by machine. Oats about the same.[30]

A farmer might experiment with a number of different plans before deciding on an appropriate model for his operation. The availability of alternative powers allowed each family to compare the costs of itinerant threshing with the expense of purchasing their own treadmill power and small separator. Men accustomed to hiring all extra laborers tended to favor barn threshing with a one- or two-horse treadmill, because the work proceeded with fewer workers and animals. A western Ohio farmer explained his choice in 1850:

> My attention has been called to the great disadvantage under which the farmer labors in threshing their wheat. . . . I was led to contemplation of the subject some years since, while assisting one of my neighbors in threshing. First he hired a large six-horse machine, with two men and two horses, for $5 per 100 bushels; then two men to rake straw, one to pitch from the stack, one to cut bands, one to get the wheat away from the machine, and a boy to fetch water, &c. two of his neighbor's horses, and two of his own, making

Six men at one dollar per day,	$6,00
One boy,	,50
Four horses, at fifty cents,	2,00
Board for nine men,	2,00
Board for six horses	2,00
	12,50

> We threshed 150 bushels that day, which was doing very well—although I have heard very large stories about threshing. Now add for machine, at $5 per 100 bushels, $7,50. Total for threshing 150 bushels is $20,00. Equal to 13 ½ cents per bushel; besides enough unnecessarily wasted to pay for threshing in the old fashioned way with a flail. We readily see that this enormous enterprise in threshing is ruinous to the farmers and consequently to the country. Now I would recommend small machines, which can be managed and run at much less expense in proportion to what they will thresh. A machine with mill properly constructed will thresh 50 bushels a day with one horse and two men and a boy, without material waste and without extra exertion and preparation attendant on the present mode. The one-horse mill will be utilized to best advantage when set in the barn and used when convenient for the farmer.[31]

Interestingly, the decrease in total labor hours and, therefore, potential wage losses to agricultural laborers as a result of threshing mechanization did not inhibit the adoption of sweep powers and separators in the Midwest. In sections of England, in contrast, generations of a sizeable group of landless laborers hand threshed the crops of farmers at the end of the harvest season. The widespread adoption of threshing machines in south and central England beginning in the 1820s denied these workers a considerable portion of their income during a season when there were few other employment possibilities. Work displacements sometimes resulted in violent countermeasures on the part of the landless rural class, particularly in some southern sections, where farm groups led by "Captain Swing" organized concentrated efforts to destroy threshing machines.[32] Few such demonstrative complaints occurred in the American Midwest, where, in general, only a minority of farmers relied on an itinerant class of workers for threshing during the period of flailing and treading. Agricultural laborers responded more vocally, and in some cases with equipment destruction, to widespread reaping mechanization in the late 1870s because a greater number of men had previously been employed to reap, rake, bind, shock, and stack the region's grain harvest.[33] A condemnation of the impact of mechanized reapers appearing in the Ohio State Agricultural Report for 1859 contains a rare allusion to labor displacements created by the adoption of threshing machines:

> Every one of the 'harvest hands' deliberately marched out of the field and told the proprietor that he might secure his crop as best he could; that the threshing machine had deprived them of their regular winter work twenty years ago, and now the reaper would deprive them of the pittance they otherwise would earn during harvest.[34]

Indeed, the region's farmers complained commonly of difficulty in finding the necessary numbers to help with the grain harvest and threshing. Rural men and families that could not acquire farms at the time of concentrated introduction and spread of threshing machines tended to find better occupational opportunities outside of their local area. They could homestead in unsettled or sparsely populated lands or emigrate to industrial employment in the region's growing cities.[35] The availability of free or inexpensive land and the drain of men due to the Civil War created severe labor shortages and high wages that spurred adoption of the threshing machine and other rural labor-saving devices. Labor rates almost doubled in many cases between 1855 and 1865.[36] In general, the Midwest rural labor pool was limited to confirmed bachelors, beginning farmers trying to raise cash to finance their own operations, men passing through the area looking for seasonal employment, and unemployed town men looking for temporary work.

The ability of farm families to employ familiar preexisting networks for reciprocating labor to meet the labor requirements of mechanization helps explain the lack of cultural and social disruption created by the adoption of threshing machines into midwestern agricultural cycles. Regional systems of mutual aid provided readily comprehensible and socially acceptable patterns that farmers managed to extend to provide the work force necessary for threshing. As a general rule, the host farmer had the authority to choose his coworkers. Although reciprocal labor systems for threshing resulted in some continuity in each locale, the group's make-up changed on every farm according to the size of the host farmer's family and the "calling in" of "short time" owed by neighbors. The diaries of Laura and Albert McKee detailing their farm operations near Murphy, Ohio, in the early 1850s reveal this dominant midwestern style. Threshing on the sixty-five-acre farm in 1851 took place on September 16 with the work of "Albert, Erastus, John Otis, James Dulin, Orvin Arariah, 2 Mormon Boys," and a machine operated by a Mr. Davidson. Of this crew, Albert is the host farmer, Erastus is his brother, and John Otis is a hired man employed at a monthly rate for the harvest season. Later entries note that John Otis threshed at the Dulin and Arariah farms, and accounts with the "2 Mormon Boys" were paid by "75 cents labor for one day each." The documentation suggests that the threshing crews at the Dulin and Arariah farms were composed differently, as only one of the three home workers on the McKee farm lent his help. The continuing participation of the "2 Mormon Boys" is not mentioned. The McKees also sent their hired man to help thresh for two other farmers, Starr and Benjamin, who do not appear as part of the home threshing crew. A "Starr boy" is listed, however, in two entries for helping to "set-up" (shock) wheat and cut oats in August, and Benjamin also owned a local sawmill frequented by the McKee family.[37]

The networks of work-exchange patterns could be quite complex. In Van Buren County, Iowa, George Duffield kept careful records of his labor exchanges during the 1868 harvest seasons. He began threshing on September 1 and finished the next day. Duffield's entry for September 2 reads: "Threshed had 209 [bushels] fall Wheat 32 Spring [wheat, and] Oats 36 bushels. Jeff Miller A. Drummond two [days each] Drineau & E. Scotten Helped one day Each. W. [the hired hand] one day." The next day Duffield sent "W." to thresh with Miller in the "forenoon" and Scotten in the afternoon. There are no reports of Drummond's threshing, but Duffield spent July 20–22 and 27–29 exchanging stacking at the Drummond farm. He also reciprocated stacking and cradling work with Scotten and Thorton.[38] Farmers always found a way to repay labor obligations, even if the nature of the reciprocal work was not similar between farms.

Other mid-nineteenth-century labor-exchange patterns are more difficult to reconstruct, as accounts were squared over long periods of time and often through complex and flexible substitutions of barter and goods. Diary and journal accounts typically reveal major differences between the names listed as supplying aid at the home threshing and those neighbors receiving labor donated by the diary-keeper's family. Yet even with all the vagaries of local exchange systems, there is little doubt that farmers viewed threshing as another rural task in which reciprocal relations played a strong role. Further, they did not regard the threshing cycle as a closed system in which all accounts for labor had to be squared by the end of the threshing season. Neighborhood labor networks were facilitated by the occurrence of threshing at a time of the year when families required mutual aid to complete the grain and corn harvests. Rural residents found it feasible and practical simply to widen local reciprocal networks to include threshing.

Other customs exhibiting individual and neighborhood variation reflect the informality and flexibility of these traditional rural patterns. One common threshing trait throughout the Midwest for most of the nineteenth century was the host farmer's authority to assign labor tasks among the local participants called in to help. In contrast, the machinery owner portioned out specific responsibilities to the members of his itinerant crew, and each of these men kept his position throughout the run. As the personnel of the host farmer's crew changed typically from place to place, each group naturally contained different combinations of accumulated skills and experiences. Delegated labor responsibilities reflected the neighborhood nuances of reciprocal obligations, as well as each man's proven abilities. The host man might ask neighbors who "owed" more labor to provide a team for the power or a team and wagon for hauling grain away from the separator. The home man did not take any set labor job for himself; instead, he worked around the machine clearing up loose or poorly pitched sheaves and directed the construction of the valuable straw pile. Farmers wanted to be near the separator, where they could anxiously watch the bushel count that finally revealed how profitable (or miserable) the crop would be for that year.

A large crew gathered for stack threshing on the T. Newton farm in northwest Iowa in 1894. Courtesy of State Historical Society of Iowa.

A small minority of rural men rejected reciprocal work arrangements and instead either employed a machinery owner traveling with a sufficient work force to complete the threshing or hired a whole gang of temporary laborers. If the thresherman brought the entire crew, the host farmer took responsibility for handling the threshed grain and providing all of the meals for the general crew. Only wealthier farmers with larger market crops chose the option and expense of hiring their own threshing gang to work with an itinerant machine crew. These landowners traveled typically to a nearby population center two to four days before the threshing to make labor arrangements. From his farm in Bureau County, Illinois, James Broughton journeyed to the towns of Sheffield and Princeton to hire an average of ten day workers for his threshing in the 1850s.[39] In Montgomery County, Ohio, James Ellis made annual pilgrimages during the same decade to Dayton for his crew, while Edwin Warren, a farmer in the Rock Island area during the Civil War, employed hired hands from nearby East Moline.[40] All of these men farmed acreages well above the norm for their respective areas and typically hired temporary work crews for other seasonal tasks.

Farmers needing only an extra hand or two employed the services of small-acreage or beginning farmers in their neighborhoods. This pattern provided younger men with an opportunity to earn cash for their own operations and introduced the process of mechanical threshing to less-experienced landowners. Temporary work on threshing crews gave non-innovators a chance to see the power and separator at work, meet the threshermen, and consider the eventual use of machinery on their own farms. A normal sequence in Midwest threshing patterns at mid-century began with the use of a machine at infrequent intervals on the larger farms in a neighborhood, with the majority of the crews hired at daily rates. As more farmers in each area adopted the same technologies, former employees and employers began to exchange work, with an elimination of the wage relationship. In Gilmer Township of Adams County, Illinois, Charles Doringh raised an average of twenty-four to twenty-seven acres of wheat and thirty to thirty-five acres of oats on his Walnut Grove Farm between 1852 and 1858. His operation was larger than the county mean, although not among the areas largest acreages.[41] Doringh paid six local farmers for help with the threshing between 1852 and 1854. Four of these men—Henderson, Moore, Toller, and Casnell—appeared in his diaries after 1854 as farmers continuing to help with the threshing, but no payments for their services were listed in the ledger accounts. Doringh now sent his hired man (or men, though never himself) to help with the threshing at these farms. In this section of southern Illinois, 1854 appears to mark the beginning of the kind of cooperative neighborhood threshing group that operated throughout the Midwest by the last portions of the century.[42]

Two striking aspects of early machine accounts are the fluid setting within the calendar year and the length of time sometimes required to thresh out a farmer's crop. Present-day grain producers acclimatized to consistent summer and early fall threshing would be baffled by the frequency of late fall, winter, and spring dates between 1840 and 1880. Many itinerant threshermen around the Midwest during these decades began work soon after the harvest and provided their services intermittently through the following spring. Late dates were particularly common in the years immediately following adoption, as farmers attempted to retain the interval sessions characterizing premechanical styles. Mechanized threshing began on the Lewis Lesher farm near Carlisle, Ohio, in the early 1840s. He arranged for machines to thresh his 1846 wheat crop in four different months: 100 bushels on September 27, 156 bushels on January 25, 1847, 206 bushels on February 11, and 117¼ bushels on March 8.[43] Thomas Page threshed the greater part of the 1845 grain crop on his Lee County, Illinois, farm between April 27 and May 7 of the following spring. Although he reported that the machine did "not seem to work like it was supposed" to, Page never again cleared off a threshing floor after this first year of machine use.[44]

Carrying grain bundles to storage in stacks or barns contributed to the lack of a set threshing period soon after the grain harvest. With the crop safely set aside, farmers could get on with late summer and fall tasks and postpone their threshing work until a quieter period. From August through November, rural families occupied themselves with the corn cultivation and harvest, hay cutting and stacking, winter wheat plowing and planting, butchering, and the harvest of apple, flax, and tobacco crops. The ability to delay threshing became particularly appropriate as neighbors began to devote two or four weeks towards cooperative help at each other's farms. To arrange a schedule to thresh one's own crops and to return the favors of assisting neighbors was at best difficult while other summer and fall chores remained largely labor-intensive and manual tasks. Finally, farmers intending to use their grain and straw as stock feed preferred to allow the animals to forage for themselves as long as pastures remained sufficient. The fresh, newly threshed crop would be a more welcome dietary addition after early winter frosts decimated forage areas.

The difficulty of estimating how long the threshing at any farm would take also contributed to some farmers' desire to postpone threshing until more lax times in traditional agricultural cycles. Threshing delays were caused by nuances of the itinerant operator's schedule, machinery breakdowns, and the unpredictability of the weather. Implement advertisements for machines able to thresh 500 or more bushels a day cloak the realities of broken gearings, sudden showers, and other delays. On the Mitchell Young Jackson farm near Lakeland, Minnesota, home threshing of the 1855 crop began on December 10. The machine crew ended up staying for eleven days, all the time sharing food and sleeping quarters with the Jackson family. A total of 651 bushels, mostly oats, were threshed by December 21, for an average of fewer than 60 bushels per day.[45] Reports of farm experiences from eastern Ohio to western Illinois also document the machinery crew's presence for one or two weeks.[46] The potential strain on anxious families caused by threshing delays can be extracted from a three-week period in the 1842 diary of Samuel Sewall of Beardstown, Illinois. Sewall purchased his first machine in 1841; his five years as a thresherman were marked by persistent machinery and weather misfortunes.

> 10–13—Threshed and finished wheat for Adkins, and moved to Richardson's, near Dr. Chandlers.
> 10–14—Finding the horse power out of order, cannot thresh until next week.
> 10–19—Threshing for Richardson. The horse power broke down.
> 10–21—Threshing for Richardson. The horse power broke down.
> 10–24—At George Bonny's repairing machinery.
> 10–26—Finished repairing machinery.
> 10–27—George Bonny and myself put the machinery together.
> 10–28—Threshed oats for feed until dinner, after which I went to work on the wheat. Son Henry who is with me at the machine too sick, and could not be here in the afternoon.
> 10–29—Had a late start, and the machine got out of order several times. The machine went well when she did go.
> 10–31—Went to Richardson's, and threshed a little.
> 11–1—At Richardson's threshing.
> 11–3—Have threshed 400 or more bushels of wheat for Richardson, and the remainder he does not want threshed at this time.[47]

In spite of delays caused by their less-than-perfect machines, itinerant operators were the essential ingredient allowing the rapid diffusion of threshing mechanization. By providing their services and knowledge on a custom basis, they enabled many farmers to take advantage of an innovation they could neither afford to purchase nor justify as a permanent on-farm item. Itinerant practices also continued a traditional regional preference for the temporary employment or exchange of labor with master workers. Most mid-nineteenth-century communities in the rural Midwest included individuals who, in addition to their general agricultural knowledge, possessed practiced ability at one or more specialized tasks. No man could be expected to perfect all trades, especially those required for only a short period each year or associated with newly adopted or complex technological devices. Varying with local needs and subregional agricultural patterns, experts could usually be found for such jobs as cradling grain, stack building, apple cider and molasses making, butchering, sheep shearing, and fine carpentry. These men were called on to lend their expertise around the neighborhood; in return, they received reciprocal labor donations or, in cases of outright hiring by more wealthy farmers, direct wages. Each master's special craft was generally well-known to his neighbors, and the informal transmission of particular skills often occurred along familial lines.

Threshermen fit squarely within this traditional pattern. The overwhelming majority were area farmers who offered their knowledge and machinery only to nearby neighborhoods. The itinerant operator's role differed from that of master stack builders or cradlers, however, in that machinery owners performed a "custom" service on a contract basis and required monetary compensation. They operated similarly, in this respect, to men hired to break prairie, dig drainage ditches, erect windmills, and, later, build silos.[48] The uniqueness of the thresherman stemmed from his use of one of the first complex machines to become a familiar sight on the rural landscape. As threshing machinery became more complex, the owner and operator assumed an increasingly overt role as a middleman between local farmers and the traditional rural complex on one side and the urban industrial and popular culture complex on the other. Community member and itinerant contractor, farmer and mechanic, insider and influential, the thresherman at times held all of these roles.

In summary, many small- and mid-sized-acreage farmers first participated in the mechanization of Midwest agriculture through their use of threshing machines. The factors that supported the transition from hand to mechanical techniques are linked to wider social and cultural patterns and are not reflective solely of economic thresholds. Minimal disruption of existing norms occurred because of the opportunity for farmers to utilize itinerant threshing machines within familiar agricultural cycles, the existence of prior work-exchange networks to meet organizational requirements, and the development of a professional class of operators that freed farmers from having to acquire a new set of skills and knowledge. In a sense, regional change required a coalescence of group rather than individual decisions. The ability to adopt innovation without major requirements for individual change facilitated a quicker and more widespread pace in threshing mechanization than that occurring in other agricultural tasks. Companies mass-produced machines to reap grain, for example, at nearly the same time that J. I. Case opened his Wisconsin factory for the production of threshing machines. Grain drills became available shortly thereafter. The expense of a reaper (which technology historian Siegfried Giedion calls the "pre-eminently democratic tool" at a cost of around $100) or drill in 1850 was less than that of the threshing machine and power, yet their diffusion occurred at a slower pace and depended more on farm size and individual economic thresholds.[49] Farmers sometimes banded together to purchase a reaper or drill or share in the use of them; however, cooperative exchanges in most neighborhoods were limited, because most farm operators planted and harvested their crops in similar cycles of short duration. The adoption lag in harvest implements is evident in the many reports into the 1880s of farmers who continued to harvest their grain by hand and thresh with a machine.[50]

IV.

TWENTIETH-CENTURY SHOCK THRESHING AND THRESHING RINGS

Stack versus Shock Threshing

The rotary and belt power produced by the sweep and treadmill limited the speed of the threshing work. In the 1870s, however, the pace of grain separation significantly increased as threshermen began using the most important power innovation in nineteenth-century Midwest agriculture—the steam engine. The application of steam power to threshing was the first agricultural task in which the energy that powered the urban industrial revolution became directly visible in on-farm work. The change from horse-power to horsepower had a significant impact on the process of the threshing work, social hierarchies within labor crews, and organization of neighborhood farmer cooperatives. Many older farmers and agricultural writers appropriately characterize steam engine days as "the golden age of threshing," because it was with the use of this technology that threshing rose to its highest levels of joint community participation.

Although some Ohio threshermen experimented with steam power as early as 1857, more widespread adoption began around 1870, when J. I. Case, Gaar-Scott, Robinson and Company, and other midwestern manufacturers initiated concentrated production of reliable horse-drawn portable engines.[1] The main transition period occurred between 1875 and 1895. During these decades, the original style of stationary engines mounted on a wood or metal frame gave way to self-propelled units whose mammoth studded wheels literally chewed their way down rural lanes at speeds of three to four miles per hour. By the turn of the century, midwestern threshermen chose among steam powers manufactured by over forty regional companies.[2] Initial adoption and diffusion of the steam engine did not follow any strong geographic or ethnic patterns. One Miami County, Ohio, thresherman's declaration in 1882 that horse-powers were "a thing of the past" is balanced by the continued use of horses on sweep powers in western Ohio and elsewhere well into the 1890s.[3] Implement companies continued to produce horse-powers for threshing until at least 1914. Steam power remained the popular choice of itinerant contractors up to 1925, although some threshermen began purchasing large internal combustion engines after 1905.

Midwestern threshing systems following the adoption of steam engines became almost wholly dependent on neighborhood labor cooperatives contracting the services of a professional local operator to provide the machinery, crew, and technological expertise to handle the engine and separator. The professional thresherman became especially crucial as the cost and knowledge to successfully use the latest machinery escalated far beyond the capabilities of most farmers. Even wealthier men could hardly justify the purchase of a $1,500 to $4,000 steam engine for personal use. The increasing reliance on itinerant operators, who by now could be found in almost every neighborhood, made it possible for smaller-acreage farmers to participate in power farming systems in threshing at the same time they retained conservative approaches and traditional techniques in other agricultural tasks. For example, there are many midwestern areas where one- or two-horse sweep powers for running sorghum cane-grinding mills and other simple devices remained in use long after farmers employed mechanical horsepowers for threshing.

This Iowa thresherman, ca. 1885, required a team of horses and driver to transport his steam engine between farms. Self-propelled models were common by 1890. Courtesy of State Historical Society of Iowa.

The greater power provided by self-propelled steam engines allowed machine owners to utilize larger, more complex separators that quickened the threshing speed. As is so often true, innovation in one component of an agricultural task motivated corresponding advancements in associated processes. Implement companies and machinery designers busily modified grain separators during the first decades of steam power adoption. Improvements in separator design included an increased threshing capacity appropriate to the twenty-five- to forty-horsepower engines and the addition of secondary innovations intended to speed the entire process. Inventors focused initial attention on devices to eliminate the duties of the band-cutters and feeders. In the late 1870s, some manufacturers placed a set of reciprocating knives at the mouth of the thresher. The blades automatically severed the sheaf bands of bundles laid carefully in the midst of the cutting area. The unprotected knives were a constant danger to the man charged with feeding the sheaves far enough to have the grain sheaf, but not his hand, grabbed by the whirring blades. Later-nineteenth-century design modifications in the pulley and power-transfer system within the threshing machine made it possible to add an endless belt conveyer to carry the bundles into the band-knife area (illus., p. 61). Most separators manufactured after 1900 included a single conveyer extending ten to twenty-five feet from the mouth. The larger-capacity machines even included a dividing board down the middle of the feeder to allow the simultaneous feeding of bundles from both sides of the separator.[4] Other contemporaneous separator improvements included automatic weighers to measure the threshed grain and the "wind stacker" to mechanically propel the straw and other discharge into neat storage stacks.[5]

Improved threshing machines powered by steam engines and the growth of a capable class of itinerant operators supported a movement to drop stacking or mowing wheat in favor of summer and early fall shock threshing. Ideally, each farmer could reap his grain, allow it to go through a ten-day to two-week "sweat" in the shock, and then carry the bundles directly from the field to the threshing machinery. The crop would be in the granary or at market before the onslaught of the corn harvest, winter wheat plowing, and other fall tasks. Adherents of shock threshing cited a checklist of reasons for abandoning the trouble of stacking or mowing. Elimination of stacking or hauling to the barn relieved farmers of an extra harvest chore and avoided potential grain loss due to shattering during transportation and handling. Supporters stressed that it took about the same time to haul the shocks to the machine as it did to bring them to the stack or barn, and that pitching sheaves to the various parts of the mow or levels on the stack required more skill and energy than pitching to a feeding table or onto a self-feeding conveyer. Farmers would also suffer less crop depredation due to what Walter Schmidt of Shelby, Iowa, succinctly called "rattage and birdage," or the grain appetites of animals squatting in or near the barns.[6] Finally, promoters of shock threshing pointed to the greater demands on

Twentieth-Century Shock Threshing

Advertisement for the Parsons Hawkeye self-feeder in *The Thresher World and Farmers' Magazine*, 1904.

available barn space due to general developments in regional farm production. Insufficient storage areas became particularly common during the 1880s and 1890s, when farmers considerably increased their cultivated grass crop levels before the widespread adoption of space-saving baling machinery.

The proponents of shock threshing waged a successful campaign. By 1900, it appeared possible that stacking would soon become a rural practice of the past. Correspondents to agricultural journals in 1903 complained that stacking experts were available only in the "good old times." A 1910 issue of *Wallace's Farmer* greeted readers with the large headline: "Stacking Is a Lost Art." The loss was no doubt more true in some locales than others and cannot be explained by a single factor. Agricultural schools and the farm press heavily promoted shock threshing during the 1880s as quicker and more efficient. Although any widespread impact of these sources on general farm practice at this time is certainly questionable, the agricultural education networks neither supported nor instructed farmers in the art of stack building. New generations of farmers were not familiar with stacking, because they grew up in areas where farmers either mowed their grain in barns or had already adopted shock threshing as an agricultural norm. The Midwest was never the home of a specialized labor group that traveled the region offering their stacking skills on an itinerant basis. European immigrants familiar with stack construction techniques tended to settle in ethnic neighborhoods, where the carefully built stack was a commonly undertaken component of the grain harvest.

Complaints about the loss of good stackers reveal that midwestern farmers periodically reconsidered their decisions to abandon the stack, particularly at those times when the apparent advantages of the newer threshing system proved to be less than imagined. Manufacturing statistics claiming new highs in machinery purchases in the 1890s were little comfort when a thresherman's promise to arrive within a week or two of shocking stretched to a wait of a month or more. Most families in a neighborhood tended to follow similar agricultural cycles, with a result that the grain in that area ripened and cured at roughly equal intervals. Farmers all threshing from the shock thus needed a thresherman at approximately the same time. Turn-of-the-century rural diaries document repeated incidents in which men promised a machine at a specific date were forced to adjust their harvest plans because of the itinerant operator's tardy arrival. A delay in getting a machine to thresh grain standing in shocks engendered anxiety over the year's profits, hindered the progress of fall tasks, and prevented the growth of pasture grasses planted to follow grain in traditional grain-pasture-corn rotations. Umphrey Stump, of Darke County, Ohio, recalled the problems of his 1902 harvest:

> A party of neighbors and myself having in all about two hundred acres of grain decided to thresh from the field. As most of us raised tobacco and the sheds had to be gotten ready for the grain, we thought it would save work at so busy a time. There are four or five machines within as many miles of here and we were almost sure of getting one when we wanted it. We had the promise of one the first week of oats threshing and waited for it until the second week and still seeing no chance of getting it we decided to get another machine which is promised within one week. We waited on it for nearly two weeks and still no machine. Then we had to fall back upon the first one and wait till it came. Of course they took on every job on the road as they knew we had to wait. The last two weeks it rained nearly every day and the grain was thoroughly soaked. Caps had blown off the wheat and the oats, having been badly lodged before cutting, was in big squatty heaps upon the ground. The machine arrived between showers and they were determined to thresh before the grain was dry enough. It was either thresh

or let them pull away so we all threshed. The grain was damp and musty and not fit for market.[7]

Threshing delays occurred sometimes because of an operator's inability to gauge the speed of work already promised, but it was also always impossible to predict a holdup due to bad weather or a mechanical breakdown. Farmers encountering unpredictable schedules often decided that stacking was the only acceptable means for saving the grain until the thresherman's arrival.[8]

The choice between stack and shock threshing involved more than a selection of technique or measure of efficiency. Agricultural evolution in the Midwest includes a variety of situations in which residents must conjoin pragmatic considerations with established community values, attitudes, and aesthetics. Farmers long used to stacking (or any other process) developed shared cultural attitudes and values associated with the agricultural cycle and judgments of an ideal plan. Neighbors evaluated the quality of an operation and, by extension, a farmer's expertise on the basis of both statistical means (e.g., bushels per acre) and the conduct of the harvest and threshing. They judged displays of carefully built stacks laid in a symmetrical pattern in the barnyard in dimension for the total yield of the crop and in form and style for the quality of the farm and farmer.

Experienced farmers held strong opinions of the color and texture of grain threshed and cured at the proper time and in the proper manner. Stacking grain provided a freedom to call on the thresherman when a few seeds rubbed from a sample bundle met with the producer's standards of moisture content and appearance. Farmers who left their grain only in shocks were more likely to thresh before or after the crops attained their optimal curing stage. Renewed interest in stacking or mowing followed especially poor seasons with excessive losses due to attempts to thresh wet grain. Farmers complained that the machine performed poorly and that considerable grain remained in the heads or blew over as "white caps" into the straw pile. Threshermen chided growers for trying to thresh wet crops.[9] Everyone recalled the advantages of the tight stack with the cured grain coming out dry and threshing clean from the chaff.

Higher-moisture cereals threshed too early and then stored for long periods in hot granaries and bins suffered "bin burn" or "chaff burn" due to the confined heating of wet grains.[10] Willard Togrim, a Norwegian-American farming in Winneshiek County, Iowa, recalled his dissatisfaction with initial shock threshing in the 1920s:

> These stacks were permitted to stand three or four weeks in order to cure and the grain, when that was cured would come out pure white, shiny, slippery [so that] it would just roll if it was on an incline. Beautiful grain. When they went to shock threshing, it probably got a little damp. It got

brown and maybe moldy and looked like the dickens. Didn't have the quality by any means compared to the stacks.[11]

Grain left too long in the shock fell prey to a different kind of damage under brilliant July and August sunshine. Prolonged exposure to the heat caused the kernels to swell and the bran coats to loosen. Direct sunlight lightened the grain seed and produced so-called "bleached" kernels. Although only slightly less nutritious or useful, the grain produced a flour with a color and quality that rural residents considered inferior to the more familiar darker wheat flour. Shock threshing thus met some resistance when it appeared to "ruin" the flour (and thus the bread and other foods).

An individual's decision to maintain or reintroduce stack threshing to complete the grain cycle had to be evaluated in the wider context of neighborhood practices. Although one or two men sometimes continued to stack after other area operators switched to shock threshing, most often everyone in a neighborhood used the same process. Shock threshing occurred soon after harvest and about the same time stack construction normally started. Farmers taking the time to carry their bundles to a stack wanted the grain to cure for at least three or more weeks before threshing. A minority stacking and postponing threshing thus disrupted neighborhood work cycles and required the thresherman to make several trips to that area.[12] Machine owners preferred to do all their threshing in one continuous seasonal run, however, and were not eager to make special trips in the late fall or winter if the main threshing run finished in August or September. Occupational differences were not as problematic in those neighborhoods where farm practices divided equally between stack and shock. The traveling rig serviced shock threshing farmers soon after the harvest and then later returned for work near the stack and barn.[13]

Farmers continuing to stack or mow their grain well into the twentieth century often did so because of ecological considerations or long-practiced cultural systems emphasizing careful construction of grain stacks or the use of large barns for crop storage. Men farming along a creek or river bottom prone to summer flash floods carried their harvested bundles to the safety of stacks built on higher ground near the outbuildings.[14] The impact of ethnic norms was particularly evident in the threshing practices in Central and North European immigrant neighborhoods. In central Darke County, Ohio, two German-American farmers continued to barn thresh long after their Anglo-American neighbors changed to shock threshing. Ira Edger, the thresherman for these men, recalls:

> Those two men [Otto Ranke and William Kunze], well they had two of the biggest barns in the area, and I used to have to go out there two or three times over the winter to barn thresh their crop. They had a lot of grain, but they never wanted to thresh it all at once, so I had to go out to their place a few times. And boy, those Germans worked hard, they always wanted their

cattle to have fresh straw and grain, and so they'd pile all their wheat in the loft of those German barns and call me out whenever they needed me.... They were about the only ones who threshed during the winter.[15]

Similarly, groups of German-American farmers in Indiana and Missouri, as well as Norwegian-Americans throughout the Upper Midwest, stacked their grain until the 1920s. Ethnic correlations in threshing patterns often involve more than a single explanatory factor. The tendency of certain cultural groups to raise crops appropriate to both their geographic location and their agricultural heritage supported particular techniques. In Missouri and Wisconsin, for example, German-American farmers raised barley for sale to breweries in St. Louis and Milwaukee. Barley producers favored the extra curing of stack storage, because the crop threshed cleanly at a lower moisture content than wheat or oats.[16]

The Occupational Practices of Shock Threshing

Threshing from the shock with a self-feeding separator easily digesting a hundred bushels an hour proceeded at a much faster clip than that possible under mid-nineteenth-century conditions. The self-feeder eliminated the need for band-cutters and feeders, but threshing from the field

Only farmers who stacked their grain could postpone their threshing until winter; Iowa, ca. 1915. Courtesy of State Historical Society of Iowa.

required the addition of two new tasks. "Field pitchers," sometimes called "spikers" or "spike pitchers," "broke down" the shocks and pitched the sheaves onto wagons, where they were systematically piled by "bundle haulers" or "bundle wagon drivers." The wagon operator then directed his team to the side of the separator and pitched the bundles onto the self-feeder. The number of workers involved in these activities depended on the level needed to provide a constant flow of wagons in the field, in transport, and at the separator. As two wagons could be unloaded at one time, each crew required a minimum of four drivers and wagons. Most groups used at least six or eight bundle wagons to ensure that a filled pair was ready to take over from an unloaded team at the thresher.

Neighborhood crews established basic labor divisions on the first day of each season's run and attempted to keep the work relationships consistent until the last bushel passed through the threshing cylinder. Each field pitcher generally teamed up with two bundle haulers, "working the sheaves" for one driver while the other wagon unloaded at the separator. The one-to-two pattern proved particularly appropriate where crews faced longer hauling distances between shock fields and machine.[17] Another common work pattern surrounded the pairing of bundle wagon drivers throughout the annual run. Most self-feeding separators handled a steady stream of bundles pitched from two wagons unloading simultaneously on opposite sides of the endless-belt feeding conveyer. Teamed bundle haulers established an alternating rhythm of dropping the sheaves onto the conveyer. As with most threshing tasks, a set of informal work rules governed the pair's behavior and work relationship. The code functioned to equalize their labor contribution and to prevent disruption of the threshing activities. The following incident near Brookville, Indiana, demonstrates that a newcomer was often not aware of traditional customs until he unintentionally transgressed some local norm:

> We had one old fellow here in the neighborhood, well he moved in here that one year. The first year he was my partner [on a bundle-wagon team]. When you started in as pairs, the same ones stayed all through the ring. You got a fellow that stayed on the opposite side of you at the machine and you stayed on your side. You was supposed to go that way all through the wheat. If you got the dust in over at a threshing, why the wind would change at the various places. And we started in and he didn't have as large a load of bundles as I did and he wasn't no fool either I found out afterwards. He got on the clean side which you had that privilege on the first time. But the second time we came in he came on my side and I thought, "Well he's just new to the ring and he isn't thinking too well. Now I'll wait till tomorrow." And the next day, the same thing. So I told him. I said, "We've got a little rule here that whichever side of the separator you start out on, you go through on that till the end of the ring." "Well," he said, "that dust hurts my eyes." "Well it don't do mine any good either," I told him.[18]

Twentieth-Century Shock Threshing

The field pitcher's work included its own unique set of skills distinguishing between proper and inefficient performance. The wagon driver who handled the tossed bundles particularly valued a good pitcher's efforts. Some threshing groups in Ohio and Indiana had a policy that drivers were serviced by the next available field man. William Miller, who threshed on a crew in Butler County, Ohio, recalls that haulers "would deliberately calculate their chances of getting a certain man to pitch on his next load of sheaves while tossing his present load into the separator's yawning gullet. How the field worker placed his sheaves within reach of the loader's fork, the regularity of his movements . . . entered into his skill."[19] Ohio and Indiana farmers with an accumulated sixty years of experience as a bundle drivers elaborate, respectively, on the finer points of handling shock bundles and the necessity for a close work harmony between the field pitcher and bundle hauler:

> Then I wanted the heads to be in the wagon, to be in facing the middle so that when I went to the separator they wouldn't fall out. Any of that grain that shattered out then would still be in the wagon. I used to say, "If the heads are out, the rabbits get fat." So I wanted that pitcher to work just right. He had to stick that fork into the bundle and then move it around, had to get it up to me just right. The heads would come down in the middle if he laid it on right. You know, you had to be pretty quick to get the hang

Field pitcher and wagon driver working together to load wheat bundles during shock threshing in southeast Ohio, ca. 1915. Courtesy of Ohio Historical Society.

of that . . . you see, also, as those shocks came off of the binder, they generally had a certain shape to them that the binder made when it tied them up. They had a tendency to wrap them bundles so that they were flat, the binder flattened them out along a side. And so if you were loading on the wagon then, if you were up there, you would want those bundles to get up there with that flat side down, on the bottom of the wagon. Then the load up there, which got quite large, would ride better. Them flat sides there would give you more support . . . and if they wasn't pitched up that way, why I'd have to bend down then and turn them over to get them just like I wanted. I didn't want to have to do that, because then I wouldn't be able to keep up with those bundles being pitched up there so carelessly-like.[20]

There's an easy way and a hard way as far as [pitching bundles into a wagon] goes. There is a way to handle that bundle. If you don't get that fork in that bundle, or "sheaves" they call 'em, it's unbalanced and that puts a strain on you up on the wagon. . . . And on top of that, if you don't twist and you put it up there and you put it upside down it will slide right off your fork. You don't have to shake it. They'd get it up there and they'd have the fork upside down and they'd have extra work. . . . Then you always want to put the bundle in front of the guy that's a-loading it. Always want to put it in front of him. And if—when you two work long enough together you know how to put the bundle up there, put the head up, so that it lays down there for him. When you'd know that you was going to go to the far side, you'd put it up there with the butt. You know he could just grab that and put it on the wagon. Then when he was on your side, you'd put the head up to him first.[21]

Threshing crew members considered field pitching one of the more menial jobs and often delegated the task to inexperienced workers or young men hired to fill a crew. The job also tended to be monotonous and lonely, as the pitcher endlessly repeated his stab-and-throw technique out in the fields with the company only of the bundle hauler.

The wagon driver's responsibilities and status were more complex. Apart from the machine crew, his contributions had the most influence on the progress of the threshing. Drivers used a variety of techniques to arrange the bundles pitched from the shocks onto their wagons. The goal was to load a large and secure pile that would not topple or shift during transport to the separator. Although the overall form of the completed load varied according to a driver's own style, the vehicle design, and the quality of the sheaves, all experienced crew members possessed a concept of the "proper-looking" pile and could determine the quality of a man's work with a quick glance at a loaded wagon. They labeled smaller than expected piles with such local derogatory nicknames as "short load," "lazy man's load," and "shyster load." "Dummy load" designated sheaves placed loosely in a pile with a hollow center, while "Saturday night load" and "evening load" were coined in honor of a driver's hurry to be done with threshing in order to get home or into town.[22] While the last two labels were often used in jest, threshing crew members singled out drivers violating the threshing work ethic by consistently loading lesser amounts of grain. Farmer Ed Barstow of Peoria County, Illinois, points out that "no one wanted to see a wagon go to the separator with a little scrawny load that looked like a tornado had just hit it."[23] A man with a "short load" rested more frequently than his partner on the bundle wagon team and caused the threshing to take longer because more trips were required between the separator and shocks.

The concept of proper construction of a solid load drew on the precepts of building grain or hay ricks. Drivers formed a consistently shaped pile of rectangular dimensions with slightly tapered sides and the center of gravity in the middle. Experience, and the evaluative eyes of other crew members, provided the best instruction.

> You'd get where you could just load her so she'd be right straight and it would be straight down the other way. You didn't have a bundle sticking out here and there. If you did, they'd get to laughing at you.[24]
>
> You always put your bundles on the wagon with the butts facing the outside and the heads turned towards the middle. Now I built my load in rows, with the butts on each inside row covering the heads on the row to the outside of it. Usually I could get three or five rows on a wagon, depending then on how long the straw was. With oats I could usually get more of them on there.[25]

Haulers laid the butt ends to the outside of the bed, sometimes overlapping the wagon's edge, so that any grain shattering from the bundles during transport fell onto the wagon bed and not the ground. The driver tramped down each bundle with his feet. Overlapping or "tying" the rows together prevented the load from shifting when the driver turned the wagon or traveled over rough ground. The heaviest tramping and most overlap occurred in the middle of the pile in order to keep the weight in the center. Bundle loaders raised the "tiers" by placing the sheaf of each new row in the gap between adjacent bundles of the layer directly below.[26] Full loads eight to twelve feet high dwarfed the vehicle as the driver, perched precariously at the top of the pile, carefully started on the trip to the threshing machine.

Fully loaded wagons contained the sheaves of 60 to 120 shocks, with the variation due to the number of bundles in each shock, the type of wagon used, and the expertise of the bundle wagon driver. The number of bushels threshed from each load also reflected the type and quality of the grain. A study of oat threshing in Illinois concluded that an average haul generally yielded between thirty and forty bushels, while three former threshermen estimate a typical wheat load at ten to fifteen bushels lower because of the larger amount of straw in the typical wheat crop.[27] The number of loads handled by each wagoner in a day's work depended on the ability of the field pitcher, the distance from the shock fields to the separator, potential waiting periods before loading, and the type of crop. Bundle haulers teamed with a field pitcher made four to seven trips daily. Higher numbers are associated with "basket racks" (discussed below), short hauling distances, and long days.[28]

Bundle haulers preferred wagons with a low wheel base to ease the pitcher's task and a tight bed to prevent loose grain from slipping out through the bottom. Most farmers also attached a wood frame, commonly called a "rack," along the front and back sides of the bed. The additions consisted generally of two or three "posts" with wide boards nailed flush to the posts in ladder fashion. The racks provided end supports for the load but left the sides open for pitching sheaves on and off the wagon. In some areas, the field men pitched bundles onto unattended "basket wagons." These vehicles contained a "basket frame" or "basket rack" that extended on all four sides to form a large open box that held bundles without the need to arrange them in any systematic order. The encircling frame resembled the temporary side walls used on hay wagons of the late nineteenth and early twentieth centuries. After loading the sheaves, the same man drove to the machine and threw the bundles onto the feeding conveyer. Basket racks were a common trait of shock threshing patterns in the Great Plains region, and midwesterners likely borrowed the practice from their western neighbors.

The choice to use basket frames or simple end racks entailed decisions about labor and the division of tasks among the work crew, although in some cases initial experimentation occurred because of a temporary labor shortage.[29] Farmers and agricultural writers favoring basket wagons claimed that the threshing required fewer man-hours, even though not as many bundles were carried in the looser loads.[30] Only a minority of Midwest crews changed, however, from the two-man system during the period of steam threshing. Proponents of a separate role for the bundle hauler emphasized his arrangements of larger loads and the help he provided to the pitcher. A pitcher laboring alone moved constantly around the wagon in his attempt to throw bundles equally to all areas of the bed, whereas a man perched on the wagon with a fork received sheaves pitched to central areas and moved them around the load. Threshermen estimated that the two-man system produced seven to ten more bushels per wagon at the threshing machine.

The two-man system persisted also because of its social and aesthetic functions. Farmers carried out the occupational tasks of shock threshing in teams or small groups. As the chart in Figure 2 demonstrates, each position involved contact between at least two crew members. Working in pairs eased the labor and relatively unchanging nature of threshing chores. Adoption of basket wagons broke cooperative patterns into individual pursuits. Moreover, one of the primary avenues for public expression of good farming know-how and taste was the bundle wagon loaded to the point where the pile appeared ready to topple over at any moment. There was

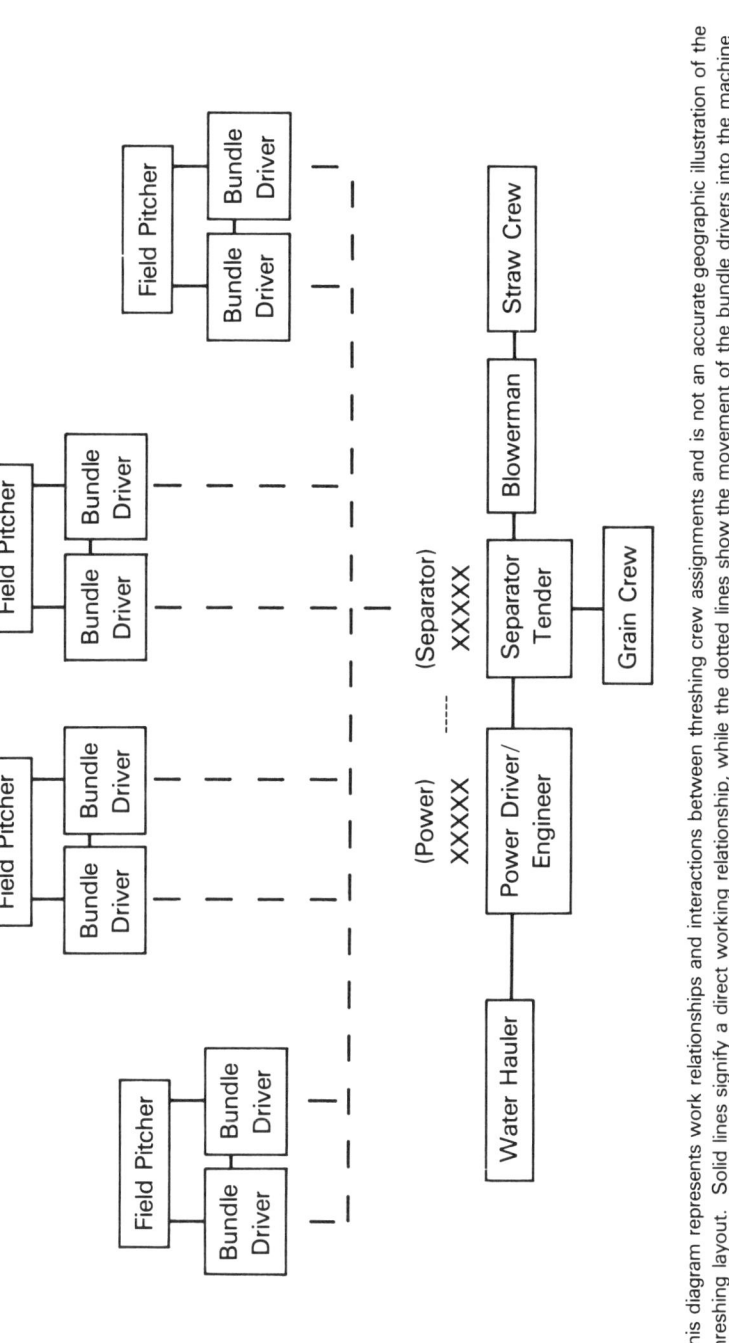

Figure 2: Work Relationships* (Shock Threshing)

*This diagram represents work relationships and interactions between threshing crew assignments and is not an accurate geographic illustration of the threshing layout. Solid lines signify a direct working relationship, while the dotted lines show the movement of the bundle drivers into the machine context. The positions shown represent all possible labor roles in shock threshing using a separator equipped with automatic feeder and wind stacker.

a fine line between carrying the largest load and earning praise from the rest of the crew, and the chance of placing too many bundles on the wagon and receiving the crew's scorn when the pile toppled. One Greene County, Indiana, wagon driver described a near-disastrous experience:

> I had a little colt, a two-year old and this other one, she was three. And Marion Keller used to give me the dickens. I just pulled them up the hill and yell "Whoa!" And get up on that wagon and just go. I had "em broke pretty good when thrashing time come. Went over here to McLaughlins' and they parked [the separator] in the barn. And we got to measuring who could put the biggest load in. I got my hitching strap, and put her on the end of my lines, you know, and oh boy I really went on up. I got up there and I couldn't get in the barn. My load was just a little bit too high. So Marian says, "You got no business going in there." So I crawled down underneath the sheaves. Moved a couple in front and I lay down in there and drove the team in there. Well the top went off and two or three layers below that. "Don't do that any more." "Well," I says, "I just got a little carried away. I'll watch it next time."[31]

Bundle wagon drivers were well aware of their audience during the approach to the center of the threshing activity. Haulers enhanced the display through the care and presentation of their wagons and teams. Wagon beds and wooden pieces were often freshly cleaned and painted before the season's run. Other men carefully cleaned and greased the horse tack and polished silver and brass pieces or used matched teams with girded fly protectors that emphasized the symmetry and form of the pair.[32]

The cardinal rules of pitching sheaves onto a separator table or feeding conveyer were the same: "heads first, butts last," at a steady pace, and without overlapping the bundles (photo, p. 73). The mechanical design of the threshing cylinder and the actions of the oscillating cutting knives on self-feeders supported these standards and illustrate the continuing influence of technological designs on regional occupational patterns. The band knives at the mouth of the separator severed the twine and pulled the bundle towards the cylinder. Heads pointed towards the concave threshed more cleanly because the friction between the straw slowed the movement of the lower portion of the sheaf. With bundles entering head first, also, the cylinder teeth would not be clogged with straw as the grain entered the initial mechanical step of the threshing process. Cylinders filled with the stems of bundles fed broadside demanded more power to keep the machine running at optimal speed. The thresherman also carefully regulated the internal air blasts used to separate chaff, straw, and grain. His manipulations of the wind gates, blinds, sieves, and screens depended on the kind and quality of grain, typical speed of threshing, and material bulk. Slack feeding permitted too much wind for the volume of materials, and good grain was blown through with the waste. Heavy feeding dammed the screens and sieves and prevented the good grain from passing through

Twentieth-Century Shock Threshing

This view from the engine shows bundle wagon drivers unloading into a self-feeder separator on a central Missouri farm, ca. 1920. Courtesy of Massie Missouri Resources Division.

them to the weigher.[33] "Feeding up in the collar," a phrase used by an Illinois thresherman, signified a grain flow allowing the separator to work at full efficiency.[34]

Automatic straw-stacking devices perfected in Indiana in the 1880s revolutionized the cumbersome and hard work of straw crews. Indianapolis lawyer James Buchanan received the first patent on a reliable design in 1884. The innovation, appropriately titled the "wind stacker," included a fan that propelled straw and chaff away from the rear of the machine through a tall metal pipe. A series of ropes, belts, pulleys, chains, and rings kept the tube swinging automatically from side to side while blasting out the waste.[35] Over the next decade, the "Farmer's Friend" or "Cyclone Stacker"—other early trade names for the device—was adopted in large numbers, and by 1910, the majority of threshing machine manufacturers equipped new machines with the telescoping appendage.[36]

The oscillating stacker mechanically formed a semicircular pile without the need for workers to distribute the straw. The host farmer, and sometimes one other crew member, worked periodically on the stack to round off edges, tramp the foundation, form the final shape, and prepare any type of cap formation. Work on the straw pile thus continued as a threshing task well into the twentieth century, especially during the early years of automatic stacker adoption, when many farmers remained unconvinced that the device, left on its own, produced a good, tight stack with water-shedding capabilities.[37] Design modifications on the blower between 1900 and 1915 gave control over stack formation to a man perched on the separator. A series of levers and wheels on the back of the machine regulated the height of the discharge pipe, and a wheel crank cabled to a hood added over the open end of the tube permitted manipulation of the length and angle of expulsion. The straw blew straight out with the hood open, and progressively downwards as the crank was turned to lower the covering. The result of these improvements was a shift in the crucial position for straw stack construction from the pile itself to the automated blower controls located on the threshing machine.

Farmers seldom practiced the manual art of straw stack construction in the Midwest after 1920. The host man still had a group-acknowledged right to work with his straw, but the bulk of stack formation rested with the "blowerman" manipulating the wind stacker's controls (photo below). He was normally a permanent member of the machine crew traveling with the engine and separator. A few threshermen asked the host farmer to either take this task himself or delegate the handling of the wind stacker to a member of the general threshing crew.[38] As farmers and machinery owners became more convinced of the stacker's ability and agreed upon an acceptable stack form, groups dispensed with the blowerman's role altogether

An Indiana blowerman in position at the cranks and wheels controlling operation of the separator's wind stacker.

and entrusted the separator tender to make the necessary periodic adjustments.

The use of automatic stackers changed the midwestern cultural landscape through elimination of one of the last expressions of individual performance within the threshing complex—the hand-formed straw pile, indicative of a good harvest and a careful, industrious farmer. Most wind stackers produced a common stack design with only some size differences due to straw quantity and form variations as a result of blower manipulations. The major difficulty of straw stack building was to design a pile with a size and shape commensurate with the amount of grain threshed in one setting and within the space allotted for stack construction. The blowerman and host farmer tried to estimate the room needed and the amount of straw contained in the year's crop.

> To my way of doing things it took a lot of planning to get them stacks built just right.... One time we was thrashing over at Joe Boren's place, oh about two miles or so east of here [near Oak Hill, Ohio]. And so they set the thrasher in the yard like Joe wanted. So then he said, "Well, you can just put my straw over there, by the barn." Well, there wasn't much space there, and I told him, I told him that I thought he'd have too much straw and he'd have to move the separator.... Anyway, they had it all rigged up to go, and I said that I'd try but I might not be able to get it all in there. So after a while that pile was getting kind of high. And you didn't want it so high, oh maybe twenty feet or so, but you didn't want to get it so high that the blower couldn't get any more on the top. Well I had that blower swinging from one end of the yard to the other, hitting all the corners as best I could. I was just hoping they'd a-run out of grain before I ran out of stack [laughter]. Well, it got all in there, you know, but I bet you we couldn't have handled another shock after that. I said, "Joe," I said to him, "Joe, how's about the next time you give a fellow a little more room." That was a tight one.[39]

Poor judgments produced long, low piles of insufficient density or the need to reset the rig when the stack could hold no more straw. Blowermen could form piles up to seventy or eighty feet long, but most farmers requested their stacks be built near the pens for livestock or dairy herds.

The ability to propel straw and chaff up in the air and a distance away from the machine revitalized interest in two regional folklife traits: the construction of temporary winter shelters for stock and the mowing of straw. Pioneer farmers in the Midwest often built straw barns framed with corner posts and a latticework of rails and poles. They then covered the skeleton with threshed straw and renewed the skin every year.[40] Straw carriers did not support the continuity of this practice because of limits on the carrier's height and the crew's preoccupation with simply moving the discharge away from the machine. After threshing, only some farmers took the trouble to carry part of the pile to cover low hog or cattle shelters.[41]

Covering temporary sheds with blown straw again became a widespread trait during the 1920s. Farmers began construction by defining the shelter's vertical and horizontal space with poles and timbers. Four basic forms are presented in Figure 3. The machine crew directed the discharge blast to a height of ten to fifteen feet around and on top of the frame. Later, farmers cleaned out one side of the pile, generally on the south or east side away from the prevailing winds. Finished sheds provided a sheltering place for stock in the winter as well as available feed during confinement due to harsh weather.[42]

Throughout most of the nineteenth century, only farmers who threshed mowed grain stored the crop's straw in barns. Many of these men raised oats and preferred the safety and convenience of the barn for the oat straw

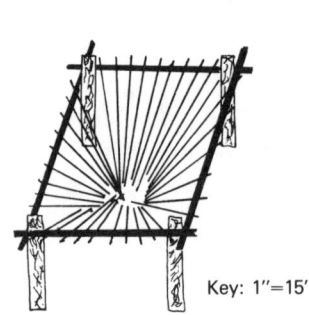

A. Darke County, Ohio (ca. 1920)
Approximate size: 15-20' x 25-30'

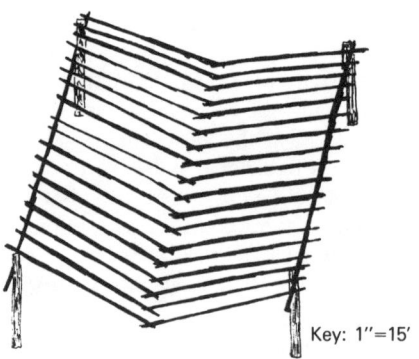

B. Jackson County, Ohio (ca. 1925)
Approximate size: 20-25' x 30-35'

C. Franklin County, Indiana (ca. 1930)
Approximate size: 15-20' x 40-45'

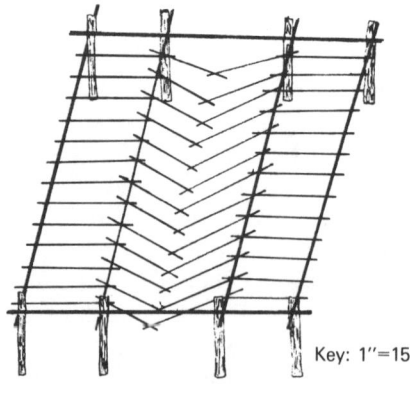

D. Peoria County, Illinois (ca. 1925)
Approximate size: 20-25' x 35-40'

Figure 3: Straw Shed Constructions

favored by stock as a winter feed. The opportunity to direct a blast thirty or forty feet permitted wind stacker operators to aim the discharge directly into a mow if the thresherman set the separator either in the barn itself or close to the structure (photo below). Depending on the barn's location and placements of the mow openings, these settings provided the ultimate tests of the thresherman's abilities. Structures were sometimes located on uneven ground, or the doors were barely wide enough for the machinery. One or two men took responsibility for evenly spreading the blown straw around the storage area. Former ring members often cite this task as their least favorite threshing experience, because it typically entailed work under a hot barn roof with little breeze to relieve the heat or blow off the choking dust. "It was like a miner's black lung," according to Iowan Carl Hamilton, "Dad would cough and spit oat dust for days afterward and his eyes would be fiery red. Grant Wood never caught that part of threshing."[43] A farmer from Greene County, Indiana, offered another understandable metaphor:

> We was threshing down there at Billy's, that's George and Dan's father, you know, and it was hot. And Billy wanted to blow some oat straw in the barn. And we had an awful time getting the machine set up to blow the straw in the barn there. There was this boy name of Earl, he was working around there in the barn about the time I got set up. I was just wringing wet with sweat, and it was steaming anyhow. And he come out, and he jumped up

Threshing at the Joe Reel farm near Oakville, Iowa, 1910. The wind stacker is set to blow the straw into a barn mow. Courtesy of State Historical Society of Iowa.

on the engine box there and set down beside me and he said, "Well, if it's any hotter in hell than it is in there," he said, "there ain't no use to send me there, 'cause I can't stand it."[44]

The grain crew cared for the threshed crop as it exited from the separator. Crew sizes ranged from two to six men, the number depending on the type of grain weigher on the machine, the host farmer's design for storing his crop, and the distance from the machine to the farmer's granary or the local elevator. By 1900, most threshing machines included elevators to lift the threshed crop to an automatic counter and holding hoppers near the top of the separator. A man stationed near the storage receptacles waited for each hopper to fill before triggering the bushel counter and sending the grain down a chute off the hopper. The fully automated weigher used throughout the region after 1915 eliminated this position entirely, as it mechanically held the grain until a preset amount was reached, usually a half-bushel or bushel, and then released the crop.

The crew directed the threshed grain into a sack or a grain wagon. Most separators produced after 1920 contained a reversing rod that enabled the grain crew to work on either side of the machine. Sacking systems required the men to wait as two to four "dumps" of the weigher filled each one- or two-bushel bag. The workers then faced the unenviable job of maneuvering two-bushel sacks weighing around 130 pounds onto flat-bed wagons, a task that earned them the appropriate title of "grain wrestlers." The crew members drove loaded wagons to the barn, where the threshed crop was either stored as sacked or emptied into cleared granary bins. Participants in groups in which sacking was the norm often agreed to provide a set number of bags for common use throughout the run.[45]

The haulers transported loose grain in tightly floored box wagons of smaller dimensions than the vehicles used to haul bundles. Whereas bundle wagons were generally around eight feet wide and twelve to fifteen feet long, most grain wagons were no more than four feet wide and ten feet long. The grain boxes were built with four walls of equal height, with a small exit door at the center of the rear wall's bottom. The wagon drivers directed their teams to barn granaries or, occasionally, to nearby mills or elevators. They opened the exit door and allowed the grain to fall onto an auger or elevator leading to the storage area.[46] Hand shoveling the grain from a wagon took too much time; thus, boxed wagons did not become popular until the widespread availability of augers to automatically elevate the crop.

Threshing Crew Hierarchies

Shock threshing participants recognized the skill required for the labor positions and informally assigned each task a place in the group's social hierarchy. Farmers evaluated both the level of occupational difficulty and the job's influence on the quality of the threshing work. Bundle wagon drivers assumed a higher role in social and agricultural orders, for example, than that given normally to the field pitchers. The pitcher's chore demanded continuous physical activity with a degree of difficulty that rose in tandem with the growing height of each load. Bundle haulers demonstrated a variety of occupational skills. The field pitcher worked solely with a pitchfork; the expert wagoner exhibited proficiency in handling a team and bundle-laden wagon as well as the crafts of building stable loads and correctly pitching sheaves into the separator. Inefficient field pitching slowed the work's progress, but the overall threshing quality was determined by a man's performance at "the business end of threshing where those bundles hit the knives."[47] Experienced farmers responsible for their own teams typically took the role of bundle drivers. The general content of oral histories of threshing provides evidence of this hierarchy. Most older farmers discuss, and relate anecdotes about, one or more men known for their abilities to handle wagon loading and pitching into the separator. They make it a point to discuss the presentation of bundle teams and the more notable experiences of work around the separator. Field pitching, on the other hand, is described only in general occupational terms.

The social standing of straw crew members or grain handlers is more variable. The host farmer normally headed the straw crew (if one was used), and his status was unquestionably highlighted during the home threshing. The remainder of the straw handlers received the lower prestige given to the position during stack threshing. Lower status does not signify any sort of punishment or ostracism, of course, but rather a group's recognition of occupational contributions and experience. Members of the grain crew took a position in the middle of the social order. Positive attributes associated with the position include responsibility for the threshed crop, the work close to the threshing machinery, and the need, in some cases, to provide a grain wagon and team of horses. Sacking grain, however, involved little more than the strength and stamina to continuously fill two-bushel bags and make round trips to the granary or elevator. Hired workers not pitching in the fields often sacked loose grain.

In addition to encouraging the shift to shock threshing processes, the adoption of steam engines stimulated significant changes in the thresherman's responsibilities and social standing. Midwestern residents always associated the thresherman with the most complex piece of technology and reserved the increasingly prestigious title for the man who most closely governed the quality of the work. The "thresherman" position thus shifted over time from directing the flail's swing to feeding bundles into the separator, and finally to controlling the power produced by steam engines. Interestingly, the movement results in increasing separation of the thresherman from the actual threshing process and the need to physically handle the crop. The flailer directly worked with the grain from initial positioning before threshing to collecting the crop for cleaning. The feeder received the opening bundle from another man and manually placed it into the machine, but he did not handle the threshed grain. The steam engine operator worked thirty or forty feet from the separator. On a good day, and with the aid of a skilled "separator tender," the thresherman/engineer seldom held a stalk of grain in his hand.

The thresherman's association with complex machinery and engines carried functional and symbolic meanings. He occupied the center stage during an era when midwestern farm families confronted the central stages of a mechanical revolution in their occupational style. The itinerant thresherman's equipment included the latest innovations in designs and materials available to the rural population. Threshing implement dealers and sales agents often sponsored exhibitions, parades, and other demonstrations to mark the arrival of a new machinery line or important innovation. Major manufacturers hired special trains to exhibit current products via "whistle-stop" tours of the Midwest. Decked with patriotic bunting and accompanied by a band (and of course a few company spokesmen), the machinery caravan touched off major community celebrations in small towns throughout the region. Present-day folk narrative traditions in Osage County, Missouri, for example, include stories about the first shipment of steam engines into the northern part of the country in the early 1880s. According to these stories, hundreds of people turned out to greet the steamboat that carried the engine up the Missouri and Osage rivers. The resulting event, which included a picnic for which one woman is reported to have baked over sixty pies, is recalled both for its demonstration of community participation and for its celebration of agricultural progress.[48] The importance of professional threshermen ranged further, however, than the display of machinery. They were the first permanent farming group whose interests and needs were aligned structurally to the traits associated with present-day agriculture. Among these identifying characteristics are special schools and educational courses, periodicals and textbooks geared towards mechanics and engineering, and specific government and legal regulations.[49] Each of these traits highlighted the special expertise and social status of threshermen.

The promotion of mechanical knowledge for farmers preceded the rise of a class of professional threshermen, but they were the first group to receive attention from formal educational networks created to serve the manufacturing industry's rural interests. The first agricultural periodicals devoted entirely to rural tasks requiring mechanical knowledge were journals published specifically for steam engine operators. Threshermen at the turn of the century could subscribe to two (sometimes combative) special monthlies: the *American Thresherman*, published in Racine, Wisconsin, with J. I. Case sponsorship, and the *Thresherman's Review*, based in St. Joseph, Michigan. The combined circulation of the journals reached almost 83,000 subscriptions by 1923.[50] Significantly, the content of both monthlies

Twentieth-Century Shock Threshing

Crew ready to thresh on the P. C. Frok farm in central Iowa, 1900. In posed photographs, the thresherman usually can be found in his special position at the controls of the steam engine. Courtesy of State Historical Society of Iowa.

A street parade of six steam engines and four separators sold in 1906 by Kriegbaum Brothers in Huntington, Indiana. This equipment was made by the Huber Manufacturing Company of Marion, Ohio.

changed from early emphasis on threshing to broader coverage of all aspects of mechanized farm operations. The *American Thresherman* eventually evolved into *American Farm Equipment: The Magazine of Power Farming and Farm Business*. The *Thresherman's Review* appended *and Power Farming* to its title in 1913, and by 1928 the monthly was simply called *Power Farming*.

Threshermen's magazines were filled primarily with descriptions and advertising of equipment lines and instructions on mechanical operations. Magazine editors also initiated and backed, moreover, several orchestrated movements aimed at the recognition of custom contractors as a distinct professional class. The journals forcefully promulgated the establishment of threshermen's associations, often called "brotherhoods," to set consistent standards and prices for labor, lobby for the operators' interests in state legislatures, and protect their rights in legal matters. The yearly dues paid by threshermen joining state organizations in Ohio and Illinois included the price of subscription to one of the two magazines. The first statewide group formed in populist Minnesota in the 1890s. Brotherhoods were then organized successfully over the next twenty years in every midwestern state. The National Association of Brotherhoods of Threshermen, established in Chicago in 1918, reported twenty-three groups in 1922.[51] Implement companies supported these organizational efforts, particularly the annual meetings of the larger groups that provided manufacturers with an opportunity to demonstrate new equipment to their customers. The impact of threshermen brotherhoods certainly varied between individuals and locales. Most former operators claim they experimented with membership in one or more organizations, although only a minority were consistent supporters for more than a five-year period. Group-set prices and other formal efforts to enact consistent occupational standards enjoyed only inconsistent impact, as there were usually a number of custom operators in each area who preferred to follow their own inclinations.

The general movement towards agricultural mechanization between 1880 and 1930 enhanced the thresherman's role as a model figure in Midwest rural society. Most farmers participated in the farm equipment revolution, even if they did not purchase every technological innovation. Implement companies continuously modified grain binders during the nineteenth century until the self-binding device gained near-universal adoption by 1900. Plows, drills, harrows, and cultivators were required on all farms; manufacturers constantly made "improvements" to these implements and peddled their latest lines through an expanding network of media, salesmen, and public demonstrations. The parade of devices for planting, cultivating, and harvesting corn and grasses was no less pervasive and, in many cases, persuasive. Within this context, farmers recognized the thresherman as a practiced mediator between themselves and the bureaucracy of companies, salesmen, banks, and government programs that agricultural historian John Schlebecker notes "may have been the most important cause of widespread and rapid agricultural technological advance."[52] Threshermen demonstrated that complex devices could be mastered and, perhaps more important, that the latest mechanized implements were an appropriate technology for midwestern farmers. Farmers conditioned to the presence and use of an industrial technology in threshing began to accept mechanical knowledge as an occupational necessity.

The Threshing Ring

The work crews used for shock threshing with steam powers were significantly larger than the groups assembled for stack threshing during the first decades of mechanization. Average labor requirements for the major systems used during the threshing period are summarized in Table 2. The chart lists the positions normally assumed with different technologies and the number of workers typically involved in each task. Variable levels for each system occurred because of differences in crop acreage, size of the social network joining together for the seasonal run, and capacity and style of the thresherman's power and separator.[53] The significant comparison is between "Stack Threshing in 1860," "Shock Threshing in 1890," and "Shock Threshing in 1920." Minimum labor requirements doubled in the shift from stack to shock systems and remained largely consistent for both shock threshing dates, although the crews' responsibilities changed because of machinery innovations. The 1890 levels assume use of a manually fed separator with web-carrier to elevate straw; the later date supposes a self-feeder with automatic stacker. At least one-third of the threshing crew manpower in 1890 was employed in tasks—band-cutting, feeding, and straw crew—unnecessary under typical threshing conditions thirty years later. The number of workers did not decrease over time, however, because the extra speed of the new threshing technology prompted assignment of the "released" men to positions as pitcher, bundle wagon driver, and grain handler.

The adoption of shock threshing systems supported the establishment of midwestern rural institutions known throughout the region as "threshing rings." These groups can be defined succinctly as neighborhood collectives annually organized to provide mutual occupational assistance at each member's farm during the threshing season. In addition, threshing rings typically included the following characteristics: (1) a consistent core membership of six to ten families and a total participation of eight to as many as twenty farms; (2) the responsibility of each member to provide at least one worker at each threshing; (3) the meeting of all labor obligations within the threshing cycle; (4) a patterned and consistent progress of members' threshing that, once begun, continued until the last crop passed through the cylinder; (5) a "threshing season" that lasted between two and four weeks; and (6) a sense of identity and a set of traditions that set each group apart from other local cooperatives. Most rings did not own their

TABLE 2 **Labor Requirements of Threshing Systems**

	Stack Threshing in 1860[a]	Barn Threshing in 1860[b]	Stack Threshing in 1880[a]	Shock Threshing in 1880[a]	Shock Threshing in 1900[c]
Stackmen	2–4	–	3–4	–	–
Mowmen	–	1–2	–	–	–
Field Pitchers	–	–	–	3–6	3–6
Bundle Wagons	–	–	–	3–6	4–8
Band-Cutters[d]	1–2	1	2	2	2
Feeders[d]	1	1	1	1	1
Straw Crew	2–3	1–3	2–3	2–4	0–2
Grain Handlers[e]	1–3	1–2	2–3	2–4	2–5
Subtotal	7–13	5–9	10–13	13–23	12–24
Machine Crew	1	–	1	1	3–4
Total	8–14	5–9	11–14	14–24	15–28

	Shock Threshing in 1920[f]	Shock Threshing in 1920[f]	Stack Threshing in 1920[f]	Shock Threshing in 1930[g]
Stackmen	–	–	3–5	–
Mowmen	–	–	–	–
Field Pitchers	3–6	–[h]	–	0–2
Bundle Wagons	6–8	6–12	–	2–4
Band-Cutters	–	–	–	–
Feeders	–	–	–	–
Straw Crew	1–2	1–2	1–2	–
Grain Crew	3–6	4–6	3–6	1–2
Subtotal	13–22	11–20	7–13	3–8
Machine Crew	3–4[i]	3–4[i]	3–4[i]	0–1
Total	16–26	14–24	10–17	3–9

[a]With use of horse-sweep power
[b]With use of treadmill
[c]With use of steam power and separator with automatic straw stacker
[d]Positions often assumed by crew members traveling with threshing machine
[e]Includes labor around the machine and in the granary
[f]With use of steam engine and separator with automatic straw stacker and self-feeder
[g]With use of small gasoline tractor and separator with automatic straw stacker and self-feeder
[h]Threshing system employing "basket" wagons or racks
[i]Deduct one machine crew member with use of internal combustion engine power

own machinery, but instead they contracted the services of an itinerant thresherman to "thresh the ring." The equipment owner provided a "machine crew" of two to four persons responsible for the operation of the power and separator.

There is no clear etymology or first usage of *threshing ring*. The phrase undoubtedly originated in the United States and is not used outside North

America. Early-nineteenth-century rural diaries sometimes describe circular treading grounds as "rings," but writers never connect the term to a work cooperative. Reports of mid-century stack threshing do not include the "ring" designation because the flexibility and smaller crews did not support a need for any formal recognition or neighborhood identity markers. The name begins to appear in the correspondence to the agricultural press in the late 1880s, or at roughly the same time as the shift by many farmers from stack to shock threshing and the consequent need for larger labor-exchange networks. Certainly, the type of reciprocal labor networks connoted by the phrase was in common use in the Midwest by 1890.[54]

While the first seasons of each collective often included some organizational difficulties, unmet expectations, and frustrations, most neighborhood groups stabilized within a few years. The diaries of Dekalb County, Illinois, farmer Fred Downer chart one early transition. Downer threshed from the stack from 1877 through 1886. The "season" stretched for two to three months, with sequences of two to five threshing days alternating with other agricultural work periods of two days to three weeks. Downer exchanged wheat- and oat-threshing work with four to six neighbors. Between 1888 and 1893, however, his threshing always began within one month of the grain harvest and was completed, with the exception of the 1891 crop, within four weeks. Labor exchanges now included eight to eleven farmers. The regularity of the work after 1888 and its occurrence soon after harvest suggest a decision by Downer and his neighbors to standardize their schedules. Significantly, there are no diary references to stacking after 1886; thus, we can assume that Downer and his neighbors threshed from the shock after that year. Annual variations in threshing dates continue according to the timing of the harvest beginning and, possibly, the schedule of the local thresherman. Once the threshing started, it dominated Downer's time until he worked at the farm of the last neighbor listed as providing help at the home threshing.[55]

Threshing rings did not all form simultaneously or as the result of some kind of spontaneous regional change. The communal groups were also not local responses to external pressures or the choreographed efforts of outsiders attempting to direct rural change. Indeed, it is impossible to answer the chicken-and-egg question of whether a change to shock threshing stimulated the adoption of larger reciprocal-labor groups or if it was only after organizing threshing rings that farmers abandoned their stacks. Perhaps more important is that rural residents initiated this change and solidified their neighborhood group practices by enlarging on an existing rural plan for the social organization of cooperative work. Further, the threshing ring functioned during its annual run as a temporary community whose members collectively oriented their activities through the definition and mediation of shared symbols, behaviors, and expectations.

The voluntary mobilization of rural neighborhoods was consistent with a long-standing midwestern cultural style. Nineteenth-century collectives

Threshing rig, including water wagon to the far left, and crew ready to leave a completed job in Ohio, ca. 1905. Courtesy of Ohio Historical Society.

of rural families met temporarily and seasonally for raising barns and houses, cornhusking, log rollings, and other tasks. Indeed, the region's farmers constantly adjusted their occupational practices and social networks in accordance with the demands of their environment—social, cultural, natural, technological, and economic. In this respect, traditional practices, and the evolution of rural customs, are not at all random events. They are individual and family attempts to derive maximum utilization of available resources and to farm in a familiar style that provides the best results (and, by extension, the best life). Mutual agricultural undertakings were possible because most rural residents had similar notions of appropriate farming patterns. The dominant regional style included the ability and right for a farmer to call upon social networks for aid and his responsibility to provide assistance when asked. If neighbors had entirely separate sets of agricultural practices and notions of community expectations, then these customs could never have been created or, certainly, perpetuated. Families in any one area did not all raise the same amounts of always similar crops or follow identical occupational cycles, of course, yet it is reasonable to suggest that the exigencies of resources and farming knowledge supported resemblance rather than difference, and coalescence, rather than divergence, of cultural styles.

The creation and continuity of the threshing ring was a significant midwestern phenomenon because it was one of those rare sequences when increasing mechanization supported the preservation of traditional cooperative patterns. As self-binding reapers replaced manual reaping, raking, and binding grain, as mechanical corn harvesters supplanted the need to husk ears by hand, and indeed as the combined harvester-thresher later motivated threshermen to scrap their rigs, the general result was a disruption of neighborhood groups with their intimacy of association and cooperative organization and a replacement by a more individualistic pursuit. The progress of threshing changes presents a mechanization enigma, because the complex passed from an individual, family, or, at most, small-group experience to a wider social participation as a direct result of the adoption of more complex agricultural devices. Individuals used and, in many cases, fashioned the tools employed in premechanical threshing. Flailing required no dependency on neighbors or outsiders for successful completion and thus had little social dimension in rural cycles. Treading opened up a slightly wider social context because of the need of one or two additional workers and extra stock. The threshing group now included family members, hired help, and perhaps one or two neighbors.

The introduction and adoption of threshing machines changed circumstances entirely for small and medium-sized farming operations. To successfully use the innovation without incurring the sizeable labor costs of hiring large crews, midwestern farmers turned to the reciprocal work patterns used in other rural contexts. Threshing exchanges with three to seven other farmers approximated the mutual-aid groups formed to stack and reap grain. The small number of participating farms in each crew and the safe storage of the crops in mows or stacks supported informal and flexible relations between farmers. Neighbors banded together along often intertwined patterns of kinship, friendship, and geographic location. The reciprocal obligations characterizing threshing rings, thus, were not newly created in the late nineteenth century, but instead they were transferred as needed to the threshing complex.

If threshing rings represented the extension of a regionally dominant cultural style, each quickly gained the status of a special bounded subcommunity with its own identity. Groups pursuing common occupational tasks with identical equipment developed overt and covert differences as a result of local customs and new traditions derived from continued group participation. No single factor accounts for all variations. Apart from Old Order religious collectives, there is little evidence for generalizations about ethnic or other subcultural predispositions. Ring members demonstrated shared expectations and behaviors in a variety of ways. Men acted in concert and collective purpose in completing the agricultural tasks. Host farmers retained a leadership role on their farms; however, the knowledge and experiences of the group dictated work patterns. Shared customs influenced the order of the threshing and work relations among bundle drivers and between field pitchers and bundle wagoners. Ring participants also developed aesthetic criteria for evaluating performances, ranging from the display of a wagon team to the construction of a bundle load or straw stack. Individual display and judgment, sanctioned by membership and strengthened with the succession of seasons, permitted personal variation while ensuring that each member's performance fell within the range of group-defined expectations.

V.

THRESHING RING ORGANIZATION AND FORMALIZATION

We are all glad to see [the threshing crew] twice, to see them come and to see them go.[1]

The threshing job needs to be systematized. Big man and little man go on a par. Tardy man and punctual man share equal dividends. There is no boss and things go at loose ends. The machine gets to Jake Thompson's at one o'clock and threshes till ten-thirty the following day and Mrs. Thompson is spared having the men for a meal. It goes from there to Steve Gallagher's, gets set by noon and does three hours work and Mrs. Gallagher has meals for twelve to provide.[2]

Midwest farmers threshing from the stack with horse-power machinery during the nineteenth century managed to satisfy their labor requirements through the work of family members, exchange work with four to six neighbors, and the help of one or two hired hands. Collectives of this size were generally easily managed by each individual calling informally upon the help of other nearby residents. Finding, organizing, and managing the larger crews necessary for shock threshing, however, presented new problems. The increasing labor complexity sometimes taxed the bonds of the small, flexible networks characterizing local neighborhood exchange patterns and required each family to take responsibility for arranging his own threshing. Farmers formed early community threshing rings to meet those challenges. Yet, as farming in the Midwest became more specialized and formalized in the early portions of the twentieth century, parallel changes occurred in fundamental components of many local threshing rings. Groups were not all subject to the same forces of change, nor did even contiguous collectives respond similarly to identical influences for altering ring structures. In those neighborhoods where major innovation occurred, the retooling of the ring was marked by a shift towards regimentation and rationalization. Changes were evident both in overt cultural practices and in the processes through which individuals made choices between contrasting cultural systems.

Host farmers needing six to ten men for threshing did not call upon every nearby neighbor for help. As a consequence, ring membership developed informally and included farmers' participation on an entirely voluntary basis. The families of each collective tended to farm similar-size operations, and the labor donated by each man generally balanced out over the run, although certainly there were differences in the numbers of bushels threshed at each farm. Unbalanced labor exchanges were either overlooked or, if problematic, were compensated for by larger farmers placing an extra worker or two on the crew. As the size of ring memberships increased in response to the need for larger labor crews, though, there was a greater likelihood of consistent major variations in members' acreages and each person's contribution to the annual run.

The threshing rings created at the end of the nineteenth century typically contained a "core" section of families united by occupational, ethnic, and geographic associations. A group north of Brookville, Indiana, on the southern tip of an area known locally as the White Plains, provides a typical example. An informal collective consisting primarily of eight families participated in annual threshing runs beginning around 1880 and continuing without major change until the 1910s.[3] Member families included Copes, Nierstheimer, Roberts, McWhorter, Swift, Moore, Younts, and Klipple (see Fig. 4). Each of these names is listed as a farm owner in the Franklin County plat book of 1873 and is represented in nineteenth-century county agricultural statistics reports.[4] The membership also includes the dominant settlement groups of German immigrants and Anglo-American emigrants. Finally, the locations of these farms indicate that participants were all a manageable distance from one another, yet there were other farmers near the core who threshed with other networks.

Decisions to thresh with larger crews and the consequent need to enlarge ring membership resulted in the rise of geographic proximity as the crucial consideration for expansion. Other social or ethnic factors were relegated to secondary, though still potentially important, status. Rings constituted solely of one particular ethnic group continued to exist, but generally only in those areas where concentrated de facto settlement resulted in close similarity between farm locations and ethnic heritage.[5] Ring membership growth in the majority of cases occurred through the addition of farms located around the core membership. Given the heterogeneity of agricultural holdings in most midwestern neighborhoods, the expansion increased the chances that shock threshing crews would include farmers with different cultural backgrounds, economic standings, agricultural operations, and concepts of social obligation.

Developments in the White Plains Threshing Ring reveal how ring growth at this time usually brought raised levels of individual economic differences between members. By 1920, the group included seventeen families participating in a shock threshing run normally lasting for three to four weeks. The additional families came from the areas between the eight core

Threshing Ring Organization and Formalization

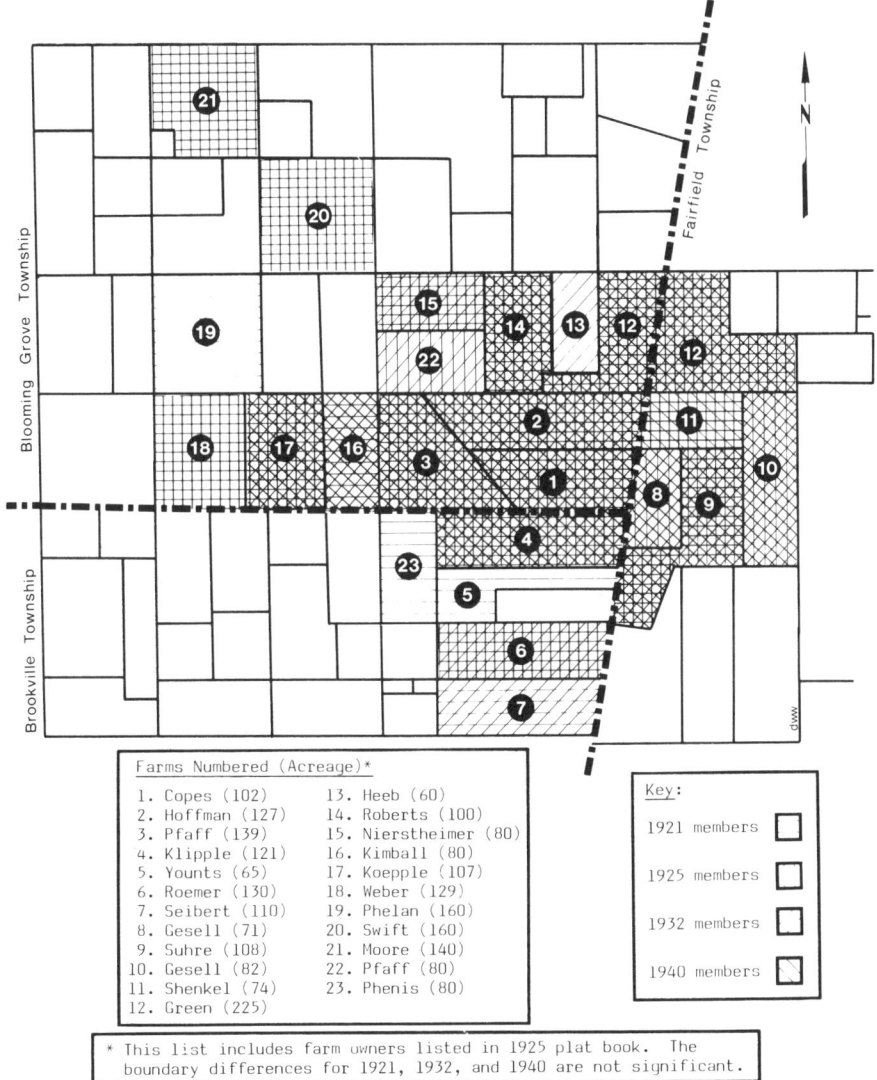

Figure 4: Farms Included in White Plains Threshing Ring during 1921, 1925, 1932, and 1940 Harvests

families. The few remaining gaps are farms that produced no grain and "a few old German fellows that wanted to stack their grain [and thus] weren't wanting to thresh when we did."[6] Ring farm locations in 1925, 1932, and 1940, illustrated in Figure 4, reveal no geographic extensions over the next two decades. In fact, the ring's membership declined through the 1930s as a result of the loss of members in the northwest and south-central areas.[7] Throughout its history, though, the ring's core area remained largely undisturbed. Farm sizes within the White Plains ring between 1920 and 1940 ranged from 60 to 225 acres, with the majority owning between 80 and 140 acres of land. Individual holdings do not reveal the range of bushels threshed by the ring in any given year, as differences in crop yields outproportion the spread in acreage. In 1930, for example, the total number of bushels (shown in parentheses) for each member was as follows: Suhre (321), Pfaff (168), Wingate (484), Copes (397), Knecht (589), Precht (455), Green (698), Gesell (508), Stang (290), Roemer (291½), Studt (89), and Pflum (174).[8] The average threshing was 372 bushels; two members threshed more than 200 bushels above the mean, and two men were at least 200 bushels short of this figure. The difference between the averages of the three highest and three lowest yields is over 400 percent.

The variations within the White Plains ring were not idiosyncratic to southern Indiana or areas in which grain raising was not a major commercial enterprise. Interviews with former ring members and farmers' correspondence in agricultural journals concur that rings throughout the Midwest included members whose farm size and grain crops typically varied by more than 500 percent. One Dearborn County, Indiana, ring reported farmers raising between 30 and 120 acres of grain and threshing a range of 200 to 1,500 bushels.[9] In Logan County, Illinois, Virgil Bratz threshed with two different rings between 1915 and 1943. A mason and part-time farmer, Bratz never raised more than 20 acres of wheat and the same amount of oats. Yet during the threshing season, when his masonry work came to a halt, Bratz "threshed out" farmers producing 2,000 bushels or more from up to 100 acres acres of grain.[10]

Differences between ring members are also confirmed by threshermen's records of bushels threshed per farm along the seasonal run. Table 3 presents threshing statistics of sample years between 1926 and 1947 for Ira Edger (Darke County, Ohio), Kenneth Tracey (Jackson County, Indiana), and Homer Holp (Preble County, Ohio).[11] The spread of farm totals each year varies typically between 500 and 700 percent, with occasional 1,000 percent differences between the smallest and largest yields. The ranges in the reported figures, however, may not reflect the actual circumstances in any single threshing ring. Tracey and Holp serviced two rings each, and Edger normally threshed wheat and oats for at least three collectives. The smallest and largest figures may thus not necessarily belong to the same ring. Further, the notation of a small crop total does not denote that it was threshed alone as a separate stop along the run. Threshing crews did not like to make unnecessary trips to a farm with a small yield, particularly if that farmer raised more than one type of small grain. Families producing a few acres of wheat and a larger oat crop often held their wheat threshing until the oats were cured so that the rig and crew needed to make only a single visit.[12]

Major crop variations within their rings prompted some farmers to begin to question the inequalities of each member's time on the run when no

TABLE 3 **Yield Statistics of Sample Threshing Runs**

Year	Total Bushels Threshed	Number of Farms	Average per Farm	Range
A. Ira Edger; Darke County, Ohio				
1926	8,564 (wheat)	23	372	76–712
	12,530 (oats)	38	330	82–684
1929	9,189 (wheat)	30	306	50–786
	16,483 (oats)	42	392	96–1057
	2,124 (rye)	7	303	88–1045
1935	16,186 (wheat)	47	344	89–760
	5,914 (oats)	23	257	75–750
	801 (rye)	9	89	15–405
1937	13,786 (wheat)	47	293	78–871
	4,285 (oats)	18	238	80–463
B. Homer Holp; Preble County, Ohio				
1926	2,143 (wheat)	14	153	72–464
	9,420 (oats)	28	336	104–771
1929	9,400 (wheat)	36	261	66–740
	6,443 (oats)	24	268	90–524
1935	8,156 (wheat)	33	247	74–684
	2,034 (oats)	17	120	48–391
1938	4,747 (wheat)	24	198	56–514
	2,262 (oats)	13	174	44–414
C. Kenneth Tracey; Jackson County, Indiana				
1938	5,738 (wheat)	39	147	54–362
	2,094 (oats)	21	100	43–271
1941	3,006 (wheat)	17	177	42–465
	506 (rye)	5	101	26–210
	292 (oats)	3	97	44–180
1945	6,668 (wheat)	42	159	36–551
	931 (oats)	7	133	52–314
1947	6,612 (wheat)	33	200	56–577
	721 (oats)	3	240	140–383
	181 (rye)	6	30	12–78

systematic equation outlined each man's labor donation. A 100- or 200-bushel job might take two or three hours of the crew's time, while one or two days could be required at the largest farms. Ring members increasingly sought to equalize differences through the adoption of new, externally derived models that included some form of intragroup mechanism to measure "differences" and provide a "leveling" solution. Most "difference systems" depended on formulas to ensure financial compensation for small-acreage farmers or increased labor or financial inputs from members raising the largest crops. Adoption of such procedures represented a departure from normal traditional patterns, in that the equalization of labor now occurred wholly within the bounds of the threshing season and through the employment of a rigid schedule to measure donated and received labors. Mutual aid in the nineteenth century involved a variety of undertakings and included work exchanged over a number of different agricultural tasks. Farmers did not continue reciprocity networks, certainly, without considered acknowledgment of time and materials lent and received.

The need for a more formal accounting system to account for differences in donated threshing labor was necessary in part because general farm mechanization resulted in a decrease in the need for labor exchanges in most other occupational contexts. Periodic events such as barn raisings occurred less frequently, and by 1910, individual families handled many annual tasks formerly completed through reciprocal aid. Almost every farmer who raised small grains owned a self-binding reaper, for example, to cut, bind, and make the crop ready for the shock. Men now harvested and shocked with the help of other family members or men hired to collect the bundles kicked out by the binder. Before the simple cutting reaper's widespread adoption between 1850 and 1870, workers cut, raked, and bound sheaves by hand. Farmers did not want the cut grain to remain on the ground very long and thus called on neighbors or seasonal laborers to rake, bind, and shock behind the reapers. The evolution of the reaper from simple grain-cutter to self-raker and then to self-binder resulted in a corresponding decrease in local needs to pool labor resources to complete the grain harvest. In contrast to the two or three persons generally working the grain harvest around 1910, four to eight handled the crop of the average farm in the premechanized period. The pattern of individualization and increasing technological self-sufficiency in the grain harvest was typical of changes occurring in planting grain, cultivating and harvesting corn, and other farm tasks. In summary, the growth of larger and more complex threshing rings coincided with a decline in contexts for mutual-labor networks in the grain harvest and other agricultural spheres. Farmers owing work found it increasingly difficult to locate other tasks in which to square their debts.[13] The threshing complex as a cooperative venture therefore became more self-contained and separated from the rest of the agricultural cycle. Farmers

Threshing Ring Organization and Formalization 95

bound the threshing season with formal or informal markers and, within this frame, sought formulas to harmonize all differences.

The adoption of larger crews for shock threshing created other difficulties, including occasional labor shortages, inefficient arrangements with threshermen, and increased pressure on the women charged with providing meals to the entire crew (see Chap. 6). Labor shortages sometimes occurred if each farmer took responsibility for making his own arrangements, because some men in the neighborhood might have other commitments and be unavailable.[14] The nature of informal reciprocal-labor networks enabled each member to "call in" his neighbors, but there was usually some degree of flexibility as to when exchanges would take place. Irregular schedules under manual or stack threshing conditions were not as problematic because farmers safely housed their grain in stack or mow. The lower manpower requirements of these systems also required farmers to gather fewer participants for threshing. Larger groups were simply more difficult to collect together. The absence of three or four men severely slowed the work process, and each delay increased the threat of decreased yields due to the loss of grain stored precariously in field shocks. As long as farmers dealt individually with the machine owner, there was always a chance also that two or three men in the same area would choose to thresh on the same day and with different threshermen. Limited labor resources in each neighborhood could result, according to Preble County, Ohio,

Members of a threshing ring near Conesville, Iowa, in 1892. The ring's threshermen, the Wall Brothers, used an engine with the less-common upright boiler design. Courtesy of State Historical Society of Iowa.

farmer Otis Aydolette, in "the danger of wire-pulling and trying to get certain persons into a certain place where it all rests with one man."[15] Severe labor shortages, in short, inconvenienced and frustrated both farmers and threshermen.

Custom operators became increasingly disillusioned with the application of older social patterns to shock threshing, because too often there was no efficient pattern to the threshing route. Threshermen found themselves crisscrossing through an area and wasting valuable time because farmers next to the man being threshed were not ready at the appropriate time or not yet committed to a specific rig.[16] The hardships of unreliable schedules included the extra wear on threshing machinery during transport and the raised anxiety of farmers destined to wait the longest period for a rig's arrival. Threshermen hesitated to visit a neighborhood where only a minority of farmers were prepared or committed to their services. Difficulties in arranging for an operator sometimes stimulated local conflict between farmers using different threshing techniques or custom contractors.[17] In areas in which most farmers favored shock threshing, neighbors brought increased pressure on the minority to abandon their stacks in favor of compressing the threshing schedule.

The Context of Formalization

Many rings resolved dissatisfactions with existing threshing traditions through establishment of a formal structure to regulate membership activities and define individual responsibility and authority. Most of these groups continued to identify themselves as threshing rings, although through formalization some adopted the more revealing titles of "threshing company" or "threshing union."[18] The identifying characteristics of these collectives included the adoption of a charter or set of bylaws, election of ring officers, use of a "difference" system to equalize labor received and donated, and participation in organization and settlement meetings marking the opening and closing of the annual run.

The main period of group formalization occurred between 1910 and 1920, although at least a few Indiana and Ohio rings initiated structural changes in the 1890s.[19] By the mid-1920s, approximately one-third of all midwestern rings worked under the authority of a charter and elected officers. The geographic locations of formal collectives do not fall into any neat patterns. No state dominates in numbers, although farm periodicals in Indiana (especially the *Farmer's Guide*) and Iowa (notably *Wallace's Farmer*) were particularly vociferous in their support for the new structure. There are small areas in which local rings organized primarily in one fashion, such as in Randolph County, Indiana, where "threshing unions" predominated in the 1910s, or Darke County, Ohio, where most groups retained informal structures until combine adoption. In general, formalized rings are noted as often in the hills of southern Indiana and Ohio as on the plains of west-central Illinois or the Iowa Corn Belt region. Innovation centers are found also in strongly bound ethnic communities in northeast Iowa and mixed-heritage areas in western Ohio. Formalized structures were rarely enacted, though, in neighborhoods where stack or barn threshing continued as a common practice into the 1930s or in communities with strong religio-cultural bases for the preservation of a traditional farming style.

Significantly, the main period of change coincides with reports on threshing by agricultural institutions and the farm press. The earliest (and only) comprehensive survey on threshing practices published by the United States Department of Agriculture is J. C. Rundle's 1918 study of "The Thrashing Ring in the Cornbelt."[20] Of the eighty formalized rings in his sample, Rundles notes that "some of the rings dated back fourteen years, but most of them were organized within the last few years."[21] Midwestern agricultural colleges were little more attentive to threshing than their federal counterparts, but the content of the few periodic publications on threshing definitely supported the adoption of formalized ring structures. The University of Illinois Agricultural Experiment Station produced a bulletin to "instruct" farmers on "Successful Threshing Ring Management" in 1925.[22] Included in the publication were "difference system" models and bylaws examples. The lateness of governmental attempts to promote specific threshing systems suggests that the land-based college experts were likely not the primary motivators for initial adoption and change in traditional patterns. Once committed, though, agricultural writers strongly supported the trend towards formalization. The statewide farm newspapers and journals took an earlier promotional lead for change. Descriptions of ring practices began appearing before the turn of the century and were common features in issues published before and after each threshing season between 1912 and 1920. At the same time, the staffs of these publications began running editorials promoting alternative ring structures and published frequent encouragements and testimonials from rings undergoing successful transformations. Although it is too late to discover the impact of popular media sources on threshing change, the support was clearly in favor of formal organization, and the timing of the promotion coincided with the main period of change.

The immediate motivations for changing the traditional complex were neighborhood reactions to organizational complexities arising from larger threshing collectives and the need to compensate for differences between ring members. Yet, local farmers did not create the concept of contractual and formally structured social orderings, nor did they base their new models on existing patterns of the threshing complex. Instead, ring participants derived the new traits from cooperative models developed in industrial and academic contexts. Farmers' use of outside-developed models reflects a general rural awakening to wider influences on Midwest agriculture and a raised consciousness of regional farming systems as part of the national scene. The last quarter of the nineteenth century and the first decades of the twentieth century in the Midwest were marked by a variety of "farmers' movements" in response to this growing awareness of the structural and economic relationships between agricultural and nonagricultural sectors. The impact of the urban industrial world reached beyond the fabrication and sales of tools and implements; cultural transference eventually included all varieties of social and cultural products.[23]

Midwest agricultural historian Earle Ross appropriately calls the period 1897–1915 the "New Agriculture . . . to signify that agriculture had passed from pioneer existence to modernized economy and living."[24] Many of the region's farmers participated in one or more cooperative agrarian responses intended to demonstrate that rural residents were not an isolated, powerless, or unorganized constituency. Orchestrated movements began in the 1860s as a reaction to speculators, monopolists, and grain brokers. Perhaps the best-known of the early rural responses is the Order of Patrons of Industry, "the Grange," founded in 1867 and joined by families throughout the Midwest during the 1870s. A variety of other organizational attempts, albeit typically shorter-lived and less popular, such as the National Farmers' Alliance founded in 1880, formed to act for the rural population in legal, economic, and political arenas. Farmers participated in meetings and activities to debate the wider interests of their formal organizations and to discuss the concerns of their communities. Farm Clubs and Farmers Institutes were convened especially with the aim of addressing specific local needs. Both of these efforts experienced a peak in interest, activity, and participation in the decades surrounding World War I.[25] Area Farm Clubs met periodically, often once a month, for primarily agricultural discussion; the Farmers Institutes were special meetings or classes organized by the land-grant college network during the off-season winter months to provide more formal instruction.

The direct impact of formally organized movements and community discussions on agricultural pratices of local farmers and their families undoubtedly varied between individuals and according to particular issues. Organized attempts to equalize economic differences between regions and industries could certainly stimulate community residents into reconsiderations of local cooperatives and mutual labor networks. Whether initial instruction and motivation came particularly from the farm press or local Farm Club meetings is not the crucial question. More relevant is the fact that some farmers acquired a worldview of occupational orderings that suggested the possibility of using contract relationships to resolve problems created by the extension of individual threshing rings. Similar assmilations of new ideas and practices supported the formation of the dairy, marketing, and farm supply cooperatives beginning in the early twentieth century. Rural economists and sociologists typically describe these structured communal efforts as examples of rural cooperative associations. Threshing rings remained neighbor-composed and neighborhood-oriented, and they lacked permanent headquarters or buildings. They never achieved the level of visibility, government support, or academic interest given to, for example, federated and centralized agricultural cooperatives. In their own way, however, threshing rings acted as an early introduction for a greater percentage of farmers to the agricultural structures of the twentieth century.

The Content of Formalization

Ring members initiated formalization with the adoption of a charter to establish the group's structure and regulate basic activities. Two sets of articles adopted between 1915 and 1920 are included in Appendix B. The origins of most charter documents are unknown. The form and style of extant samples do not suggest local or internal creation, and the diffusion of charter models was influenced greatly by the popular agricultural press. Generic bylaws suitable for adoption within any neighborhood were periodically presented in full detail in many general midwestern farm publications. Between 1917 and 1919, for instance, the *Indiana Farmer's Guide* and *Wallace's Farmer* printed identical ring charters a total of seven times.[26]

Ring bylaws reveal the extent to which threshing activities were formally regulated and withdrawn from individual initiative. Reorganization typically spelled an end to basic occupational differences' between the crews at each member's farm. Host farmers organizing their home crews under informal systems also took responsibility for partitioning out labor tasks among the participants. As noted, this custom reflects the traditional rural notion that a man who calls for donated labor is entitled to place and utilize the workers as best suits his plans. The practice promoted the continuity of individual styles and differences between neighbors who had their own idea of the proper divisions of labor and responsibility. Further, the composition of the labor force changed between farms according to the ability of the host farmer to provide workers from his own family and the varied patterns of obligation in effect with his neighbors.

Dramatic shifts followed the adoption of a formal structure, because procedures previously left open to annual and personal variation were now formally systematized, specified, and placed under the authority of a centralized committee or elected official. Although local standards were sometimes used to initially define labor formulas, the move to place group practice under schedules formally protected against individual variation marked a shift from a folk to an official cultural process. Charter rules (e.g., one laborer per twenty acres of grain) became sanctioned threshing traits changeable only through a majority vote. All formal rings adopted fixed procedures for apportioning and regulating labor tasks. Members received specific labor responsibilities at the beginning of the season and maintained their positions throughout the entire run. The major systems for delegating work tasks were selection by the elected captain (if the position existed) or president, by lot, or by a committee of two or three men chosen by the president. No custom gained any special regional status, though a majority of groups placed the responsibility in the hands of a single individual. Of 46 references to job selection in signed correspondences to the agricultural press between 1915 and 1925, almost two-thirds (30) noted the use of a ring officer, while choice by lot (9) and committee (7) garnered near-equal percentages.

The rationales for unchanging labor positions stressed the bywords of "modern" farming: systematization and regulation. Consistent positioning allowed participants to know exactly their obligations for the season. Each farmer prepared appropriately for his day's work, arriving at a set time and instantly assuming his place within the labor complex.[27] The change to shock threshing supported this development. Almost all of the work in stack or barn threshing occurred around the machine. The four to six field pitchers and perhaps twice that many bundle wagon drivers in shock threshing performed much of their labor away from a centralized area. A more efficient work plan resulted when pitchers went directly to the bundles in the fields. Wagon drivers left their day's last load by the separator so that the machine crew would not wait for a new cycle of loading to begin the next day.

The memberships of formalized groups collectively selected a thresherman and agreed on the season's prices. A committee chosen to represent the entire ring made arrangements, sometimes tendering the ring's commitment as early as the autumn before the next year's run.[28] The rigidity of a group's decision and strength of the bond to a proven thresherman are demonstrated in the experience of a thresherman and ring participant living near St. John's Creek in north-central Missouri in the 1920s. He joined the neighborhood group before the purchase of his rig and never threshed his own crops "for the simple reason that the ring in which he was living had engaged an outside machine for several years."[29] The bylaws also often set out the threshing order. The most common plans specified successive beginnings on alternate ends of the membership area, reverse orders for wheat and oats, or the demarcation of three or four rotating positions for beginning each annual run.

Regulations for selecting labor positions and threshermen and for establishing the threshing order had wider consequences than the simple structuring of the threshing work. Farmers participating in a fixed order of threshing could better predict the arrival of the machinery at the home farm. Yet, systematization also forced some families to alter agricultural activities to conform with their position in the threshing for that year. Farmers near the end of one run sometimes found it necessary to stack or mow their grain, whereas members near the beginning had no choice but to thresh from the shock. Threshermen generally approved the new arrangements because they could set their schedules more quickly and avoid delays due to unprepared crews or uncommitted farmers.[30]

The typical hierarchy of formalized rings included the elected positions of president, secretary, treasurer, and, in some cases, captain.[31] The president took responsibility for calling meetings and presiding over business activities, selecting members of various working committees, and, in some cases, apportioning labor tasks to ring constituents. The secretary, in addition to his normal task of documenting meeting activities and decisions, had the important job of compiling labor and crop statistics for each threshing day. This information was needed for figuring "difference" at the end of the season. The treasurer kept account of the ring's funds and made payments as specified by the ring membership. The captain's role paralleled that of the union shop foreman or steward and is further testimony to the industrial imitations enacted through formalization. The captain typically selected labor positions for the membership, directed the season's threshing route, decided on the starting and ending time for each day's activities, and chose when and where the ring meals would take place. He thus occupied the most important and unique position on the general labor crew. The captain's decisions affected both the wider framework of the threshing run and the day-to-day activities of ring members. As in the experience of one southern Indiana ring, it seemed as if at times the membership looked to him to resolve all possible ambiguities:

> Only the captain had a hard job [of the officers]. Of course, like now if you'd be a-thrashing and it looked like it was going to rain and here you didn't want no half-dozen or eight loads sitting around to get wet. Well he had to decide if it was going to rain or not. He'd have to tell you you better wait awhile to see if it's going to rain before you loaded those loads. Of course then he had a lot of responsibility. If he missed and it didn't rain, they'd say, "Well, you ought to have sent more men out." If you got all the loads cleared up before the rain, then of course they were happy.[32]

The captain took no fixed labor task for himself. He usually worked around the separator, where his main occupational contribution was to feed bundles of grain that fell from the bundle wagons or were errantly tossed towards the feeding conveyer. The location near the machinery allowed him to regulate the ring's activities and serve as liaison and arbitrator with the rig crew. The president assumed many of these responsibilities in rings without an elected captain.

The election of officers to regulate the ring supported the ability of the core membership to maintain a form of centralized control over intragroup activities for periods stretching to thirty or forty years. Ring membership rolls were often quite remarkable in their continuity, although there was usually some change in family memberships between seasons due to renters, tenants, and changes in farm ownership. Delegating significant roles through majority votes enabled core families to annually reelect members of their own group and thereby perpetuate local styles and preferences. The minutes of the White Plains Threshing Ring contain over fifty family names on the membership lists between 1919 and 1942. Only two men not belonging to the core membership of nine families were ever given ranks of authority, however, in twenty-three years of elections with four or five positions voted each year.[33] Bylaws seldom restricted a man's tenure in office, and the same men tended to occupy official positions year after year.

Difference Systems

All formalized threshing rings adopted formulaic mechanisms, known as "difference systems" or "settlement systems," for equalizing variations in members' labor contributions, the amounts threshed by participants in the run, and the time spent at each man's farm. The difference equations specified the variables, along with attendant values, to be used for comparison of each man's contributions and obligations. One ring officer, generally the secretary but sometimes the president or a designated "timekeeper," kept close account of activities throughout the run. He tallied the results at the end of the season and employed the accepted formula to figure the amount deserved or debted by each man. A single reckoning at the run's close negated the need to account for differences occurring each day or between each member's work, because the official could cancel opposing debts.

> I remember that, well there was one time I remember, must have been around 1923 or so, we had just gotten married when I had just come onto that ring. And Joe D-, he was the one to see, the one who was supposed to tell us all what we owed there at the schoolhouse [where the settlement meeting occurred]. Well, I had a fair crop that year but didn't think I could have owed nobody anything. Me and my brother had threshed everybody out. So we go there, and here comes Joe saying we got to pay this money to these people and such. But then he says that, well others got to pay us too. . . . So by the time we was all through paying and getting, and giving and getting, what was coming to us, well between us we had something like thirty-two cents! Now, I'll tell you something. I never worked so hard in my life for that money. Yes, thirty-two cents is about all we got. You see what I mean, it was all messed up then "cause you had to have it all figured for each man. That was all messed up, but it didn't take long to figure something better.[34]

Settlement system models were proposed in the popular farm press and were protected against change by the simple parliamentary procedure of conducting ring business. The only significant differences between settlement system practices were the variables used for the reckoning.

No single measure dominated a majority of rings, and even the bulletins published by the land-grant college network exercised caution in suggesting a regionally appropriate system.[35] Among the commonly employed variables were the nature (e.g., one man, two men, one man and a team) and time of labor donations, grain acreage, total yield, and time spent on each farm. A number of rings also charged for meals taken at each farm or provided by the host family.

Difference systems used by rings in Indiana and Illinois illustrate a range from a typical simple accounting procedure to a most thorough and complex reckoning. The Union Center Threshing Ring in Huntington County, Indiana, figured difference on the amount of labor provided by each member throughout the run against the charges for paying an entire crew at the home job. In 1921, for example, each man providing labor received a credit of 30 cents per 100 bushels for wheat and half that amount for oats. With sixteen men involved in the run that year, the debt for home threshing was figured on the basis of $4.80 for 100 bushels of wheat and $2.40 for the same amount of oats. A farmer raising 350 bushels of wheat and 400 bushels of oats accumulated a threshing bill of $26.40. If this same man helped to thresh 6,000 bushels of wheat ($18.00 for his labor) and 4,200 bushels of oats ($6.30 for his labor), he ended the season owing the ring $2.10.[36]

The Illinois example comes from the border of Tazwell and McLean counties, where rings used a settlement system initiated by two brother preachers, N. B. and S. W. Crabtree. The plan became locally known as the "Concord Plan" because of Nate Crabtree's pastorship at the Concord Church in Tazwell County. A farmer as well as a preacher, Nate Crabtree participated in such "progressive" rural activities as the organization of local Farmers Institutes. His accounting system for threshing typically included notes on crop rotations, yields, and "soil treatments." A page from the "Director's Book" of 1920, shown in Table 4, demonstrates the exactness of Crabtree's threshing recordings. Ring members hired a "director" to be "boss of the whole crew and timekeeper as well. He saw to it that grain was supplied to the machine, and directed the movement of the teams."[37] For his work in 1920, the director received five dollars a day.

The comprehensive Concord system figures labor donations to the minute and charges members for both their meals and the feed supplied to the horses. The rates in 1920 included the following: $6.00 a day for a man and team, $4.00 for a man alone, 75 cents for each dinner or supper, and 25 cents for horse feed per day. A meal furnished on the job with fourteen men present earned a credit of $10.50 on the farmer's account; the same number of horses were worth $3.50 for the provision of feed. The sample page of Nathan Williams's threshing documents the work for threshing twenty-two acres of oats. Each member's contribution is noted. The "Balance" reflects the difference between the value of the labor provided to Williams and his donated work at each member's threshing. The

TABLE 4 **Sample Difference System Page (Illinois)**[a]

Nathan Williams										
	Wheat				Oats				Total	Balance[b]
	Team	Men	Hrs.	Amt.	Team	Men	Hrs.	Amt.		
B. Stubblefield	—	—	—	—	1	2	2:35	3.61	—	4.99
G. Springer	—	—	—	—	2	1	2:35	4.13	—	2.09
W. Lee	—	—	—	—	1	1	2:35	2.58	—	4.32
J. Humphries	—	—	—	—	1	1	2:35	2.58	—	4.37
O. Tyner	—	—	—	—	1	1	2:35	2.58	—	1.02
C. Tyner	—	—	—	—		1	2:35	1.03	—	.92
H. Irwin	—	—	—	—	1		2:35	1.55	—	.95
C. Holam	—	—	—	—	1	1	2:35	2.58	—	4.74
M. Holam	—	—	—	—	1		2:35	1.55	—	2.55
H. Lee	—	—	—	—	2	1	2:35	4.13	—	5.47
H. Armstrong	—	—	—	—	1		2:35	1.55	—	1.50
L. Stubblefield	—	—	—	—	1	1	2:35	2.58	—	—

Date 8/19/20 acres   wheat   bu.   average   30.45   32.92
                                                    less[c]   .21
Time Began 8:20   due for labor   32.71
     Quit 10:55   meals, etc.   14.67[d]
           2:35   Check $47.38
Dinners 26 @ .75 = 19.50
Horses 24 @ .25 = 6.00
  22 acres   oats 1014 Bu.
Crop Rotation
Soil Treatments   Lime   Phosphate   Other Corn
                     Clover   Alfalfa   Soy Beans, etc.

[a]Documentation by Nate Crabtree, Ring Director, Tazwell County, Illinois.
[b]Balance of Williams's labor donation to each man vs. their contribution to his threshing.
[c]This figure is not explained.
[d]Balance of Williams's contribution of $25.50 (see left) vs. his meal and horse expenses throughout the run.

accounting is based solely on labor provided and time worked rather than bushels threshed or acreage. Williams's contribution to other members always outweighs or equals the time and labor given to him (a fact that reveals the ring's location in a strong grain-raising region). The last sum entered in the balance column, for "Meals, etc.," is the balance credited to Williams for hosting the threshing crew minus charges against him for food and feed provided to him during the season.[38]

Organization and Settlement Meetings

Formalized rings marked the beginning and ending of the annual run with the organization and settlement meetings. The opening session occurred "when the grain was in the shock," or one to three weeks before the anticipated commencement of threshing activities. Members gathered during the evening at the president's house or at a local meeting space such as a church or school. Only the male ring members attended, and there were no planned social activities. Typically, the current ring president chose the date and place and reigned over the discussion. The main task was to take care of matters essential to conducting the year's run. Meeting participants voted on the admission of new members into the ring, elected officers, apportioned labor tasks, specified the threshing order, and considered any new business or amendments to the bylaws. They also discussed the need to hire extra workers, the rates of paying difference, and the current charges of the thresherman.[39]

Settlement meetings typically combined business and social functions and were held during an afternoon or evening one to four weeks after the last ring threshing. The gathering provided a symbolic close and appropriate metaphor for the threshing season. As entire families often participated, the ring normally gathered at larger public sites, including schools, churches, or centrally located picnic areas and groves. The meeting began with participants and activities spatially segregated. The men met privately to settle differences based on the season's account. Some rings contracting with an outside thresherman also invited him to attend the meeting and paid him during the opening business section. Members also paid any hired hands, heard the treasurer's report on the year's activities, and discussed potential threshermen for the next season. The business segment of settlement proceeded rapidly as members completed the few organizational chores necessary to close the season's business.

While the men "settled up," the women prepared for a "social time." Some rings celebrated threshing's end with a full meal or picnic, but most groups feasted on ever-popular ice cream and cake or perhaps watermelon and other special items. A ring in Randolph County, Indiana, stipulated in their bylaws that the event should include "a good ice cream social or watermelon carving."[40] The closest parallels in rural culture to the "social time" at settlement meetings are those events known as ice cream socials or cake socials. Interestingly, participating families did not prepare all of the foods for settlement events. Particularly in the case of ice cream, which gained regionwide popularity as an appropriate settlement fare, either the ring's treasury or the thresherman bore the financial burden. Traditions calling for the itinerant operator to provide food are especially noteworthy, qualifying as a sort of midwestern potlatch and equalizing exchange between the thresherman and his "customers."[41] Whoever supplied the ice cream, the women always contributed the cakes. The men rejoined their families for the social segment after completing their business. The reunion signified the end of the threshing season, the return of the absent male members to their families, and the beginning of the celebration for a harvest completed. Clarence Pyle summed up the feelings of his southern Indiana neighbors: "We ate to our heart's content . . . the crop was in, we all had money in our pockets—there weren't any soreheads."[42]

A few rings did not include a "social time" at their settlement meetings, but instead they added a wholly social event later in the fall. Postseason events were also started in rings that had no formal structure or scheduled gatherings to mark the end of the grain threshing. The affairs ranged from informal male-only parties centered around a keg of beer or whiskey to planned meals involving whole families.[43] Extra social events of formal rings always included entire families and were designed to promote intragroup solidarity and continuity. In Parke County, Indiana, the custom in the 1910s was the "grand jubilee picnic" held in a convenient grove. Each family brought special dishes, and the meal ended with the crowd-pleasing ice cream and cake.[44]

Cooperative Ownership of Threshing Machines

Only a minority of rings cooperatively owned and maintained their own equipment. While no regional statistics are available, it is unlikely that more than ten percent of midwestern rings consistently operated without an itinerant thresherman between 1900 and 1930. The low number reflects a general midwestern rural tradition (until recent decades) of owning most items individually used and "contracting" or sharing special equipment with limited application. One or two farmers in most neighborhoods generally owned such devices as sorghum mills, ensilage cutters, and silo fillers. Rings usually purchased a complete rig as an effort to gain more control over their threshing. Difficulties in soliciting the service of a thresherman close to the time the shocks cured motivated members to seek their own rigs as a way to avoid losses due to an itinerant operator's delay.[45] Farmers without the barn space or stack-building expertise to store the grain over an extra period had a particular need for immediate threshing. A group with its own equipment began work on members' crops as soon as both men and grain were ready.

Rings that included one or two members with experience working with the appropriate power type and separator were more likely, of course, to agree to the expense of a machinery purchase. A combination of complex machinery and a lack of technological expertise often proved disastrous as ring members became frustrated with the threshing quality and lost time as a result of their own mechanical inexpericnce.[46] Ownership of the threshing technology always raised consciousness about machinery operations and responsibilities:

> Of course we took a lot more interest in the machinery than we might have before, because now we were the ones who'd be responsible for it. Like if that separator would break down, everyone would lose time. You couldn't

just wait for someone else to fix it, or blame someone else for getting it fixed. There wasn't no one else there running the machinery. . . . I think maybe we all got more careful then because if things went bad, like I said, there wouldn't be no one else to look after it. Like with the throwing in the bundles, you always wanted them heads first into that separator. Else you'd lose some with the straw. You didn't want to see grain going out with the straw. That would be our money going out there, You always got a bit more concerned when it was your money laying out there on the straw pile.[47]

Some rings evolved towards eventual threshing autonomy by purchasing a rig and hiring a proven thresherman to run the machinery for a limited time. Two or three members served as apprentices and then took over the machinery's operation after one or two seasons of instruction.[48]

In comparison to the flexible relationships characterizing informal collectives, the structures of machine-owning rings represent the extreme of formal organization. The initial steps towards threshing rig ownership parallel the organizational phases of farm supply and marketing cooperatives organized in the 1910s and 1920s. Consensus agreements were necessary for planning membership obligations, cash inputs, investment returns, dividends, and schedules for maintenance and operation. The process followed by a ring in Douglas Township in Madison County, Iowa, is representative. Farmers frustrated with the "chance arrivals" of a thresherman decided in 1919 to purchase a used steam engine, a water wagon, a machine shed, and a new separator.[49] Group members estimated a need for $3,520 to finance the purchase, pay an engineer and separator man for the first year, and cover other expenses. They formed a fourteen-man stock "company," with eight men purchasing a full share of $320 and six men opting for a half-share. Members adopted bylaws specifying procedures for returning investments and elected officers. During the threshing run, each man paid the prevailing rate per bushel into the treasury. The ring also threshed for a few farmers outside their membership and added the earnings to the group's accounts. The treasurer settled all bills for supplies and paid wages to the engineer and separator man at the season's close. The remaining funds were then divided among the membership according to their shares. Although one group member considered the first year's crop "harder than usual" because of low yields and heavy straw, each farmer owning a full share received a dividend of $69.

Cooperative threshing rings were chartered as small for-profit stock companies. Successful ventures normally benefited from the leadership and management of one or two farmers with proven business acumen. Near Hortonville, Indiana, the Munday Thrashing Company was organized by James and Zeno Earl Munday, two brothers who were active in other farm organizations and the later creation of a farmers' elevator. The company began by raising $2,500 for machinery purchases and other supplies through the sale of $100 shares. They also borrowed over $1,000 from the Hortonville Farmers Bank. Threshing with the new equipment began in 1915, and the treasurer's reports from the years 1916–1922 reveal that the Munday Thrashing Company did quite well during this period. The ring paid off its bank note in 1918 and returned dividends to its shareholders after each season. Dividends paid averaged over 12% for the seven years, with the best returns being 29% in 1920–21 and 16% in 1921–22.[50]

Rings owning threshing equipment typically contracted the use of the machinery to nearby farmers with no group affiliation. Members then hired themselves out as a custom crew to take care of all labor tasks except handling the grain. Their main clients were wealthy farmers, infrequent grain producers, or the occasional man who stacked his grain and threshed when most shock ring members were busy harvesting corn.[51] Custom crews charged double the rate received by a thresherman providing only a machine crew and, after paying members for their labor, returned any surplus to the general treasury. The quantity of custom threshing varied between groups and seasons. "Outside" work occurred only after ring members completed threshing their own crops and never approached the levels of travel or personnel characterizing the itinerant threshing crews in the Great Plains or Northwest. Free-lance work could entail, though, a considerable percentage of the ring's annual activities and reward participating shareholders with a sizeable supplemental income. In 1918, a group organized only two years previously and located a few miles south of Columbus, Ohio, threshed approximately 20,000 bushels of grain. Over 9,000 bushels of this total were wheat and oats raised by non-ring members.[52]

The Significance of Formalization

The enactment of formal ring structures resulted in important departures from the traditional sociocultural traits characterizing nineteenth-century manual and stack threshing patterns. New systems created initially to standardize labor and economic partnerships stimulated changes in social relations and orderings. The most overt and embracing consequences were the systematization of the labor exchange and the use of more complicated social orderings with new symbols of prestige and status. The impact of a choice to change, however, ranged from formal bounding of rings and employment of a closed season for equalizing differences to election of officers, from specification of labor positions to settling of differences, and from votes on new memberships to official sanctions for individual deviations from charter regulations.

The movement to formally regulate the threshing event signifies a shift in the pattern of cultural development from a "folk" to a "rational" process of evolution. To state that change becomes more rational is not to imply any inherent changes in the agricultural practices of farmers or their perceptions of a quality of life. Purposely avoided are such misrepresentative terms in cultural evolution as *progressive, scientific,* or *efficient,* because these labels name pragmatic methodologies appropriate to any technology. *Folk* and *rational* refer to the process through which cultural patterns are learned and transmitted and to the orientation of value systems towards tradition and custom. Cultural products are the result of the cooperation between physiological and cognitive energies. Formalization, and the attendant weakening of local folk culture, is characterized by the ascendancy of three trends in decisions about cultural change: the turn to external cultural models and agents as a source for new models, the rise of consciousness of the individual and individual life-situations, and the consequent abandonment of traditions and shared behaviors as patterns for innovation.

Sociological studies of innovation adoption distinguish between changes emanating from in-group motivations and initiatives from those reflecting response to forces originating in external contexts. Internal-based processes, best characterized by Charles Loomis's use of "immanent change,"[53] dominate folk cultural continuity and evolution. Whether it is a ballad singer changing the content of a song, a craftsman experimenting with a new form or material, or a farmer developing a new way to stack loose hay, the important unifying features of folk culture are self-direction and the motivation from individual and group experience. Innovation diffusion in traditional society generally divides along existing cultural boundaries, as intragroup acceptance is necessary if any act of cultural change is to continue and gain wider acceptance. Evolution is unplanned insofar as there is no formal directive for change (although the innovators may themselves be very conscious and deliberate in their work).

Externally motivated change begins with an individual or group who "consciously attempts to bring about change within a social system or upon a social system."[54] A classic example of this process occurred in England when scattered peasant holdings were transformed into large fields through officially prescribed redistribution and exchange of parcels. Changes motivated by outside influences generally have a high correspondence between the level of planned direction and the likelihood of cultural conflict. Judgments about potential innovations in folk culture are made on the basis of attitudes towards traditions maintained by, and within, a group. In contrast, directed change typically requires individuals to make conscious choices between at least two cultural models—their own and the one introduced from the outside. Both processes require conscious decision making, but the need to select among competing cultural patterns becomes more crucial in situations of group contact and outsider-motivated innovation.

The first generations of midwestern farmers to adopt threshing machines used a single dominant model to generate the neighborhood groups required to successfully complete the grain cycle. No new systems were proposed, or at least none gained any widespread acceptance. In effect, nineteenth-century cultural changes were largely spontaneous sociocultural responses occurring along predictable lines. As "outside" models became increasingly available in the early twentieth century, the predictable future (because of the continuities with the past) became unpredictable on account of the conflict of contrasting patterns. Cultural resolution now entailed increased discourse about alternative systems, and farmers began to depend more heavily on outside specialists for information. Eventually, the spontaneity and local base of folk processes were replaced in some locales by the adoption of patterns developed by outsiders, who often were not familiar with neighborhood customs. This shift carried no inherent negative impacts on the threshing work, but change occurred only with the loss of local customs that formerly supported the integrity and identity of each rural neighborhood. Midwestern threshing remained a distinctively cooperative affair, but with fewer occupational differences between organized rings.

A significant motivation for formally regulating the threshing complex was not the mechanization of the activity itself but the development of a wider worldview and different value orientation. The initial use of mechanical devices did not result in a shift in the region's overall cultural patterning, because farmers used existing models to solve the crucial problems of adoption. Threshing patterns through the last decades of the nineteenth century remained largely undisturbed as farmers employed mutual-aid networks that paralleled and supported other rural cooperative efforts. In the early decades of the present century, and long after mechanization, midwestern threshing style began to reflect the covert signs of a wider cultural change. Threshing formalization signified a weakening of the traditional local culture and the increasing impact of regional and national trends promoting greater personal and institutional similarity between rural neighborhoods and the urban-industrial complex. Debates over conflicting models were carried to the popular agricultural press and into the pages of land-grant college bulletins. Writers and defenders of formalized structures continuously stressed that the new models were efficient and, importantly, geared to the needs of each individual farmer.

An important component of the rational process is a consciousness of the individual. Although cultural-studies scholars agree that the individual is the ultimate source of change in folk culture, they also recognize that personal creativity and change are strongly limited by shared group membership and the conservative force of tradition. The cohesive network of shared attitudes, values, and beliefs underlying traditions acts as a buffer against idiosyncratic change. The strength of tradition refers to the sanction given to specific practices through repeated performance. The strongest traditions are those customs that reflect the most widely held and central cultural norms. Folk culture, rooted in the past and based on shared traits, therefore depends on a fragile compromise between individual variation and subservience to group patterns. Subordination does not deny innovation but assumes the greater importance of maintaining the aims and equilibrium of a wider social network.

During the nineteenth century, farmers developed cooperative plans appropriate to their particular needs and relations with neighbors. Each neighborhood system included a system of checks and balances ensuring conformity to local patterns and negating the need for institutional controls. Formal rules were not necessary because of the strong expectations of group participation and the power of extant value systems. Informal group pressures and "safety valves" in occupational flexibility reduced incidents of individual nonconformity or displeasure with local social and cultural practices. Farmers did not consider threshing to be a closed system, and they squared labor inequalities in other work contexts. Further, a sense of neighborhood, family, and obligation prohibited excessive misuse of the status quo, because the members of neighborhood threshing rings often interacted in other social and occupational contexts.

Threshing formalization movements indicate a rise in individual consciousness to the point that personal expectations, objectivity, and abstraction take priority over local group traditions, consensus, and social ties. This shift did not (and cannot) occur without prior weakening of supports for group conformity and maintenance. The redress of traditional patterns of mutual aid coincided with the loss of other contexts for equalizing labor differences, the demise of shared group views of labor obligations in relation to grain acreages, and the realization that informal group controls could no longer compensate for individual differences. Farmers seeking to regulate labor donations and job responsibilities could not resolve their needs by reworking local customs. Dissatisfied members increasingly viewed themselves as separate participants of a collective temporarily formed for a specific agricultural task and within a bounded time frame. The shift in priorities is critical. Rather than conforming their behaviors to ensure group continuity, these men now viewed the threshing group's function as the formal satisfaction of individual situations. The ascendancy of the individual was reflected in bylaws standards that included monitoring each member's crop and labor donations, charging for meals eaten or cost of animal feed, and electing officers with specific responsibilities throughout the run.

The evolution towards a rational process and away from folk culture signifies a reorientation of value systems. Farmers no longer viewed local traditional customs as the most appropriate source for providing answers to contemporary problems and concerns. Folk culture depends on custom and social pressure to regulate change and provide models for the future. Rural residents increasingly restructured threshing rings through formulaic models borrowed from presentations in the popular media and agricultural press. Some of these new ideas were first proposed by the region's farmers; others were the idealistic creations of editors, cooperative specialists, and other "experts" who rarely sat down at a threshing meal. In general, though, the new models supported local acceptance of formerly nonrural social and cultural traits. Timekeepers to monitor each day's threshing, charges for meals, officially voted hierarchies and centralized authority, and formal occupational regulations were practices appropriated from the urban-industrial complex. The use of a general structure with little basis in the shared culture of a group's membership limited the continuity of local traditions. Agricultural practices tended to homogenize between groups as farmers abandoned individual and neighborhood customs in favor of standardized popular forms.

VI.

"THRESHING WAS SOMETHING SOCIAL, TOO"
FOOD AND PRACTICAL-JOKING TRADITIONS OF THE THRESHING RING

> If you want to know what came from this threshing ring, you might say a federated church came from it.... Threshing fostered a spirit of cooperation which made it easier for our schools to consolidate.
>
> Gladys Pyle[1]

> Threshing was like a big family in a way. You had your good ones, and sometimes not so good I'll tell you, but you stayed together in a family way.
>
> Herman Enslinger[2]

Farmers established threshing rings to successfully achieve an agricultural goal. Yet, the scope of activities occurring during the annual run indicates clearly that "threshing time" provided contexts for the expression of other cultural practices and social displays. Performances of such customs as threshing meals and practical jokes explored interpersonal relationships between participants and served as evaluations and, usually, affirmations of wider community networks, aesthetics, and expectations. The wider cultural functions served by activities occurring on the threshing run linked the Midwest to traditional rural societies in other regions of the world that attach a variety of social expressions and practices to cooperative agricultural tasks. Some researchers emphasize the "license" for special behaviors during mutual-labor undertakings that are prohibited or inappropriate in everyday situations. In Matti Sarmela's study of Finnish Karelian reciprocity systems, for example, he notes that normal social life was restricted by a conservative religious system and the difficulties of meeting life's basic needs. The existing moral and economic limitations were overcome, though, during communal agricultural pursuits that included times set aside for social liberalness and consumption.

> Joy in life was not forbidden for the people formerly, but its forms were adapted imperceptibly to practical daily pursuits. "Work and diversion" were closely linked in the life of early static society. Work gave sanction to amusement, which without the veil of "practicality" would have been considered sinful and condemned by the church as well as society.[3]

In the Midwest, the timing of the threshing season in the context of the yearly work schedule contributed more to the social significance of the activity than any possible limitations of a religious ethic. The intensive work period of traditional agricultural cycles began with spring plowing and oat seeding in March or April and ended with the harvest of the last bushel of corn in November or December. Between these dates fell a continuous run of planting, cultivating, harvesting, caring for animals, and the dozens of tasks occupying the good-weather months. Threshing occurred typically between July 15 and September 1, or during a time when farmers were engaged also in reaping, shocking, and perhaps stacking the grain crops, cutting and stacking hay, and cultivating corn. Rural residents did not have much time for purely social affairs during busy summer schedules of long workdays. Further, the mechanization and technological innovation of most farm tasks between 1870 and 1930 resulted in the ability of farmers to carry on with crop production and stock chores through individual or family efforts. Special chores that continued, or developed into, cooperative ventures, including silo filling, corn shredding, and butchering, took place after the threshing season.

Midwestern rural families anticipated threshing not only for the completion of the grain harvest but also because it provided a break in a long period of isolated and intensive family work. They viewed the opportunity to assemble together as a chance to meet social needs largely abandoned over the previous four or five months.[4] The gathering of twenty to thirty people provided opportunities for the spread of information, news, rumor, and gossip of family and community happenings. Threshing was not any easier than other tasks, but working together "allowed you to catch up on the news and pass a little besides," it "gave you a chance to see how your neighbors were doing and maybe even to learn something from them."[5] Cooperative ventures affirmed social bonds and perhaps created new ones. Although memories of threshing rings are somewhat romanticized, it is the social experience, rather than the agricultural process, that rural residents usually emphasize when they talk about threshing as a symbol of a previous way of life.

Changes in everyday patterns during the crew's visit to each farm testified to the wider significance of threshing days. The opportunity and activity

"Threshing Was Something Social, Too"   115

More than forty individuals assembled for this threshing in Leatherwood Valley, Guernsey County, Ohio, 1898. Courtesy of Ohio Historical Society.

affected families differently, yet most created markers symbolizing the specialness and consummative nature of the event. "The threshing crew was like guests coming," noted a woman from south-central Ohio, "and you wanted to put on your best for them."[6] Prethreshing preparations included clearing and cleaning all spaces in the house and barn likely to come under the scrutiny of the visiting crew and neighborhood women. Farmers devoted special attention to granaries and carefully repaired any holes or cracks through which grain could exit or vermin could enter. The men readied all the necessary equipment, perhaps adding some fresh paint to a wagon bed or polishing horse tack. Children attending school were excused from educational participation to help their family. The day was special to kids, who anticipated the presence of so many neighbors, the visibility and enticement of the machinery, and the opportunity to share in moments of rowdy behavior. During threshing, children circulated through the fields carrying water to the crew, helped out in the kitchen and around the meal table, pestered the engineer for machinery instruction, and played around (and on) the irresistible straw stack.[7] They were also given more chores to do around the farm because of the absence of the leading male worker(s).

Family preparations and displays were conducted within a range of performance standards sanctioned by local aesthetic evaluations of proper behavior. The guiding norm was the presentation of order and beauty within the limitations of available resources. To perform well within traditional bounds demonstrated a family's recognition of local preferences and the ability to present themselves at superior levels without overstepping neighborhood standards. This process was nowhere better manifested than in the planning, preparation, and serving of threshing meals.

Threshing Meals

> This gal down the road south of here . . . was so high-falutin' and bragging on her threshing dinners all the time. She'd say that her meals were *always* eaten up, you know that the men were *always* eating up everything she put out. And, my gosh, we always felt like it was better to have food left over. If they ate everything, why how could she be sure they'd had enough to eat. We always wanted to make sure they had enough . . . than blowing off all the time like she did. . . . And this gal I was telling you about down to the south, she *never* called on any of us to help her like we did each other. No, she was one to hire girls to work *for* her, she'd pay them to do what she wanted.[8]

Providing food for the crews participating in cooperative labor is a rural agricultural tradition with origins predating the documentation of harvest customs. In England, where hired gangs of itinerant laborers or local "cottagers" provided the bulk of the work force on many larger farms for hundreds of years before mechanization, it was usual for the farm owner to supply labor gangs with a final harvest or "hawkey" supper.[9] Early travelers in the Midwest discovered the continuation of the tradition during the pioneer period. The English visitor William Faux witnessed a corn-husking near Washington in Daviess County, Indiana, and chronicled the event in his usual ridiculing tone:

> My host had a large party of distant neighbors assembled to effect a corn shucking, something like an English hawkey, or harvest home. All gentle, and simple, hard work till eleven at night. . . . After I had retired to bed the hawkey supper commenced; all seemed fun, created by omnipotent whiskey, with which they plentifully supplied me, although in bed.[10]

Other reports of early midwestern cooperative tasks describe the persistence of celebratory meals at log rollings, corn shuckings or husking bees, house raisings, and reaping.[11]

The opportunity for display during threshing meals and the consequent evaluations of the performance often led to a (usually) friendly competition between the women in a threshing ring. Host families tried to meet the expectations of the threshing crew; at the same time, they attempted to provide a meal experience that would be recalled later as both appropriate and unique. The audience for each display reached beyond the immediate participants, as threshing crew members quickly reported the success or failure of any effort to their families and the larger community. Experience passed rapidly into local anecdotal and narrative traditions, strengthening local aesthetic judgments and supporting a consciousness of performance on threshing day.

Negative reports typically singled out individuals setting themselves apart by extravagant behavior, such as the "high-falutin'" gal in the text above or families that shirked expected responsibilities.[12] Women charged with meal preparations walked a narrow line between traditional notions of cooperation and individuality. On the one hand, ring members expected women to provide special meals with a content and form appropriate to local aesthetic norms. Yet, to prepare the quantities necessary for the crew, the wives of ring participants exchanged kitchen work with one another. The amount of mutual aid requested by any family depended on the number of cooks already present at the host farm, the size of the threshing crew, and the length of the expected work. Three to five women were typically needed to prepare the meals, and only rarely did one woman help more than three or four neighbors during an entire threshing run.

Ring members evaluated meal performance on the basis of content, quantity, and the eating context that included the table setting and meal area. "Content" suggests the use of foods with the appropriate social prestige for threshing gatherings, as well as the quality of each preparation. Although rings variously set their own preferences for specific foods, the kinds of meat served were a consistent measure of prestige throughout the region, perhaps because they form the centerpiece of the meal.

> Chicken was not one of our favorites. There was a belief that a farmer who served chicken saved up all his tough old roosters just for threshers. Beef, preferably steak, was the favorite, with roast pork a close second.[13]

> Sometimes a stingy housewife would skimp on the beef or pork and slip in some wieners, which we held in low repute. She got a bad name if she tried it too often.[14]

> To begin with, the meal preparation had to begin a day in advance, with a trip to town to buy a roast beef, since the meat you canned yourself just wasn't fancy enough.[15]

While freshly slaughtered chicken or lamb, pork, or even "wieners" were acceptable foods in a few areas, beef is commonly acknowledged by ring members as having the highest social prestige. Roast beef or some other special cut is the most cited item of all products purchased in town for threshing dinners.[16]

Beef is a high-prestige food within most American cultural and regional groups, and there are many European counterparts. Eighteenth-century laborers in East Anglia ate beef, "rarely eaten at any other time of year," provided by farm owners at the harvest supper or *largesse-spending*. Pork was the common fare of the working classes because of their low wages and the inability to raise cattle on small holdings.[17] The use of beef for guests, special occasions, and Sunday dinners has a long history in American midwestern traditional culture. When the Carpenter family in DeKalb County, Illinois, hosted forty men for a barn raising on their homestead, Lena Carpenter wrote in her diary that it was "clean and cool. Father went to town. bought 50 tin cups & Beef & Buns & Bread for Barn Raising. We have a very large barn."[18] The association of beef with threshing meals is not, then, a custom reflective of this specific agricultural task; rather, the meat's significance stems from the community's attachment of high social prestige to beef in most public performance contexts and at celebrations. At a time when most meat was produced and slaughtered on the farm, a trip to town to purchase special beef cuts demonstrated an investment of money and a recognition of social obligations.

The status attached to "store-bought" or "town" foods differed between items and neighborhoods and often changed over time. Some rings considered purchased bread a positive sign of generosity and an appropriate item to serve guests. Other groups, during the same period, felt that fresh home-produced bread symbolized a family's hospitality and effort. In general, the substitution of purchased products for foods perceived to be part of the rural domain, and hence home-produced, commonly sparked negative responses.[19] Former ring members also recall the "snickering" and "bad reputations" following the use of paper plates, paper napkins, or other items that rural people perceived as a reflection of a family's laziness or refusal to recognize the meal's higher social status.

On the other hand, host families received neighborhood recognition for providing a quantity of some item associated with on-farm scarcity and festive occasions. Before refrigeration and home freezers, farmers normally acquired and stored large blocks of ice for use through the summer. Family members rarely used the ice to cool everyday foods or drinks; thus, ring participants viewed the use of chipped pieces to make "real ice tea" as evidence of the meal's high prestige.[20] Special additions to average threshing dinners were often store-bought or purchased through catalogues and therefore contrasted sharply with the central rural practice of providing home-grown and self-prepared foodstuffs for the bulk of the meal. Distributing soda pop, ice cream, cigars, potato chips, canned salmon, or prunes to meal participants raised their awareness of the meal's status and highlighted the performance context.[21] Farmers purchasing high-status items displayed a hospitality based on their acknowledgment of contemporaneous preferences and expectations. The popularity of threshing rings coincided with a time when goods and services of urban or industrial origin were becoming increasingly popular in rural settings. Ironic as it may seem from the present-day return to "home cooking," mass-produced items were often accorded an initially high social prestige in rural contexts.

Many women established their reputations by fixing a special dish recognized by the participants as an individual creation and contribution. Local identification for pot pie, chicken and dumplings, or berry pie defused potential competitive difficulties by establishing a cook's status for a unique dish. This egalitarian solution did not require participants to compete for superiority in a limited range of preparations; rather, it gave each individual a distinct reputation for her particular preparation. As with beef, only rarely did any dish have a particular association with threshing other than that the event provided a context for public performance. The traditional dishes, including such items as beef, potatoes, gravies, and pies, were preparations that rural families identified as foods appropriate to cooperative social meals in general. Women could offer their special contribution at a church supper or other neighborhood event and receive the same commendations.

Accounts of the kinds and quantities of dishes prepared for the communal meals are now legendary among older rural residents. As a Johnson County, Indiana, woman recently wrote, "No farm wife worth her salt wanted to set a skimpy table."[22] Offenders of local aesthetics in most accounts are often wealthier women whose attempts to be "extra fancy" did not satisfy basic midwestern palates or ideas of neighborhood cooperation, or stingy farmers who skimped on generosity and hospitality. Not all meals included the varieties listed in the following description, but the range of preparations suggests the energy and planning required to feed a large crew, and in such a way as to leave a lasting positive impression:

> My mother was one of those who prided herself on the culinary arts. The main course of meat usually consisted of roast capon, baked ham, roast beef, to which would be [added] mounds of mashed potatoes, potato salad, sugared sweet potatoes, fresh peas, right from the family garden. To this would be added applesauce, strawberry preserves, currant and grape jellies, that had been so carefully prepared months before for just such an occasion. All these good things would be topped off with pies galore: apple, peach, berry, gooseberry, and a half-dozen kinds of cake.[23]

A final area of aesthetic judgment centered around the meal setting and included evaluations of the layout of the table, overall sanitary conditions, and atmosphere of the eating area. Women enhanced their table settings by using "guest" cloths, special tablecloths and tableware, or by arranging freshly cut flowers as centerpieces.[24] Ring cooks viewed passage between the kitchen and the dining area as a move from a private, work-oriented space to a public, social context. Some women marked area boundaries by saving special clean aprons for girls serving the threshing crew, while other

Grant Wood, "Dinner for Threshers," 1934. Perhaps the most famous portrait of a threshing meal, this tempera on masonite painting is criticized by some former threshing participants as showing the meal activity in too clean and orderly a fashion. Courtesy of The Fine Arts Museum of San Francisco.

participants split their responsibilities, also with appropriate dress, between work "in the kitchen" and "at the table."[25] Midwestern stories about threshing meal disasters often focus on unsanitary conditions in the eating space and the inability of host families to keep distinct boundaries between occupational and domestic contexts.

> I threshed at a place. My brother was with me. I threshed at a place with *great* big bank barns, built on the backside of a hill. We set down [the threshing machine] behind the great big bank barn, got in there. We went to dinner. They had a place out there in the yard to wash, with tubs and everything. And then we went around the corner of the house to a dining room. There was an old couch pulled up to the backside of the table. Now this was supposed to be a *fine* place. And there was some chairs along the side of the table. But there wasn't no screen door. The door was open. The first couple of fellows that came into where the table was, it was setting there, here come half-a-dozen, or ten or eleven young chickens off the back of that couch and ran across the table and out of that door. In the butter and everything else that was on the table. Well, I could drink the coffee and eat burnt bread. So I had bread and coffee. My brother hurried up and got out of there. He didn't stay long. I don't think he ate much of anything at all. I ate some beef, they had some cooked beef. Now I *knew* that was cooked. So, I ate some beef and some bread; I ate two or three pieces of bread and some coffee. And when I went out back to the barn, back down to the side of the barn, my brother went on his hands and knees and was bent over. He just couldn't hold it down then anymore. He was down on the ground, carrying on like that you know. And as long as they lived there, well I always tried to thresh for them when they lived there, between the meals.[26]

In contrast to the dirt, dust, and nature's intrusions into the threshing area, regional norms called for the dining space in the house, on the porch, or in the yard to be neat, clean, and orderly. The crew passed from the dirt of threshing to the (anticipated) cleanliness of eating via use of wash basins, soap, and towels placed in a transitory location near the house.

Threshing meals are today best remembered for their culinary aspects, but they also provided the most important contexts for social interaction between male and female participants. Each man on the labor crew occupied a set task that brought him in contact with a limited segment of the entire work force. Women spent most of their day in or near the house and away from the threshing activity. The entire group gathered together only during the meal periods. The functions of threshing days widened considerably during these hours. Although other appropriate events existed in rural society for courting and meetings between unmarried adults, for example, some future matrimonies began, or took giant leaps towards completion, during time set aside for threshing meals.[27] Manipulations by self-professed "match makers" in at least some rings resulted in the continued meeting of single adult males and females. "Social planning" included the invitation of particular women to help out at specific farms, the announcement of a marriageable woman's responsibility for certain meal preparations, or the placing of an unmarried son on the crews working at selected farmsteads.[28] These activities were recognized by the participants and contributed to their anticipation of the social dimensions of neighborhood threshing runs.

If mealtimes (and other stolen moments) provided a chance for intergender socializing, women devoted the entire day to meeting intragroup needs. The dissemination of family and neighborhood news occupied only a portion of the activity. Experienced participants instructed younger

Threshing ring members washing before going inside to eat dinner on the August Stille farm in Nashua, Iowa, ca. 1920. Courtesy of State Historical Society of Iowa.

women in techniques of meal preparation and the norms of proper behavior within threshing and, by extension, larger rural contexts. The lessons were sometimes as purely pragmatic as the demonstration of the quantities of food necessary to feed twenty-five or thirty people. No woman wanted to undergo the embarrassment of a young Indiana wife who "didn't bother to get the advice and help of one of her more experienced neighbors." To her surprise and despair, a local legend relates, her estimates of "just how much food she should fix" proved inadequate "when the first thresherman took two-thirds of the potatoes."[29] Sara Jane Kimball, in Jones County, Iowa, thought enough of this danger to carefully note a near-miss in her diary on August 4, 1895: "Friday we had the threshing done and the men here for dinner, 18 in all and the last table nearly ran short."[30]

Only rarely did the male work force sit down and eat with the women and children. Instead, the participants organized "settings," or groups eating in shifts. Decisions about who would eat in each setting and the order in which participants moved to the main table typically revealed general social hierarchies among the individuals present. In Spencer County, Indiana, threshing crews in the 1920s often included Black Americans who worked for members of the "threshing company."

> And we had a few black men. In those days the white men wouldn't eat with the black men, couldn't eat at the same table with them. They just wouldn't have it that way. At our house, my mother said that sometimes that made it bad for the threshing. Their wagon load of wheat might be ready to come up to the separator and if they had to wait for the last table they was slow. We had a big long back porch where we always ate, and a big long table. So she put a small table at the end of the porch. They ate at the same time then but not at the same table.[31]

Invariably, the men ate first, and the women and children took their food only after the entire work crew finished at the table. This sequence is traditional and is found both at nineteenth-century harvest meals and at some contemporary rural gatherings for Sunday dinners and other special occasions. If the men could not all sit together because of space limitations, ring decisions as to who would eat first were often made on the basis of local perceptions of the value and responsibilities of each labor task. Men occupying positions with the highest prestige always rated a place at the first table. In most rings the machine crew ate before the field crew, especially when the members of the itinerant group were not immediate neighbors and thus received primary guest status. Martin Tew recalled that the feeder and driver on their Minnesota horse-power rig in the late nineteenth century were "honored as the threshers" and given "the best eating and sleeping places."[32] Conversely, the hired men in most rings ate at the second table because of their rather low social standing.

Changes in Threshing Meal Patterns

The significance of threshing meals in the Midwest is revealed in responses to twentieth-century efforts, particularly between 1915 and 1925, to alter traditional practices. Former ring members recall a variety of motives for changes, and only a minority of rings voted for innovation. The most common reasons for reconsidering the traditional meal complex were the requirements—fiscal, physical, and mental—of feeding large shock threshing crews and the competition to "provide a better meal than your neighbor did." In 1916, an Indiana woman suggested to readers of the *Farmer's Guide*:

> The threshing meal is said an old-time custom, and custom is a hard task master. While most women see that it is a foolish practice they fear being thought lazy or lacking in means if they don't come up to their neighbor in setting a groaning table. Now we all know that a lazy woman in the country is as scarce as the proverbial needle in the hay stack and everybody in the country has an abundance to eat, but time and bodily strength to do what is required of them are what they lack. . . .When the men form their threshing rings, let the women also form a ring to consider the threshing dinner. Cold lunches have been tried but no one relishes a cold lunch. A simple, wholesome meal would be appreciated by the workers in the field. Let some more leisurely time be the occasion for the elaborate and intricate menus.[33]

The amount of food and time needed to prepare meals that met the appetites and expectations of shock threshing rings taxed especially the small farmer, renter, or tenant. "Sometimes I think it cost more than Dad got for his wheat crop [in the 1920s]," noted one Ohio woman, and an Indiana resident commented in 1912 that "often a farmer's profits are literally eaten up."[34] The cost of meals and decisions to include purchased items were not always left to individual choices as to the appropriate content of a threshing meal. In some cases, a ring's aesthetic norms compromised family preferences through pressures to purchase certain specialty items. The penchant for beef and a growing taste for store-bought ice cream are examples of group-sanctioned customs that individuals found difficult to resist. Formalized rings in three states recognized the additional hardships and provided meal allowances by 1930 to cover the cost of purchasing ice cream for threshing dinners.[35]

Reconsiderations of traditional meal patterns also resulted from inequalities in the provision of meals due to irregular schedules and manipulations by the threshing crews. Unpredictable weather and unforeseen mechanical breakdowns or illnesses tested the host family's patience. One local legend with a clear lesson concerns a Catholic family expecting the crew on a Thursday and thus stocking up on beef. The family is forced to get rid of the beef and buy fish when a breakdown causes a one-day delay.[36] Lena Carpenter, whose diaries of farming in late-nineteenth-century Illinois are generally a model of midwestern rural taciturnity, described an exasperating sequence of one week's threshing activities that prompted her to pen one of the few emotive lines in her entire journal:

Fri.	July 29 Thrasher Came this evening
Sat.	July 30 Cloudy 60 It rained hard last night. Of cours cant thresh. Maschin Men went to town to get the self feeder fixed. Cloudy and damp till noon.

Mon.	Aug 1 Setting out oats to dry this morning. Threshers here for dinner—did not thresh any
Tues.	Aug 2 Commenced threshing about 8 AM. Had a hard rain at 1 1/2 PM—all hands and maschin men went home. Mrs. Ballarby[?] was here until eveny—about 2/3 done. It has commenced raining again this even.
Fri.	Aug. 5 Clear 64 Deg. Threshers came at 11 AM. Lena and Minea took Edna home after dinner. Commence Thrashin afternoon and soon after a monky wrench in a bundle of Oats went into the Cylinda an mad a bad Break-up. So I give up.
Sat.	Aug. 6 Cloudy 66 Deg. Boys hauling in Sheaf Oats this morning- 3 Thrasher Maschin Men here for dinner and then finished out. Boys helping Brow Thrash this afternoon.[37]

Many former ring participants remember times when the crew either slowed down or accelerated their pace of work to influence the location of the next meal. Almost every group included a member with a reputation approaching Albert Britt's description of a farmer in Warren County, Illinois, who "sold what he could, what he couldn't sell he gave to his family, and what the family couldn't eat he fed to his hogs... what his hogs declined he saved for the threshers."[38] The crew's eagerness to eat at a certain place complimented families with a reputation for excellent performances, but such actions could easily burden households faced with a disproportionate share of preparations.

In addition to complaints about irregular schedules, extra expenses and worry, hot kitchens, and heavy work, some individuals (generally men) expressed dissatisfaction with the time spent at the meal itself. Complaints about lost threshing time were raised particularly in rings with formal structures. Members called for changes in meal patterns so that the threshing proceeded more "efficiently" and with less interruption. "Where dinner is served warm to all present the machine must stop at least one hour," claimed one Indiana ring member in 1915, "and more frequently two hours are taken for the men to arrange and feed their teams and eat their dinners."[39]

Other motivations for change stemmed from wider developments within and outside rural life that carried implications for the continuity of traditional social customs. Although neighborhood women typically exchanged labor, each farm's ability to provide meals for the threshing crew depended on the participation and aid of family networks. Cooking crews were easily assembled when large families lived and worked together and extended families resided in close proximity. The host woman generally depended on the help of daughters, sisters, aunts, or cousins at times of need. By the early decades of the twentieth century, however, the family labor pool was decreasing as single women increasingly left the farm for jobs in nearby towns and cities.[40] An interesting external influence in some locales was World War I and attendant slogans calling for food preservation and conservation. Indiana County Councils of Defense called for the adoption of "dinner pails" carried by men to replace communal patterns. One council claimed the practice would "result in less work for the women" and "avoid considerable waste, for where large meals are prepared as has been customary at threshing time, there is more or less food left over." While few farms ever let any food go to waste, the consciousness of participating in wartime responsibilities provoked some people into criticizing traditional components of threshing meals as noncompatible with patriotic efforts.[41]

Rings adopted a variety of solutions, each of which addressed different problems and reflected the level of formal organization within the group. Between 1920 and 1930, most formalized rings restructured their meal practices. Some groups adopted mechanisms to better predict meal locations and to diffuse the chances either that an unsuspecting woman would face the sudden arrival of the crew or that a household would be saddled with uneaten preparations intended for men deciding to eat elsewhere. Rings achieved minimal control by agreeing to a custom typified in an Illinois ring: "It was understood by all of us that if the rig pulled away before ten-thirty [for dinner] or by three-thirty [for supper], the following meal was on the next farmer."[42] Firmer direction resulted when the captain, president, or thresherman set each day's route and then warned, as accurately as possible, each farmer of the crew's arrival at his farm.[43]

Moves to specifically defray the costs incurred in meal preparations occurred primarily in rings with an accounting system for equalizing labor differences. Bylaws specified that a member's obligations included a set cost of twenty-five to fifty cents per meal. Meal debts were then taken into account with other expenses at the end of each season. "Charging by the plate" for harvest meals represented a significant break with previous tradition, but it provided a logical mechanism to allow continuity in the host farmer's responsibilities. Not all "company" rings took this step, and many former participants recall that this innovation was followed by a period of disgruntlement during which some farmers called for a return to the older patterns.[44] Once the new plan was implemented, however, the group rarely abandoned the practice of paying for meals.

Informal rings also initiated change by limiting the host farmer's responsibilities and specifying appropriate participants at each meal. Typical patterns between 1900 and 1920 included providing dinner and supper to the entire crew and breakfast to the machine crew present for early morning preparations. Some groups altered their schedules to end the threshing earlier in the evening so that farmers would not have to supply supper to the entire threshing crew. The machine crew still received morning and late meals if they remained with the threshing rig. Women later benefited when their threshermen switched from steam to gas power, as the internal combustion engines required far less time for the engineer's preparations and did away with the continuing presence of the machine crew before and after each day's work.

The most sweeping change in meal patterns was the decision by some rings to drop the requirement to provide communal meals in favor of either carrying dinner to work in the morning (with beverages generally provided by the host farmer) or using a self-contained cookwagon to accompany the threshing rig. The "chuck," "cook," or "grub" wagon was a common component of threshing crews on the Great Plains, where the traveling group constituted the bulk of the manpower required to thresh at each farm.[45] The neighborhood base of midwestern threshing rings inhibited widespread adoption of cookwagons because most of the crew were local farmers who usually ate breakfast, and often supper, at their own homes. More important, midwestern rural residents never accepted the traveling cookwagon as an appropriate change in the traditional cultural style associated with harvest meal patterns. Carrying dinner presented a change parallel to other structural changes in the organization of threshing crews; in other words, the individualities of practice in labor and meals corresponded to one another. Cookwagons, on the other hand, presented a cultural enigma; the crew ate a communal meal, but one not prepared by participating farmers or taken in the host man's house.

An early regional experiment occurred in 1911 in Washington County, Indiana, where a ring found that the cookwagon relieved the women of "fretting and sweating."[46] By the beginning of World War I, a small pocket of innovation had spread through some southern sections of Indiana, although at least two rings used the wagon for less than four years.[47] A standard system marked the arrangement and method of paying for meals wherever mobile cooking units were used. The thresherman took responsibility for providing the wagon and purchasing the necessary foodstuffs. He also hired one or two people to operate the wagon and provide meals throughout the threshing run. A shift in threshing participation occurred, as men typically worked as cooks for the work crew. The itinerant nature of the run and cultural expectations concerning the presence of women in the kitchen, but not with an all-male work force, account for the change. Threshermen charged for wagon service by adding an extra one or two cents to the price of each bushel threshed.[48]

Midwestern attitudes towards fundamental changes in the meal system suggest interesting aspects of threshing, worldview, and rural life. Ring members opting to perpetuate traditional host responsibilities emphasized the social functions of meals, the preservation of older patterns, and a sense of local obligation. Continuity in meal patterns supported the persistence of a basic rural worldview aptly summarized in 1915 by Dearborn County, Indiana, farmer Oliver Heck: "Anyone who doesn't think enough of his neighbors to fix them up a meal once or twice a year to get his stuff threshed isn't worthy of the name of neighbor."[49] Heck's attitude is typical of that of other male participants voting against radical change.

> It was back around 1926.... And some of the people around here wanted us to carry meals every day. They wanted to get rid of those big dinners we

had because it was a lot of trouble for the women and such. And there was a few rings around here that'd already done that, and some thought it would be better if we did it that way. But you know I never could see doing it differently then we had been before. Some rings you know would follow every new fad like that that come along, every year they'd be doing something different than the year before. Seems like some people always got a notion to change. But I couldn't see it; I liked those meals and I think the women did too. . . . It was a bother for them even when they had a lot of help. But back then it was their duty to fix those just like it was our duty to work out in the fields. And I think they respected that. We all sure liked to get together when that whistle blew for dinner. And like I said, I sure wanted my good home-cooked meal when I worked so hard. And I think others did too, anyway, because we never did get away from the dinners until they brought in those little combines.[50]

We used to call that ring [that carried their own dinners] the "bucket ring" and I, well, we always felt kind of sorry for them men in there, taking them buckets to work. . . . One time we tried it. It was no small bother to pack your dinner along each day. Besides, the ants got in it and the dogs got in it and by around noon then, you'd be wondering if you had any dinner to eat. We never had so sick a crew on the threshing deal as we had that year. . . . And eating at your own meal, why it didn't seem like that was real neighborly. It always seemed like that dinner helped us to get through those hot days, it got real hot, and that work was hard.[51]

Implicit in these statements is a worldview distinguishing work in the fields, or economic pursuits, from activities of the home and family, or social activity. Discussions of pragmatic considerations mark debates over the usefulness of new mechanical innovations to speed the threshing process or to relieve the drudgery of agricultural tasks. Decisions to adopt occupational innovations are then justified by the goal of "improving" practices and taking advantage of appropriate new ideas and techniques (although "appropriateness" may include some degree of consideration of social and customary practices). Ring members rarely recall dissatisfaction with the alternative of carrying their dinners on the grounds that the practice was more expensive, time-consuming, or somehow detrimental to agricultural ends (unless it was through less efficient work due to less satisfactory meals). Rather, farmers' judgments towards continuity parallel what anthropologist Anthony Wallace terms "perpetual rationalistic" revitalization, or the preservation of older patterns based on a rational association with a chosen, practiced lifestyle.[52] Clearly, many midwestern farmers distinguished between cultural styles associated with home and hearth and those viewed as purely agricultural.

Women's attitudes towards ideas for changing meal patterns were generally more complex and difficult to categorize. Most former members of midwestern rings claim to have favored retention of older patterns as a matter of respect for existing sociocultural roles and the labor of their husbands and older male children. Yet, women also recognized the difficulty of their task and the savings of time and work that might follow a change to carrying dinner or using a cookwagon. For the majority, the pull of older social roles and cultural expectations was stronger.

> Well, it wasn't because women didn't sympathize with the men; I'm sure that most of them did. Because, my you'd see those men out there laboring in the heat, in the dust, in the dirt. It was hard work. And you did feel that if you were a woman that they should have good meals. And they ran the risk of carrying those meals in the hot sun, and of spoilage. Really, to be a self-respecting woman, it was your job to cook a meal. Do the best you could, even if it was nothing more than fried potatoes.[53]

The subject of threshing meals would not be complete without brief mention of the contributions of this activity to regional proverbial sayings and comparisons. Folk speech terminology related to occupational practices of threshing groups has passed from active use because of its specific reference to tasks and jobs now long abandoned in most midwestern locales. "Grain wrestlers," "stackmen," and "spike pitchers" are almost incomprehensible to the present generation of farmers. Expressions associated with meals are more persistent because of their connection with an often-recalled aspect of threshing ring experience and their continued appropriateness in contemporary rural contexts in which eating a communal meal is a central activity of larger social get-togethers. The lasting proverbial comparisons generally focus on the quantity of the food or a particular participant's appetite:

> Eating like a thresher with a hollow pit for his stomach
> Eating like a thresher with a hollow leg (stomach)
> A meal fit (made, like) for threshers
> Table groaning like it was set for threshers
> Just like feeding threshers
> Sloppy as a thresher
> Hungry as a thresher
> Starving like a thresherman who missed his breakfast

Practical Jokes

The gathering of ten to twenty neighbors and the itinerant machine crew created a context for interpersonal ritual jokes to create, explore, and solidify relationships between the participants. Some pranks were intended simply to mark the end of the threshing run or test the patience of their victims. All members of the threshing crew qualified as targets of a prankster's disconnection of a wagon's running gear moments before a driver set the team in motion or the substitution of a soiled diaper or rag for clean towels seconds prior to a blind reach from a soap-filled wash basin.[54] Practical jokes functioned also as a form of social control and elaboration of sociocultural roles. Ring members carried out pranks as symbolic gestures to comment on each other's personality and work, to instruct novices about proper ring behavior, and to mark the acceptance of newcomers into the neighborhood.

Threshing participants found appropriate times for the creation and performance of practical jokes within the frame of the threshing run. Short lax times occurred when equipment broke down or bad weather halted operations, over the Sunday rest, before beginning or after ending each farmer's threshing, and, especially, during the last job of the threshing run. The dinner table also provided an appropriate forum for highlighting individual food habits and matrimonial status. Young single men and women, and also the local confirmed bachelor, were the common targets of mealtime pranks. Members of one Ohio ring often delegated an "old maid or widow" to stand with a fan behind the oldest determined bachelor. She fanned until her target's patience wore out, generally around dessert, according to recountings of these incidents.[55] Other groups set up single women by forcing them to wait on eligible men; jokesters mixed pepper in the coffee of particularly eager and often naive bachelors or hid foreign (and often embarrassing) objects in the food of a male participant trying his hardest to impress a young woman.[56]

The idiosyncratic personality or behavior of ring members provided a popular nexus for intracrew pranks. Many jokes emphasized a nonstandard action or trait in a mischievous manner intended more to test and embarrass than to ridicule or punish. The following incidents occurred in rings in west-central Ohio:

> Charlie Garber was an Old Order man, and he wore a wide-brimmed hat. Well, Charlie had this habit of giving his hat a throw at dinner time. The hat he wore for threshing was an old one and was rotten around the sweatband. So, one day some of the guys found some old rusty spikes and nailed Charlie's hat brim to the ground. Well, when he came out after dinner and grabbed his hat off the ground, he ripped the brim right off.[57]

> Now Bud S—, he worked for Uncle Rob, you know, he run the separator for that threshing rig. But he was driving that threshing machine up the road. You know how they used to jump up there and sit down on the tank. Well, he was going on up the road and Virgil, my brother, and Carl S—, they'd do anything to get him. They had done—They had a pasteboard box in the side, it was sitting aside it. Bud jumped off and grabbed this pasteboard box and put it to set on. And Virgil, my brother, and Carl S—, Uncle Rob's grandson, had put bees, a swarm of bees in that thing. And he said that he didn't know what to do. He said that those bees commenced coming out of there and he said that all he could do is he just grabbed that throttle; and pulled the throttle open and opened the firebox. That's all he could do.[58]

"Threshing Was Something Social, Too"   131

Practical jokes carried out between the thresherman and members of the general threshing or machine crew carried more serious connotations. Some pranks were thinly veiled tests of the thresherman's authority or his ability to perform as an itinerant contractor. The custom operator maintained a fragile balance between his responsibilities as an occupational "foreman" and his obligations as a community member. An experienced thresherman did not always exercise his control over the crew through direct and (possibly overly) harsh criticisms, but instead he sometimes used his own joking abilities or one-upmanship to diffuse potentially troublesome situations. Two Indiana anecdotes illustrate the abilities of threshermen to deal with violations of the widespread interdiction against drinking while working on a threshing crew:

> Well, we was threshing over at a place called Elmer F—'s over there. And the boys—well, there wasn't that much to do that day, and so Dutch S—and Casey H—, they went to Lyons and they got them a pint of Cuban Rum. They brought it back and neither of them had ever drunk any of it. They brought it up to the engine where I was. I was running the engine at that time. So, they opened it up and they took a little of it and it was pretty hot. It was about 100 proof and so they didn't drink any to amount to anything. It was on a Saturday and so we always had to clean the engine and wash the boiler out. So I told "em, "Well, I,ll just put it in the engine box here and you can get it back Monday morning." Well, when I got ready to leave, I just put it in my pocket and stopped down at Marco. Smitty W—, he was setting out there in front of the filling station. I stopped there and, oh it was hot, and I said, "Smitty," I said, "bring us out a couple of cokes and we'll have a drink." So, we poured out about half the cokes, and then filled them half full of rum. And we drunk about all of it up. Well, Monday morning when we went back, why Dutch he come to the machine first. He came and he looked in the engine box, and he said, "Where's the bottle at?" And I said, "Well, I don't know," I said, "didn't you take it with you?" "No, no," he said, "I never." He said, "I bet that Casey got a hold of that bottle." And so it went. After a while, Casey he come. He looked in the engine box and he wanted to know where the bottle was and I said, "I don't know." And he said that Dutch went and drunk all of that up. So after a while they got together, and neither one of them knew where it was, you know. And I thought there was going to be a fight. They got right into it. So when it got hot, I went out and I told them, "Well, you left it here. I thought you left it for me, so I just drunk it up." They never got into that stuff any after that.[59]

> We was a-thrashing and I done a lot of thrashing for this guy. His name was H—. And they got a case of beer when we was there and they tried to get me drunk. Of course I didn't allow no drinking around that machine. But I knowed better. I run that machinery. Pulled into that last job and got it done. They had two cases of beer and a tub full of beer and ice on it. So I took two bottles and I went back to the tractor and I put them in the tool box. They thought I drunk them. So I went to the separator and there's a

step on it. So I missed that two or three times and I grabbed it and missed that again two or three times. And they were laughing, they thought they had me drunk then, and me always talking against drinking. Then I got up there and pretended like I was holding on. So then I just walked up to them, sober as can be, and I said, "It's time we moved this rig out of here." And they were just as surprised as ever.[60]

Local farmers carried out practical jokes against threshermen to remind them of ring expectations of the contractor's job performance and the operation of the engine and separator. Common concerns about the machine's performance included the possibility that good grain exited with the straw and that improper sifting screens allowed foreign materials to pass through with the grain to the weigher. Joking exaggerations reminded threshermen of farmers' worries in a way that also lessened economic tensions. During a slow period, a farmer might call the thresherman over to examine a sack of grain. Opening the stitched bag, the prankster pulled out a rabbit, tool, or other object that could not conceivably pass through the separator unscathed or unnoticed.[61] Alternatively, a man with sleight-of-hand abilities might hide cleaned grain in his fist. After gaining the thresherman's attention, the jokester held his hand in front of the straw blower for a split second. He then displayed a fistful of the secreted seeds and chastised the operator for blowing good grain onto the strawpile.

Practical jokes functioned also as ritualistic means for indoctrinating older boys into the secular and, at times, profane world of the all-male labor force. A popular prank involved the water boy and the water jug he carried to men in the fields and at the machine. The water carrier qualified as a choice target because the position was normally filled by boys too young to be full members of the threshing crew but old enough to desire acceptance by the men.[62] And the jug served as the perfect vehicle for jokes centering on the substitution of various "dirty" liquids for the normal fare. Jokes with water jugs played off the additional sobering question of the quality of the water and drinking spout after making the rounds of five or ten thirsty field laborers. Most rings included one man with a fastidious reputation for either carefully wiping the jug before and after using it or pouring out a small dribble prior to drinking.[63] These individuals were a perfect foil for entangling a boy in a scheme to simultaneously test the water carrier's manhood and call attention to the prudish crew member. Near Frankfort, Indiana, a feisty ring member challenged each new boy with "I betcha can't hit the hole in the top of that water jug whenever you have to take a leak." Floyd Whitinger, who recounted these episodes, followed his father's strict admonitions never to initiate such an incident. His hesitancy to trick others, though, did not prevent him from falling prey to the same prank years later.[64]

"Threshing Was Something Social, Too" 133

Ben Shahn photographed this thirsty worker drinking from a water jug during an Ohio threshing, ca. 1934. Courtesy of Ohio Historical Society.

Dissecting important community events into their economic, occupational, and social components does not reveal the potential influence of the whole activity upon the participants or the impact of engaging in cooperative efforts year after year. Threshing events were significant as more than simple expressions of isolated sociocultural norms. Successful ring continuity required a coalescence of individual patterns and group symbols and thus served potentially as one model for evaluating other neighborhood activities and concerns. The statements at the head of this chapter suggest the function of the threshing ring as a community organizational exemplar. The opening passage is from a participant of a ring in Marshall, Indiana, that involved eight core families from around 1890 to 1940.[65] The community's rural population began to decline during World War I as a result of emigration to nearby urban areas, increased mechanization of farm operations, and a significant rise in the size of average land holdings. According to Gladys Pyle, one result of these trends was a decrease in rural church congregations to the point that the neighborhood residents could no longer support separate institutions. "So since people had learned to work together as neighbors in the ring, they were able to work together and compromise to create a federated church." She goes on to add that the successful cooperative venture also eased the formation of Turkey Run High School, one of Indiana's first consolidated schools.

Although the veracity of this folk history is impossible to test, Gladys's connections suggest a group-defined belief in the social function of ring participation. The widespread organization of fifteen to twenty families often brought together people who might otherwise have remained apart because of ethnic, religious, economic, or social considerations. Participation in cooperative threshing did not negate or end individual differences, but each annual run demonstrated that mutual aid for a common purpose was at least possible and necessary. Herman Enslinger's connection of threshing and family may reveal another romantic sense of threshing and rural history viewed from the contemporary perspective of an elderly retired farmer. Yet, his comments underscore the compromise and sharing required to complete the grain harvest before the introduction of the combine. These same sentiments are expressed over and over by former ring members in discussions of the social dimensions of the threshing ring. The emphasis signifies the importance of threshing both as a social experience and as a symbol of social evolution and change. If threshing days were hot and full of hard work, they were at least experiences in which significant cultural goals and positive social experiences reached a most fruitful coexistence.

VII.

THE CONTINUITY AND DECLINE OF THRESHING RINGS

Claims about the continuity of midwestern threshing rings seem almost unbelievable in light of statistics on contemporary rural population movements and popular stereotypes of farmers as strong individualists. William Miller reports that his family's ring in Butler County, Ohio, retained its basic membership from 1870 to around 1940.[1] One former member of a group that threshed together in Marshall County, Illinois, as late as 1939 remembers his grandfather describing a similar ring pattern that was "already old" by 1895.[2] Although most rings did not keep records of their membership, larger groups organized at the outset of the steam threshing era usually stayed in existence until dissolution between, in most cases, 1935 and 1945. Farmers' testimonials to ring continuity acknowledge periodic changes in the constituent family members and shifts in occupational practices in response to technological innovations. Former ring participants distinguish, though, between changes in specific tasks required to complete the threshing work and the preservation of the overall cooperative structure as an expression of local cultural style. When older farmers talk about "threshing," they use the term to name a whole complex of traditions, symbols, and values woven together in an agricultural and social event.

The cultural style of the threshing ring centered around the mutual exchange of labor and the social organization of the work. A major reason for the remarkable consistency in ring histories is that farmers solved the labor problems of technological innovation with cultural systems familiar to Midwest rural residents since the early settlement period. Alternative solutions were widely known, especially the common practice of Great Plains farmers who hired entire crews to thresh.[3] Yet, with the exception of the custom threshing crews discussed in Chapter 5, midwestern rings retained the same basic social structure until combine adoption. Machinery innovations did not inherently require changes in ring structures, as members could maintain the older social networks even while altering occupational practices in response to wind stackers, grain weighers, and other secondary threshing inventions. The lesson of the midwestern pattern is that the ability to preserve networks governing work exchanges can allow for occupational change in the task itself without disruption of local social systems.

Threshing ring continuity is attributable in part to member participation in wider community activities and other cooperative agricultural tasks. During the threshing ring period, a variety of other rural, nonagricultural activities took place on a local or neighborhood level. Some important changes were already occurring by the 1920s and 1930s, including school and church consolidations and increased leisure and social mobility due to automobile travel. Yet, the majority of institutions and activities in rural areas remained primarily local in scope, location, and participation. Table 5 shows the participation of members of the Stateline Threshing Ring (Butler County, Ohio) in four non-threshing activities around 1930. A great deal of intragroup contact occurred outside the threshing ring, even though not every person participated in all networks. The chart is not complete, moreover, in that it does not list the participation of subgroups of the ring in such other activities as the local Grange chapter, cooperative butchering, holiday celebrations, church suppers, and school programs. Kinship and friendship ties of male and female social groups also contributed to group cohesiveness. Sociometric networks of the entire neighborhood cannot be reconstructed forty years after ring dissolution, but two former members recall some of these constellations. A kinship relation existed between the two Meachems (brothers), Hughes (the sister's family), and Williamson (cousins). The Meachem homestead farm shared boundaries with the Williamson and Longman farms. These three families were quite close socially,

TABLE 5 **Other Associations between Members of the Stateline Threshing Ring (Butler County, Ohio)**

Threshing Ring Member	Church Membership	Farm Bureau Members	Children's School	Silo Ring Membership
D. Longman	A[a]			A
B. Williamson	A	X[b]	A	
C. Ellsworth	?	X		
W. Meachem	B	X	A	A
P. Kuhlman	C		A	
A. Hughes	A	X		A
T. Abbott	A		A	
W. Warner	C	X	B	B
J. Chipp	?	X		
D. Cass	B	X	A	A
H. Bradt	C			
P. Mills	A	X	A	
T. Meachem	B	X	A	A

[a] A letter (A, B, or C) signifies participation, with members listed with the same letter all belonging to the same institution or organization.
[b] An X signifies membership.

as were two German-American families (Bradt and Warner) settling in the area in the late nineteenth century.

The interpersonal networks underlying ring organization fed, paralleled, and resulted from other social systems. For most ring members, cooperative threshing work was just one of a variety of local efforts involving joint effort and participation. The concomitant existence of similar groupings in other contexts supported the solidarity of threshing ring social structures. The social pressure to continue with the same group should not be underestimated. One could possibly withdraw from a ring; it was more difficult to leave the community. In general, then, the strength of the threshing ring structure derived from the vigor of the wider community structure. Threshing groups were more likely to survive as long as ring members and families remained in close order and contact in other areas of rural life.

Other factors that supported unbroken ring histories are revealed in the activities of collectives that resisted formalization. These groups shared a combination of at least some of the following characteristics: low geographic mobility of member families, high percentage of farm ownership, general similarity in farm sizes, presence of two or three extended family networks, use of an itinerant thresherman who lived within the ring's general geographic boundaries, and a conservative nature towards farming practices. Although most threshing cooperatives encountered similar difficulties during the shift to shock threshing, these rings avoided formalization by widening existing neighborhood bonds and social norms to incorporate new agricultural practices.

The Rock Creek Threshing Ring operated in the southwestern corner of Lincoln Township in Harrison County, Missouri. The group's members farmed rolling prairie and brown loam soils ten miles south of the Iowa border, raising corn and oats as staple crops and feeding beef cattle as a principal stock activity.[4] The eastern and northern portions of Lincoln Township are dominated by, respectively, Lot's and Muddy creeks and their tributaries. Larger agricultural enterprises, especially stock farms, developed along the rich bottomland in these areas around 1880. The southwest is more hilly, with the majority of its most productive land confined to sections along the creek bottoms. The township was settled primarily by Anglo-American emigrants from Ohio and Illinois.[5]

A plan of the farms included in the Rock Creek Threshing Ring between 1910 and 1940 is shown in Figure 5.[6] Although member families changed over the years, the ring maintained its basic L-shape outline throughout its 30-year existence as a formally bounded group. The strength of the collective derived from local custom and shared familial heritages. According to former ring participants, six families—Rankin, Armstrong, Blanchard, Bram, Adair, and Tarlton—made up the core membership. Each of these families owned their farms and had settled in the county before 1890.[7] The Rankin, Armstrong, and Bram families trace their settlement to the Civil War period, when they joined a group of emigrants arriving in north-

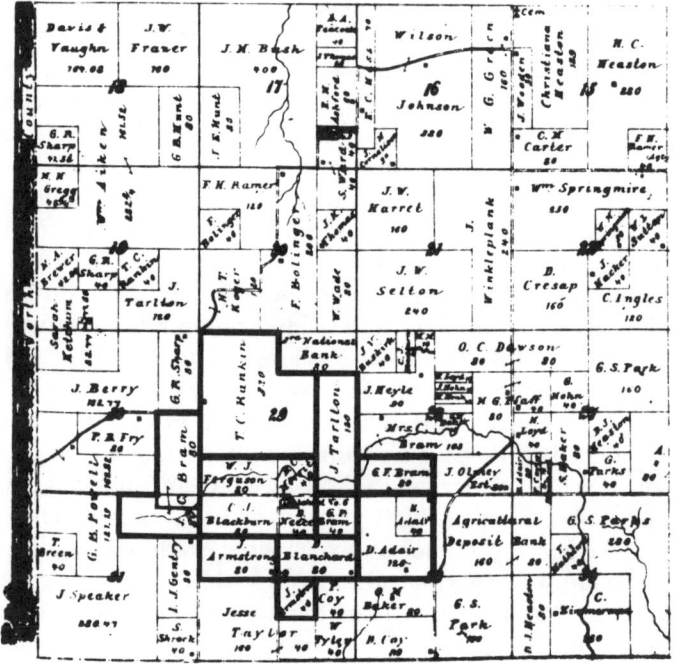

Core Membership Farms, ca. 1925-30 (Acreage)*

1. Rankin (320)
2. J. Bram (160)
3. Armstrong (120)
4. Blanchard (80)
5. Adair (120)
6. Tarlton (120)
7. G. Bram (120)

*Information based on township plat map of 1923 and interview with Oscar Bram, September 7 and 8, 1983.

Figure 5: Core Farm Memberships, Rock Creek Threshing Ring, Lincoln Township, Harrison County, Missouri

east Missouri from Perry County, Illinois. There is no oral or written history of nineteenth-century threshing practices, but Oscar Bram, 86 years of age in 1983, remembers his father describing horse-power threshing with a sweep unit owned by one of the Rankins.[8]

As in the case of the White Plains Threshing Ring, however, a shared historical frame was not always sufficient cause to retain traditional threshing patterns. An important mitigating circumstance in the Rock Creek area was the ownership of the threshing machinery by a member of the ring. The Rankin family always managed their schedule to include their close neighbors and fellow ring members as well as formal collectives in western Worth County and northern Harrison County. Members of the Rock Creek

Threshing Ring did not need any mechanism or committee to annually renew their commitments and reaffirm their expectations to an outside custom operator. The group also never included more than twelve families. Organizational chores were simplified through an informal norm specifying a contribution of two workers per participating farm. As Figure 5 indicates, the equity of labor donation roughly paralleled a similarity in farm sizes. Finally, continuity for the members of the Rock Creek ring became a persistent and conscious choice to maintain carefully considered boundaries between their neighborhood and other nearby areas dominated by large stock farms. Notes Oscar Bram:

> Our ring was different. Of course, now, we had our own thresherman, the Rankins I was telling you about. And so we always knew where they was going to be. And then we didn't worry about so many things. Like those rings up there [in the northern parts of the county] where they had *big* crops, and those farmers still have the *big* operations. You see what I'm telling you. We didn't have so much worry. We weren't big. Now, maybe we're better off now down here. We aren't losing our farms yet anyway. Back then, of course, seems like everyone wanted a car, or wanted to get a tractor, or something. But we just kind of went along, I didn't have a tractor until about 1947. Turns out now maybe we knew more back then than we know now. Now you go up there, they'll tell you a different story. Maybe they're right, but this is *our* story. . . . And I'll tell you this. When we thrashed it was family coming together. Now I'll tell you it wasn't family, wasn't our family, but it was. I'd just tell you what to bring, like maybe I needed your team to haul from the fields, and then you might come back and get mine. [There] weren't any questions asked, not then anyway. Seems like everyone just knew what to do.[9]

Threshing ring stability depended on a group's ability to satisfy occupational needs with social practices grounded in local customs and appropriate to the relationships between the individual members. A similarity of technology promoted an identifiable regional occupational style; the nuance of neighborhood traditions and settlement promoted wider variation in social organization. The quality of the soil southeast of Sharpeye in Darke County, Ohio, is marginal by midwestern Corn Belt standards. Until the years following World War II, generations of farmers wrestled with the heavy clay base to establish mixed agricultural operations on 40 to 120 acres. Only the present farming generation has had access to the tillage methods and heavy dosages of chemical fertilizers that support commercial row-crop rotations. A large ring involving close to twenty families living mainly along the Greenville-Nashville Road threshed continuously from around 1890 to 1950. The thresherman for most of the twentieth century was "Uncle" Rob Clemens. He owned a farm in the ring and also threshed one or two other nearby collectives. Clemens was one of the few Black American threshermen in the Midwest. His customers and ring comembers included the Black American, German-American, and Anglo-American settlers in the area.

The Rob Clemens Ring never formally organized; instead, members gave the thresherman responsibility for most organizational chores. No special group meetings were required, as communication between ring members passed informally within two major constituent families—Clemens and Bass. One former ring member recalls, "We'd usually be watching the wheat, and then come some Sunday Rob would tell us all [at church] that he was going to start in at the threshing."[10] Each member farm contributed one man to the ring, and the host next in line notified participants if he needed a team, grain wagon, bundle wagon, or other special equipment. Variations in crew make-up and individual responsibilities thus occurred between farms, although the members with the largest acreages always provided a wagon and team. All participants threshed from the shock and stored their grain in barn granaries. Rob Clemens set the threshing order according to his determination of which ring area was farthest along with the wheat harvest. From that point, the direction of threshing followed the lay of farm location. A reversing of the wheat schedule for oats ensured equalization. Families assumed meal responsibilities as they fell along the progress of the neighborhood run, and "if you got away with [having to serve dinner] one time or another, why they'd soon catch up to you, and maybe they'd expect more besides."[11]

Maze Clemens's statement on meals reflects basic assumptions linking rings that remained informally organized. Members in these groups viewed each year's run as just one event within a larger cycle of ring participation. Instead of bringing pressure to equalize all contributions within a bounded frame, farmers in the Rob Clemens Ring expected a "settling" across seasons. No member kept an exact accounting of labor or meal donations, but each man expected, by virtue of experience and shared custom, an eventual leveling of any excesses. If circumstances allowed one to avoid providing a meal one year, then the next year, or two years later, the separator "arrived before dinner and left just after supper." Membership in the ring acknowledged a family's willingness to accept local norms even if their origins were unknown to new participants. Since the majority of Clemens's customers were from only a few extended kinship networks, a farmer who challenged ring mores risked the reputation of his family and the solidarity of the neighborhood.

Midwestern farmers maintained traditional patterns through choices grounded in the social norms of family and community networks. Presented with structural alternatives, ring members judged the social bonds of existing systems as too important, or at least too entrenched, to risk upsetting. Social continuity was rarely, though, a question of maintaining practices "for tradition's sake." Farmers in informal rings remained conscious of labor and yield variations among members of their groups. But because families tended to be more permanently aligned and cooperative in other spheres, they were less likely to highlight differences within the neighborhood and less prone towards formalizing methods for compensating inequalities. Rings continuing to reject change, even as they witnessed the restructuring of neighboring groups, developed pride in their conservative tendencies. The positive identification of mutual cooperation without the stigma of a time clock or need for official regulation is foregrounded in the statement of a former member of a Miami County, Ohio, ring:

> We couldn't have ever had it like that ring around Tipp City [that had a formal structure]. What with their men to order others around and such. They were called, they called that a "Company Ring" and I guess it was. We couldn't understand why they did it. It just didn't seem right to us, you know, to have to pay your neighbor for helping you out. You just helped your neighbor, and then he'd help you, and every other man in the ring. And the women helped each other too [in the cooking]. I don't believe we could have got the wheat or oats in any other way. I suppose, well that was the *old* way of doing things, to help your neighbor. Anyway, that's how we did it around here until we got those little combines around '40 or so.[12]

Conflicts between group members tested the bonds of the threshing ring's social core. It is a testimony to the strength of ring relationships that participants resolved almost all internal troubles in short order and without the dissolution of the group. Oral historical narratives concerning intragroup dissensions emphasize typically a problem created by new or young members unable to perform according to ring expectations of proper behavior. In conflict with the antagonist is the host farmer, thresherman, or other group participant with a high degree of authority. The offender in the incident eventually conforms to the existing pattern or else leaves either on his own initiative or through dismissal by the general membership. The enmity in the following Indiana anecdote surrounds a poor performance within accepted norms of straw-stack work:

> On one occasion a farmer put a boy whom some neighbor had sent to do the stacking. The boy went about the work carelessly. Finally the owner went up to right things. Before long both came tumbling down by the stacker in a rough and tumble, but they were separated and the work went on. At dinner, as was the custom, the farmer wanted to ask the blessing but felt he should make amends for the trouble. "I think before I proceed I should apologize for what happened this forenoon," he said, and continued that it would have been all right but when he got on the straw the boy insulted him. At this the boy jumped up and called him a liar and another fight started, but it was stopped and the meal proceeded without a blessing. That was that boy's last day of threshing.[13]

Serious flare-ups between ring members and threshermen occurred infrequently because of prior screening of the operator's worthiness and the usually long association between a ring and its thresherman. In the following account from Franklin County, Indiana, the combative crew members confronting the thresherman are area newcomers. The sentiment of the majority lies with the itinerant operator.

> One time they had a fight here. Two boys, now, by name of F—, who had just moved into the area, they didn't like the thresherman and one morning they got into a fight. They hit him, hit his arm, with a poker that they used to stir up the coal in the steam engine and so then he called a halt. And then these fellows got throwed out of the ring and they formed a new ring.[14]

Ring solidarity is the topic of one of the few threshing legends related throughout the Midwest. The story concerns a disgruntled farmer who sabotages a separator by placing a heavy piece of metal or a tool in a grain bundle. The protagonist is a farmer frustrated with the thresherman or a vindictive man out to damage another person's threshing. The hidden object passes unnoticed into the machine and ruins some of the cylinder and concave teeth (and sometimes other parts as well) before the belt is stopped. The "sabotaged threshing" legend is a third-person account, told as a true story, and usually identified with a specific ring in a neighboring township or county.[15] The narrative content reveals the sometimes tenuous relationship between local farmers and the thresherman forced to balance roles of community member and custom contractor. While one might doubt the veracity of each individual legend, the aggressive action suggests a high degree of apprehension and frustration on the part of some farmers. Perhaps more important, the narrative functions as a measure or metaphor of intragroup solidarity. Equipment sabotage by a ring member suggests the most negative performance of cooperative labor. The thresherman suffers immediately and faces repair costs, but the entire neighborhood work is also delayed. Relating this story as a true experience occurring in some *other* group highlights the trouble-free existence and neighborly cooperation between the narrator and his fellow group members.

The flexibility and dynamism of folk culture supported the continuity of a dominant midwestern threshing form through the period of steam engine threshing. Specific traditions varied from group to group and season to season, yet farmers recognized and perpetuated the threshing ring as the core of a regional response to the available threshing technology. The principal form of the complex remained relatively stable even within those rings that opted for formalization between 1910 and 1925. Farmers held fast to this style as long as threshing remained a stationary agricultural process requiring the labor of cooperating neighbors. Not surprisingly, the adoption of new agricultural technologies, specifically the small multipurpose tractor and the pull-type combine, was the major cause of the threshing ring's demise. Individual ownership of tractors did not in itself result in an end to cooperative practices but supported a change to smaller

The Continuity and Decline of Threshing Rings 143

rings of four to eight farms. Pulling a combine behind his tractor, however, released a farmer from any mutual labor requirements, as he could now harvest and thresh his grain in a single sweep through the fields.

The Decline of the Threshing Ring: The Tractor's Impact

The Hart-Paar Company of Charles City, Iowa, offered gasoline tractors for sale to midwestern farmers as early as 1903. Most of the first internal combustion models were as large as steam engines, and the single- and double-cylinder models remained practical purchases for only professional threshermen. More widespread adoption of tractors did not begin until the 1920s, when major manufacturers produced reliable multi-purpose machines and farmers received higher prices for their grain. The 1920 census lists 63,071 total tractors on farms in Indiana, Ohio, Illinois, and Iowa. The figure increases to 135,027 in 1925 and 230,839, or about one tractor for every five farms, in 1930. Many farmers thus still relied on horse-power through the early Depression period. By 1940, however, when the census returns charted 517,805 tractors, the majority of farms in the four-state region used a machine purchased from one of over fifty tractor manufacturers in the Midwest.[16]

The small tractor was the most important innovation in on-farm power since the steam engine, and it quickly proved more appropriate for use for a variety of farm tasks.[17] Companies produced models suited to the average midwestern operation and modified a host of field devices to enable operators to attach the implements to the tractor's rear hitch. Farmers in the 1920s and 1930s could purchase a new Fordson, Case, or Allis-Chalmers model for five to eight hundred dollars, or less than one-fifth the price of most steam engines. The tractor's ability to power separators promoted a fundamental development in neighborhood threshing rings. Most manufacturers equipped machines with takeoff pulleys rated at sufficient belt horsepower to drive small and mid-sized threshing machines. Implement manufacturers responded by increasing their lines of small separators as tractor adoption accelerated and as farmers expressed increasing desire to abandon their use of itinerant steam threshing rigs.

The primary impact of the shift to threshing with small tractors and separators was a decrease in the size of the threshing crew (see Table 2 in Chap. 4) and the consequent formation of small "tractor rings" of four to eight farms. Tractor threshing completed a cycle in threshing ring development: from the small crews of stack threshing around 1860, to the largest groups during the heyday of shock threshing with steam engines, and then back again to the original size of the horse-power years (see Fig. 6). Major reorderings of neighborhood groups seldom occurred, however, because farmers accustomed to threshing with each other formed tractor rings along preexisting social networks. In many cases, the participants of large steam

Fordson Tractors were popular in the Midwest between 1925 and 1935. This 1925 advertisement shows the multi-purpose abilities, including threshing, of small farm tractors.

threshing collectives split successfully into two or three groups.[18] The smaller capacity of "tractor separators" lowered the number of bushels threshed per day, but farmers contributed less time to the ring because the work occurred at the most optimal moments, at fewer farms, and required minimal organizational chores. Instead of the average three to five weeks of the larger neighborhood runs, members "threshed out" a small ring in one to two weeks. Interestingly, the increased adoption of automobiles during the same period had little effect on decisions of ring membership. Car ownership provided residents with greater flexibility in choosing other

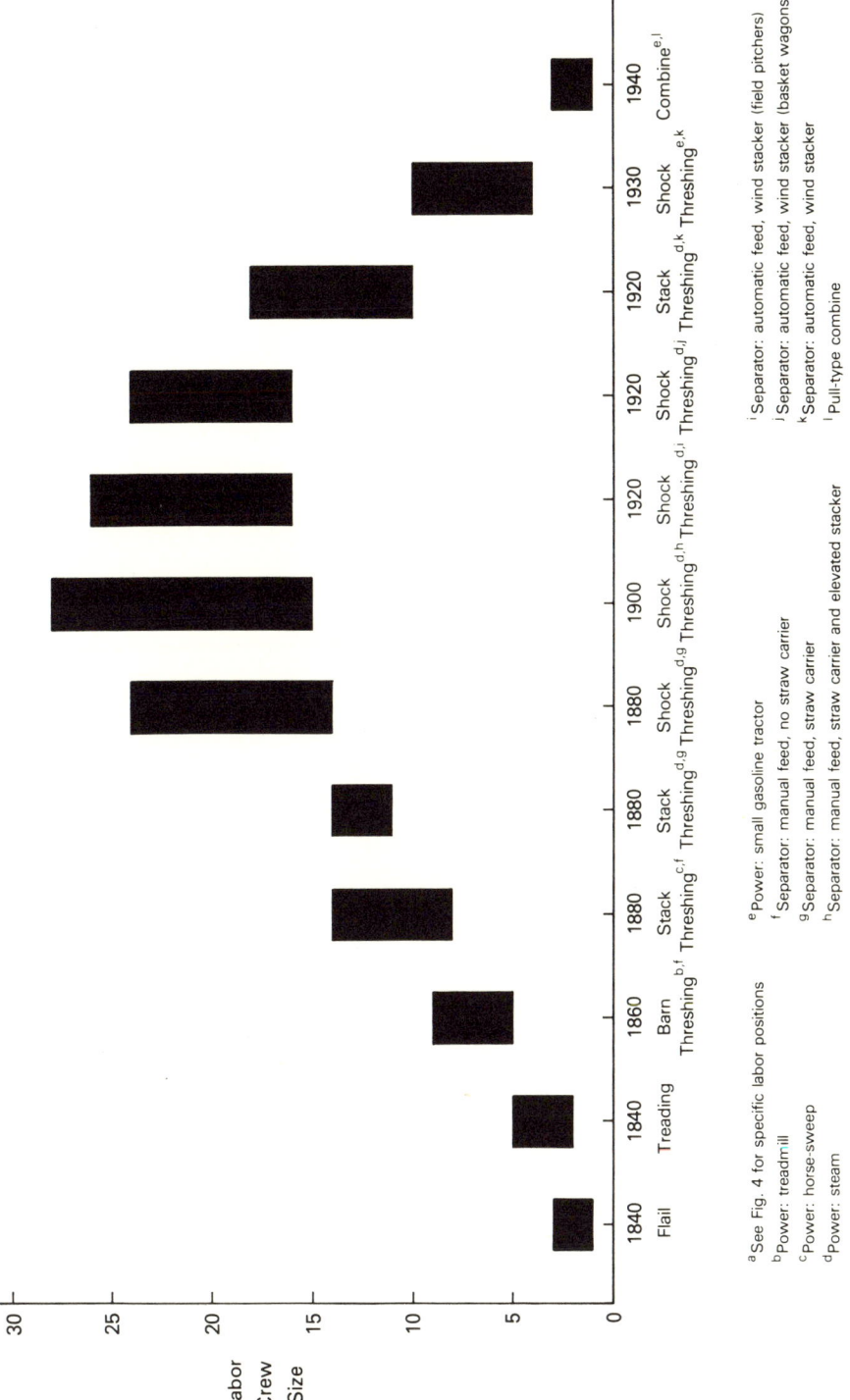

Figure 6: Labor Crew Sizes, from Flail to Combine[a]

group memberships, but farmers still used teams to transport shock bundles and grain.[19]

Belting farm tractors to separators returned threshing to a wholly neighborhood activity without the presence of "outsiders" or custom contractors. The new "little" separator required only initial and periodic adjustments, thus negating the need for professional machine tenders. And the efficient tractor, largely maintenance- and trouble-free, demanded little attention after the fuel tank was filled and the belt was set in motion. The small multi-purpose tractor thus freed farmers from reliance on the thresherman's schedule and initiated the demise of professional itinerant operators as a special subgroup. Many tractor groups chose their most mechanically inclined member to "tend the outfit." Some rings cooperatively purchased a separator and hooked it up to tractors provided by each farmer at his home threshing. In other groups, one participant owned the power and separator used by all members and charged a small fee, typically one-half of the thresherman's bushel rates, as tractor rings did not have to pay the wages of any machine crew.

Farmers in tractor rings streamlined occupational efforts with the goal of keeping the thresher operating with the minimum number of laborers. Many groups adopted basket racks for transporting shocked bundles to the separator and gave little special attention to their straw stacks. Basket racks negated the need for field pitchers, and the absence of a worker on the straw stack saved an additional laborer. A Sac County, Iowa, farmer summarized a common plan:

> It takes only seven men and a boy to run our small threshing outfit. The boy watches the grain wagon, while one man who hauls is away from the separator. I tend the outfit myself and the other five men run bundle teams. We always leave two loads in the evening so we can start in the morning without delay.[20]

The percentage of midwestern farmers participating in tractor rings is difficult to establish because of the informality of ring organization, the lack of written records, and the typically short-lived span of many groups. The first small rings formed between 1920 and 1930 and lasted only ten to twenty years.[21] Many of these initial efforts served as a transitionary occupational style between the large shock threshing ring and the adoption of the combine. Tractor threshing received support from the editors of farm publications, who pointed to the creation of the small independent threshing groups as one of the benefits of tractor adoption. Thus, the first group of farmers to abandon large threshing rings were larger-acreage operators desiring to use the tractor's drawbar capabilities to pull a variety of agricultural implements. These same men were the most likely innovators to buy the initial combine models of the 1930s that required a tractor to pull them through the fields.

No more than ten percent of midwestern farmers threshed as members of tractor rings in the 1920s. The level of participation increased, possibly to a crest of twenty percent, in the mid-1930s with more widespread tractor adoption and the demise of steam engine popularity. Interestingly, the small tractor rings beginning in the middle or late 1930s often continued to use threshing machines long after the combine's acceptance into mainstream Midwest agricultural patterns. The trend was particularly commonplace for those middle- and small-acreage farmers who tended to participate in technological innovation sequences as late adopters. Having established a successful tractor ring in the middle or late 1930s, these farmers were more likely to eschew or postpone individual ownership of combines as long as their fellow ring members agreed to continue existing mutual efforts.

The Decline of the Threshing Ring: The Combine's Impact

The introduction and adoption of the small combined harvester-thresher finally eliminated any need for threshing rings. Initial experiments with machines that could simultaneously reap and thresh small grains began in the mid-nineteenth century. Early devices satisfactorily harvested crops in grain sections to the west long before being successfully accommodated to midwestern occupational styles and environments. Large combines pulled by teams of twenty to forty horses prepared grain for market in California and the Pacific Northwest throughout the later decades of the nineteenth century.[22] These mammoth harvesters were too large for use in the cultivated fields in the Midwest, with their limited size, odd shapes, and poor access. Early combines were appropriate also only in those semiarid areas where the grain, particularly winter wheat, ripened all at once during summer weeks of continuous low moisture and humidity. The vagaries of midwestern weather patterns, field drainage capabilities, and land contours promoted an uneven crop maturation that prohibited harvesting and threshing in one operation. Finally, the region's farmers needed grain straw for bedding, stables, and feed. The western combines, including the popular models used in the Great Plains region until 1920, cut the straw close to the grain head and left the stalks standing in the field.[23]

Manufacturers introduced a suitable solution to midwestern problems with the introduction of a small combine designed to be pulled by the all-purpose lightweight tractor. The first models made available in the 1920s included their own self-contained power source, as power takeoffs on tractors were not yet commonplace. The combine reaped, threshed, and held the finished grain in a small storage area until a man unloaded it into a truck or wagon. Standard machines cutting a four- to six-foot swath cost between four and seven hundred dollars depending on the model, size, and manufacturer.[24] Although advertisers promoted the combine with illustrations of farmers individually harvesting their crops, more often early combining required three persons working together. One man drove the tractor, a second worker rode on the machine to regulate the cutting height and make other adjustments, and the third participant drove the loading vehicle between field and barn. Combine harvesting thus completed the cycle of threshing manpower requirements by returning the average number of workers on each farm to premechanical levels (see Fig. 6).

Adoption of the combine proceeded at a slow and sporadic pace through the 1920s. The first combine in Illinois, for example, harvested the 1924 crop; by 1928, only 300 machines were in use in the state.[25] The primary innovation period in most midwestern locales was from 1930 to 1940, especially during the second half of the decade, as market prices slowly rebounded from the Depression and the international demand for American grain rose as a result of the deteriorating economic scene in Central Europe. By this time, Allis-Chalmers and other manufacturers advertised small, reliable combines for less than four hundred dollars.[26] Initial adoption by one or two neighborhood farmers between 1925 and 1935 did not usually cause a ring to disband. As members increasingly purchased their own harvester-threshers in the late 1930s, however, the remaining ring participants faced more acute manpower shortages. The number of member farms in the White Plains Threshing Ring in Franklin County, Indiana, dropped from seventeen in 1930 to twelve by 1940, largely as a result of combine purchases. The group managed to stay together through the decade by hiring temporary employees to complete a standard shock threshing crew (see Table 6a). Additional membership declines by 1942 convinced the remaining ring farmers to divide into two tractor rings. Many other midwestern groups never attempted to replace lost members with seasonal workers, but instead the members disbanded within two years of initial combine use in their area. A farmer who did not then combine his grain either joined another nearby ring or tried to convince some of his neighbors that cooperative tractor threshing remained the best possible alternative.

Farmers who wanted to combine their grain did not necessarily go out and purchase the required machinery, though they could clearly not band together in "combine rings" similar in style to the older threshing groups. Neighborhood social networks for mutual aid were simply not necessary with the low labor requirements. Further, as one Indiana farmer expresses it, "When a stand [of grain] needs to be combined, it needs to be combined now."[27] Farmers curing their bundled grain in shocks or stacks were able to delay the home threshing while helping their neighbors. Fields ready for the combine, in contrast, cannot be left too long without overmaturing and the consequent danger of crop loss due to shattering and lodging. The replacement for the itinerant thresherman was the local "custom combiner." Enterprising farmers, including some former threshermen, purchased equipment and then hired out their services to local farmers.[28] The practice of custom combining began soon after the machine's availability and con-

TABLE 6a **Threshing Statistics, 1928–1940, White Plains Threshing Ring***

Year	Farms	Hired Men	Total Bushels Threshed	Average Bushels Threshed per Farm
1928	16	1	5,105	313.4
1929	16	1	5,247	327.9
1930	15	1	4,754	316.9
1931	15	2	10,100	673.3
1932	15	2	5,400	360.0
1933	14	3	4,600	328.6
1934	14	3	6,133	438.1
1935	13	4	8,200	630.8
1936	14	3	5,000	357.1
1937	14	2	5,000	357.1
1938	13	5	4,300	330.8
1939	13	6	4,000	307.7
1940	12	7	4,419	368.3

TABLE 6b **Error Computations Using Labor Rates**

Year	Wage Rate (per 100 bu.)	Wages Paid (per man)	Bushels Threshed Based on Labor Rate	Report of Bushels Threshed	% of Error in Labor Rate
1928	25 cents	$12.69	5,076	5,015	.012
1929	35 cents	18.69	5,245	5,247	.000
1940	25 cents	10.75	4,300	4,419	.027

*BASED on "Minutes of the White Plains Threshing Ring" (see Appendix B).

tinues today. The degree and scope of midwestern "custom combining" does not approach the Great Plains patterns described in detail by historian Thomas Isern.[29] Midwestern operators rarely work outside their local community, and most custom operators in the region own only one combine, although some men run two- or even three-combine operations. The region's practices seem almost feeble in comparison to the large multi-combine and truck caravans that follow the harvest trails from Texas to the Dakotas and Canada.

A few practical problems had to be resolved before farmers fully benefited from the combine's abilities and accepted the machine as the most appropriate harvest technology. Grain producers threshing from the shock harvested their crop and allowed it to cure for at least one or two weeks before threshing. Combines could not be put into the field, however, until the grain was close to full maturity, because all mechanical operations occurred in one pass. The small cereals planted in the 1930s, particularly wheat and oats, tended to lodge before reaching "combine maturity." Farmers who combined too early found that their high-moisture grain brought a lower price at the elevator or molded in the confines of a barn granary. Initial experiences in western Ohio sometimes proved frustrating:

> Well, you can't do a good job with the combine. The grain has to lay there and dry first. We didn't have the dryers then. [The farmers] wouldn't want to leave their wheat stay there so long cause nothing would grow underneath it.[30]

Experimental breeding of stiffer-stalked grain plants and, later, hybrids less susceptible to early lodging solved most of the difficulties by the 1940s.[31] The construction and use of mechanical drying facilities also allowed farmers to harvest crops with a higher moisture content.

Some rural men held out against combine adoption because of the machine's poor treatment of the straw and grain. Dairy farmers and men with diversified operations criticized the device because it left the valuable straw standing in the field. They later resolved this problem by adding a straw harvest after the combine's work. Farmers began to mow the stems and bale the straw before storing it in barns or in stacks built near stock pens. Finally, there were complaints, often confirmed at the elevator, that the combine's threshing performance was simply inferior to that of the separator. Early combines tended to crack and bruise the grain. The crop graded lower at grain markets and performed poorly as seed grain. Until the mid-1930s, farmers in many areas of the Midwest earned a penny or two less per bushel than their neighbors still using threshing machines.[32]

The concomitant adoption of soybeans as a replacement for feed grains supported the use of combines on midwestern farms. Farmers initially raised soybeans in the 1920s as a supplementary hay or feed crop.[33] Until World War II, a man's choice of how he would conduct his bean harvest depended on his planned use of the crop. Soybean producers looking for an additional hay crop simply cut and dried the entire plant. Early adopters quickly discovered that standard grain binders were not successful in the low, tangled mass of soybean growths. Moreover, plants cut early for hay and then tightly bound had a tendency to mold. Trial-and-error harvest plans eventually resulted in a common sequence of mowing the crop, letting it dry in the swath a day or two, raking it into windrows, and then allowing a few more days of curing before bringing the yield to the barn. Roscoe Deller, of Steuben County, Indiana, recounts a miserable experience bringing in his first planting, sown unfortunately in a "muck field of about three or four acres that had been used to raise onions."

> Yes, they went down [lodged] and it was a job to mow them and we finally got them what we felt was fairly decently dry and we raked them and they just rolled up like a rope. And we tried a hay loader to load them and you couldn't get them up to the hay loader. So we had to tear them to pieces

and put them in bundles and let them dry a little more and then pitch them all on by hand and it was terrible.[34]

Other farmers raised beans in order to use the seeds as a high-protein feed additive, and, later, a cash crop for sale to soybean oil processors. These growers let the seeds dry in the stands two to four weeks longer than if they intended feeding the entire plant as a supplementary hay. Drier beans were more easily cut with binders and then shocked or stacked.[35] Threshermen called on to use their separators then had to devise a workable modification of the machine's small-grain design. Most operators slowed the cylinder's speed and removed some of the threshing teeth in the concave because soybeans are larger, yet more fragile than most grains. Thresherman Ira Edger of Darke County, Ohio, recalled some of the early experimentation in threshing beans:

> I thrashed soybeans when they first came out.... [To thresh them] you was supposed to, you was supposed to have a great big pulley on your cylinder, to run your cylinder slow and then have another great big pulley out there to run your blower faster. But I didn't have nothing to change anything with. Probably put in a couple of boards in the place of the concaves and just used the cylinder for spikes. I thrashed some soybeans that way, yes sir. Didn't do too bad.[36]

The production of soybeans rose significantly between 1935 and 1945, and they eventually replaced oats and barley on most Midwest farms. The low Depression prices farmers received for their stock and the search for new market crops fueled the trend to increasing bean acreages. Soybean market forecasts promised a brighter future, and, importantly, acres of beans were more suited to combine cutting than oats. Soybean plants remain standing in the field for a long period without shattering or blowing over after their leaves have withered and died. The low stands lodged towards the ground and therefore were more successfully harvested with a combine than cut with a binder. Oats, on the other hand, grow higher off the ground, but the types then used tended to blow over and shatter if left standing until proper combining time. Farmers introducing soybeans into their crop rotations looked more favorably on the use of a combine, as the machine could successfully harvest both beans and cereals.[37]

Rural views of technology and change often depend on the stage of development from which the perspective is formed. As with most of their decisions to adopt new agricultural technologies, midwestern farmers rarely gave up their place in the threshing ring with feelings of regret or remorse for the end of a particular set of social patterns. Just as European romanticism for the common man and peasant culture did not begin until after the rise of industry and industrialization, so also did midwestern rural residents lack any public or symbolic expressions of the positive aspects of the threshing ring period until after combine adoption. Farmers regarded the invention of the small combine as a development in support of the family farm and average man because individual ownership provided the ability to harvest and thresh on one's own schedule. Combine manufacturers were well aware of the popular rural trend towards independent agricultural operations, and they promoted family individuality in their advertisements for new harvester-threshers. A 1938 McCormick-Deering photo advertisement for their No. 60 six-foot combine included the following copy:

> This one man machine makes the harvest a family affair—cutting and threshing small grains and seed crops in one field operation—No twine to buy, no shocking, no stacking, no waiting your turn in the thresher "ring," no thresher bills to pay, no crew to feed, no extra work for your wife.[38]

This message connotes a common assumption about production self-sufficiency that should not be confused with the self-sufficient pattern characterizing the rural Midwest 100 years earlier. The "self-sufficient" trait of traditional agricultural systems applied to the neighborhood rather than to each individual farmer. Rural communities survived largely (though never entirely) on their own because they contained the necessary means to produce and consume the goods required for continuity. Larger-manpower tasks, including mechanical threshing, required neighborhood cooperation and aid. The idea of production self-sufficiency implies that each farmer possesses the necessary tools for an independent undertaking of all labor operations. The facts that the tools required to be an individual family farm in twentieth-century Midwest agriculture include equipment produced in urban factories and that the power is fueled by the yield of foreign oil wells (and the majority of agricultural products are raised for nonlocal consumption) do not inherently contradict this attitude. They suggest, though, the absurdity of applying a "self-sufficient" label to modern Midwest agricultural systems, including family farms.

Contradictions between popular concepts of the self-sufficient or tradition-oriented community of the settlement period and a technological self-sufficiency of farm production underlie a basic ambiguity embraced by both rural and intellectual-outsider views of agricultural systems. Confusions between the two rather incompatible constructs are evident in the writings of Thomas Jefferson, who expressed support for the small, individual farm, while at the same time he praised the merits of such contemporaneous technological developments as Eli Whitney's cotton gin. Jefferson and other nineteenth-century thinkers failed to recognize the social consequences of mechanization.[39] Unfortunately, the correlations between increasing individual self-sufficiency, decreasing bonds between rural residents, and a growing dependence on the industrial sector that controls machinery production have not been recognized until quite recently. American programs stressing the adoption of new ideas and practices, conducted both in the United States and around the world, tend to emphasize immediate gains over long-term social and cultural impacts. Only in the past two decades have rural sociologists turned some of their attention from figuring out how to get people to adopt innovation to measuring the consequences of planned change. Not surprisingly, researchers are finding that the potential benefits of a new crop or machine are only one of the many factors that the farm population uses to evaluate the value of change. Midwest farmers may raise more crops with a new hybrid strain or herbicide, but if the rippling effects of innovation include lower prices, farm foreclosures, and decreased community harmony, then the older way may be perceived by families as the better way of life.

Midwestern rural residents rarely offered resistance to ending the threshing ring pattern on the basis of a preference for preservation of local custom or an ideological cultural conservatism. Rather, the positive forces for continuity were the existence of small neighborhood rings of small or mid-sized farms, diversified agricultural operations, and local ownership of a small separator and tractor. Threshing rings still functioning after World War II were normally tightly knit groups of contiguous farmers who believed that the older patterns were economically equal or superior to the costs of ownership of a combine or hiring a custom operator. Some rings survived until the mid-1950s, but not because the participants refused to be modernized.[40] Indeed, the members of these small groups were able to continue threshing only because they possessed the necessary machinery and technical knowledge to manage and maintain their equipment. The group of last threshing participants, as a whole, can be labeled "conservative" only in the sense that they weighed the financial cost of innovation and concluded that older practices still provided the most efficient way to complete the grain harvest.

CONCLUSION

There is a constant and perhaps irreconcilable tension between rural efforts to maintain traditional cultural patterns and farmers' participation in major changes in agricultural styles and structures. A family works hard and long to develop a farming style that provides the means to attain social and economic goals. Many of the values, attitudes, beliefs, and expectations bound up in favored rural lifestyles are based, though, in patterns developed over generations of community life and under very different occupational and social circumstances from those existing today. As average farm sizes increase and family sizes decrease, for example, it becomes difficult and impractical to maintain familiar community institutions, because there are simply not enough schoolchildren or churchgoers to justify and support local educational or religious institutions. Particular agricultural styles and social patterns are thus inextricably intertwined with the abilities of rural residents to create and perpetuate a chosen style of life.

The tenuous relationship between the occupational benefits of technological change and the desire to perpetuate cultural norms is one aspect of a growing anxiety about contemporary rural life in the United States. The by-products of the farm crisis of the 1980s include general concern over the relationship between agricultural structures and the quality of life in rural areas and a renewed interest in the plight of the family farm. Specifically, many rural residents and concerned outsiders share a basic belief that the family farm—itself only one component of the American agricultural structure—is threatened by forces ranging from corporate marketers-producers to the farm programs of the United States Department of Agriculture. Although there is little agreement over such concepts as "family farm" or "quality of life," the assumption of those who promote the protection of independent farm families is that this unit is the active carrier of cherished American values. Idealized portraits in which our agricultural producers are associated with the preservation of special social benefits or democratic values are not, of course, born out of the present rural crisis. Similar views have been expressed by rural and nonrural leaders since Colonial times. Unfortunately, two centuries of idealism have not yet produced the kinds of qualitative studies that might demonstrate how individual agricultural styles are perceived by rural residents or how the pursuit of a particular style relates to specific social or cultural goals. Most studies of rural development are either so quantitative and general that they reveal little about individual life and experience, or so couched in

Conclusion

theory and rhetoric that we tend to learn more about scholars of rural life and those who support this research than we do about the people who actually live and work on the farm.

In spite of our desires to see midwestern rural history and culture neatly addressed and summarized, a reliable comprehensive portrait eludes us because of the lack of individual case studies necessary to construct more general statements. The technology used to complete the grain harvest is one crucial variable of an occupational style that forms part of the agricultural structure of midwestern rural communities. This study is an attempt to chart and analyze occupational, cultural and social changes tied to the development and use of specific threshing systems. Interpretations of a single sphere of agricultural activity cannot account for all aspects of regional evolution. Yet, the impact of mechanization or the formalization of the threshing complex parallels and reflects wider rural developments occurring at roughly the same intervals. We know, moreover, that threshing was a common occupational task and an important agricultural event. Many of the activities occurring on threshing day were motivated by occupational needs, yet threshing work after mechanization became a community activity. And as a significant event shared by neighborhood residents, such components as the organization of the work and the demonstration of group-defined labor obligations reveal a great deal about commonly held community values and perceptions of proper farming styles. Detailed discussion of a specific rural development, with analysis grounded in the experiences and opinions of rural residents, might lead to the kind of general synthesis that can both explain the past and provide some basis for constructing a viable model for predicting the impact of various future programs. This work is not an applied sociological treatise intended to inform governmental or economic action (or inaction). On the other hand, attempts to understand rural evolutions are not idle academic exercises. The horizontal and vertical integration of agriculture into nonrural sectors too often gives agricultural policy-making responsibility to individuals who regard history and tradition as obstacles to be hurdled during the implementation of orchestrated change for the highest capital return.

Threshing machines are not inherently "good" or "bad" for farmers or communities. Handled according to "manufacturer's specifications," a particular device will have more or less capacity than some other model, but design and form are not informative about cultural use or impact. The adoption of a particular tool or implement may or may not result in the creation of tension with an individual or group's perceptions of a "good" or "bad" quality of life. Rural residents usually regard agricultural change as a cultural "good" insofar as the particular occupational practices resulting from that change reflect positive aspects of rural worldview and increase an individual's ability to perpetuate the traits associated with their chosen lifestyle. The problem facing farm residents (and researchers and planners) is to determine which cultural and social complexes are important to maintain, and to gauge, as much as possible, how particular changes in occupational practices will affect one's ability to continue those patterns.

It is almost impossible to predict the exact cultural and social patterns that will result from adoption of, and adaptation to, a new farming practice or idea, Part of the problem lies in the fact that few tools and devices are "socially deterministic"; in other words, a specific technology may require a minimum number of workers, but it is up to the adopters to decide what level of manpower will actually be used and how the organization of that work will occur. Farming style and regional ecologies are two of the variables defining particular systems of use. A comparison between midwestern and Great Plains threshing patterns demonstrates these influences. Although many farmers west of the Missouri River, particularly those raising vast quantities of winter wheat, adopted combines in the 1920s, families in both regions favored the use of similar styles of steam engines and separators in the late nineteenth and early twentieth centuries. In the Great Plains region, most grain crops were threshed by custom operators who provided the entire work force and employed a cookwagon. Machinery owners covered a wide territory, beginning their runs in the southern portions in the summer and moving north with the ripening grain harvest until winter.

Interregional variations demonstrate that similar threshing technologies adopted into contrasting farming systems result in different occupational styles depending on variances in settlement patterns, eco-zones, agricultural cycles, regional concepts of reciprocal labor, and existing systems of neighborhood cooperation.[1] Great Plains threshing patterns were appropriate to the larger, more uniform fields of that region, the advantageous nature of a predictable and dry climate, and the greater distances between farms. Western farmers also depended on cash crop farming rather than diversified agricultural operations, and they engaged in fewer occupational tasks requiring neighborhood work-exchange groups. At all stages of technological development, threshing machines and the powers to run them did not in themselves determine the final form of assimilation or local response. At most, we can say that a specific technology bounds or limits the possibilities of use. Virtually all grain separators, for example, required four tasks: bringing the grain to the machine, feeding the bundles, removing the threshed crop, and clearing away the by-products. The variety of cultural patterns created to accomplish this work, however, demonstrates clearly that mechanical design is only one occupational determinant.

Cultural and social impacts of change are difficult to predict also because mechanical innovations often have rippling consequences extending far beyond the immediate function of the new technology. Anthropologist George Foster suggests that we use the term *sociotechnical development* in place of *technological development*. He writes:

> Development is much more than the overt acceptance of material and technical developments. It is a cultural, social, and psychological process. With every technical and material change there is a corresponding change in the attitudes, the thoughts, the values, the beliefs, and the behavior of the people who are affected by material change.[2]

Few people, including the designers of agricultural machines and the farmers who welcomed every technological advance, recognized the broader impacts of mechanical changes within the threshing complex. Certainly most rural residents did not analyze the shifts in values and attitudes that had to occur prior to an acceptance of each major innovation. Techniques, values, and attitudes are so tightly bound up in each other as not to be immediately perceived or distinguished by farmers or any other group. Covert or intangible cultural changes are subtle; they are often overlooked, or their significance is underestimated. Further, it is one of the ironies of traditional culture that the strongest patterns are usually the ones continued with the least amount of conscious awareness or critical thought. At those moments when cultural and social norms are threatened, families must quickly set their priorities. The development of midwestern agricultural styles in general is characterized by a high level of technological change. A person viewing the amazing development of agricultural implements used on Midwest farms over the past 150 yards might expect major social shifts to have accompanied such drastic changes. In truth, it is remarkable that until recent generations, midwestern communities effected material improvements with minimum disruption of other aspects of regional culture.

The region's threshing styles reflect an uncanny ability of farmers to assimilate new technologies into familiar regional farming and neighborhood patterns. The guiding principle of the accommodation sequence was the decision of rural residents to use existing cultural systems to define the fundamental occupational and social order of the threshing work. This process remained the regional norm until the formalization of threshing rings and the later adoption of the combine. We should not underestimate the assistance that existing norms provided in contexts of technological transitions. Local traditions provided farmers with a pool of accumulated knowledge and experience for completing occupational tasks and meeting organizational needs. The maintenance of customary patterns eased adoption, because the new systems retained shared group expectations and thus enabled families, neighborhoods, and communities to conserve familiar functional and symbolic orderings.

A family's desire to farm in a manner that reflected existing concepts of work and neighborly obligations did not prohibit innovation. Traditional patterns and personal expectations are dynamic, and both also require periodic decisions concerning adaptation and change. Given the shared basis of traditional culture, however, no farmer could simply abandon or alter his practices without prior recognition and acceptance of a new method and some ability to consider the impact of innovation. A man did not discontinue stacking his grain before threshing unless he first decided on another technique that he believed to be a more efficient way of conducting the harvest. He also had to consider the impact of his plan on both other aspects of his agricultural style and the practices of his neighbors. Under traditional agricultural systems, farmers could not afford to consider occupational techniques as isolated procedures. Nor could they view innovation as a simple pragmatic testing of diverse methods or technologies. Stacking was more than a method of storing unthreshed grain; it also denoted a cycle of harvest, of labor, and of farm management.

The sanction and power of shared tradition account for the particular nature of the social units organized to complete the threshing work. Midwestern farmers displayed a consistent (although not surprising) ability to assimilate new threshing technologies into specific and precise systems grounded in extant sociocultural patterns. Initial mechanization in the nineteenth century, for example, required farmers to organize small labor groups to provide the necessary number of workers. Rather than appropriate any external models, midwestern farmers extended the familiar and similarly sized reciprocal-labor networks already used for the grain harvest, butchering, corn shucking, and stacking. These threshing systems remained informally based because they included social norms widely accepted and practiced by the members of the groups formed in each neighborhood. While farming systems within each area were rarely homogeneous, the opportunity to join together in groups of five to eight families allowed operators with similar practices and notions of work relationships to band together.

The threshing ring of 1880–1930 represented the peak expression of threshing as a community-based activity. These collectives of ten to twenty farms functioned as folk groups of limited annual duration. Each ring developed a coherent social identity through shared participation in the seasonal run, and each perpetuated group traditions across successive yearly cycles. Repeated expression of commonly held attitudes and values provided a sanction for individual custom and intergroup evaluations. The conscious perpetuation of a shared occupational practice supported the continuity of a midwestern threshing style. Group memberships and specific agricultural practices changed during these years, of course, but the existence of core membership farms in each ring facilitated the maintenance of group identity through the preservation of essential social relations and cultural norms. The wide scope of shared behaviors during the threshing event, from occupational techniques to meal patterns, allowed rings to transform single traits without complete dissolution of the group's identity or overall style. Some rings altered meal practices to carrying dinner while retaining closing social celebrations and systems of mutual labor donations.

Other groups shifted labor responsibilities as a result of new mechanical technologies, but this movement did not require a break in the continuity of the standards by which they evaluated work performance or in the cooperative nature of the seasonal planning. Many ring activities were simply not amenable to regulation or standardization because of their anchor in wider community norms and relations.

The major result of initial mechanization was thus a neighborhood reorganization rather than the disorganization or disintegration that is commonly thought to be the social consequence of the transition from manual to mechanical processes. The adoption of threshing machines, sweep powers, and steam engines neither determined the social impact on rural neighborhoods nor prohibited the continuity of traditional social and cultural norms. An understanding of midwestern rural evolution is far from complete if it does not go beyond simple observations of overt cultural changes. It is true, for example, that flailing and treading did not continue on the same farms where itinerant operators were invited to set their threshing machines. More important to an understanding of cultural development is the task to discern if existing norms supported or inhibited change and, further, to chart the process of adaptation as a result of innovation.

The cultural traits existing at the time of agricultural innovation include inventories of agricultural practices and a notion of the value of change. Farmers' attitudes towards innovation as a normal occupational endeavor range from perception of change as a positive cultural goal to the view that new practices are a general threat to cultural continuity. Farm operators are generally selective and conservative in considering, implementing, and reacting to innovation to the degree that they perceive a specific change as antithetical to the continuity of basic values, beliefs, and attitudes. An excellent modern example of this relation was farmers' resistance to the introduction of government programs for crop reductions. In essence, many producers viewed the restrictions on crop acreage as irreconcilable with their basic rural philosophy of maximum production.

No single value dominated midwestern attitudes towards the array of threshing devices introduced between 1820 and 1940. Certainly, rural residents discriminated between the potential fallout of various innovations. Notable across the 120 years charted in this study are both a sweeping acceptance of innovations to speed the threshing process and a shift in the reference systems for learning about change, disseminating information about new ideas and practices, and evaluating the importance of maintaining existing community norms and expectations. In general, midwestern rural families throughout most of the nineteenth century looked to their neighborhoods, community leaders, and cultural heritage for definitions of appropriate values towards technology and for the criteria for evaluating competing farming styles. Local models were important as designs for cultural behaviors and as esoteric tools for measuring the perceived impact of change. Shared patterns provided a barometer for defining ranges of innovation, creativity, and competence, whether manifested in a style of stack construction or in the organization of a cooperative work force. In contrast, the attitude towards change that is summed up by an "agribusiness" style of farming includes the valuing of innovation as a mark of progressiveness and the reliance on broader geographic and social frames of reference.[3]

The formalization of cooperative threshing rings marked the beginning of a structural departure from a tradition-based orientation for organizing the threshing complex. Up to that point, the bureaucracy and agribusiness interests associated with threshing were confined largely to the activity of the custom thresherman. In essence, the itinerant operator allowed threshing to remain a local activity, because he took responsibility for those aspects of the work that entailed interaction with nonrural institutions. The positive acceptance of the thresherman's role by farm operators, however, shadowed an increasing rural awareness that reliance on traditional patterns as a mode of thinking and problem solving could no longer satisfy all of the demands of a modern agriculture. The threshing ring's shift to a farm style characteristic of twentieth-century agribusiness began with the assimilation of modern-organizational traits to govern occupational and social relations within the group. Captains performed as foremen, and secretaries functioned as timekeepers and monitored labor contributions. Personal organizational responsibilities, formerly based in individual preferences, local relations, and shared custom, were now outlined in group charters or bylaws and placed under centralized authority of elected officers or delegated committees. Formalization of the occupational procedure represented a calculated effort to make cooperation a more efficient and equitable partnership. The formal arrangements allowed rural families to maintain a quasi-democratic form of self-control over their work, yet the regulations also required ring members to surrender their active involvement in making some of the decisions affecting occupational patterns on their own farms.

The expanding complexity and power of the threshing technology that motivated shifts in the organization of the labor groups also increasingly separated each worker from full participation in the actual work. Thus, it is one of the special traits of Midwest threshing systems that mechanization—at least until the adoption of the tractor and combine—supported both a need for wider neighborhood cooperation and a conscious acceptance of labor specialization in the work context. Each man participating in a flailing or treading session was involved in all phases of the threshing process. Workers carried out the sheaves, laid them on the floor, held the flail or led the horses, turned the grain, and removed the seeds, straw, and chaff. Initial mechanization and the process of stack threshing brought labor divisions into the occupational arena, as each man took only a single job each day. The use of small, informal work exchanges and the authority vested in the host farmer, however, resulted generally in a rotation of work responsibilities between farms. As neighbors adopted shock threshing with a complete separator powered by a steam engine, they increasingly appropriated external industrial-based models to structure their work responsibilities. Among the traits of this new structure were the delegation of occupational tasks by central (though elected) authority figures and the retention of specific labor tasks throughout the annual run.

Formalization of the cooperative relationships was not necessary until the adoption of larger labor collectives made it necessary to compensate for competing cultural systems and agricultural styles within each group. Some farmers were able to extend existing traditional models to resolve the organizational difficulties and provide an equitable economic solution. In general, however, the potential for threshing change coincided with a wider rural movement towards formally structured associations based on joint participation to attain common goals. The main period of threshing ring change coincided, for example, with the formation of many agricultural cooperatives. In the 1910s and 1920s (although not for the first time), farmers and farm organizations rallied against perceived injustices of corporate entities and middlemen and pushed for special legislation to support the establishment of farm supply and marketing cooperatives.[4] The "Magna Charta" of cooperative legislation, the Capper-Volstead Act, passed into federal law in 1922. With a normal coalition of input from farmer-members, a board of directors, and a hired manager, the bureaucratic processs of farm cooperatives parallels the organizational structure of many formalized threshing rings.

The quality of life in rural areas includes a farm family's perceptions of their ability to govern their own affairs and, if they are successful producers, to maintain their chosen lifestyle. Farmers developed larger threshing rings and employed formalized structures in an attempt to be more efficient utilizers of the power potential of available technologies. Similarly, farm cooperatives grew from small, community-based organizations into large business firms because larger groups could cut margins by buying and selling goods in greater bulk. Both of these examples demonstrate that the quest for increased efficiency often leads to growing structural complexity in a corporate and capitalistic economy. Unfortunately, the price for the small or average farmer is usually a decrease in personal power and control over the organizations created to act in his behalf.[5]

Over the past twenty years, the many major changes in rural life have led people to question whether the farmer's integration into the organizational-modern structure will lead to the end of the "family farm" as an independent operation.[6] Some individuals believe that it will be only the inefficient and marginal full-time operators who will have to give up their farms. Unfortunately, this attitude equates efficiency with a capitalistic economic structure under which farmers prosper through specialization and integration. Rather than a Midwest of diversified operations, the region will develop into a large factory operation or extension of marketing corporations. Some farms will specialize in farrowing and then sell the young pigs to operators who will fatten them for market. Others will employ automated setups for preconditioning calves, feeding cattle, or finishing beef to slaughter weight. Livestock producers will be supplied by row-crop specialists who require thousands of acres to make efficient use of available technologies.

The relationship of efficiency to a better style of agriculture is open to question; the equation of efficiency with a better quality of life is, at best, naive. Farming efficiency is often measured in the formation of larger units, the establishment of closer relationships between marketers and producers, and the increased employment of automation and specialized technologies. There is evidence, however, that independent "small" operators produce better-quality products, practice more effective soil and water conservation techniques, and often earn higher profit margins for their products.[7] Moreover, we need to realize what some rural residents have learned only through trial and error: efficiency of farm style and technology is not solely an occupational variable. Particular farm styles and techniques are intertwined with cultural values, social norms, and perceptions of the quality of specific lifestyles. Therefore, changes in the name of "efficiency" that result in alterations of agricultural styles are bound to have important social consequences.

When former ring participants "talk threshing," they are engaged in the debate over change and the impact of current agricultural structures on the ability of rural residents to maintain cherished cultural and social norms. Commentaries about developments in midwestern threshing serve a number of functions and are expressed in a variety of ways, from oral discourse to printed memories, and from annual threshermen's reunions to the statements about the past displayed in the noontime machinery parades at regional steam engine shows. In today's world, to "talk threshing" is, on one level, an attempt to educate new generations of rural residents (many of whom are not agriculturalists) about farming systems now near-extinct. Some of the lessons are oral and visual histories of processes, machinery, and techniques that must appear primitive to young operators only two generations removed from participation in a threshing ring. And although rural neighborhoods still unite at times of emergency, disaster, or local functions, annual cooperative efforts in occupational contexts are no longer a regional need or norm. Technological improvements and other innovations have drastically lowered the time needed to raise grain or fatten feeder steers and have enabled those farmers able to acquire the latest devices to handle their chores independently (and perhaps work in town, as well).

"Talking threshing," however, is not simply a didactic enterprise. Farm residents do identify their occupation as "a way of life" or "expression of life." They recognize that the social components of a community's agricultural style reflect dominant rural norms. And, importantly, those men and women who have lived through the stepped-up phases of mechanical

Conclusion

(and now chemical and genetic) revolutions clearly feel a sense of decline in the quality of rural life as a result of their abandonment of traditional cultural traits. This perception is a complex issue that should not be confused with nostalgia or selective memory. The impact of giving up important cultural traditions can be felt like the loss of a relative or friend. After stages of denial, remorse, and anger, one gains an acceptance of that loss and an appreciation of compromise. Men and women do not associate the "good old days" of the threshing ring with easy work or high profits. Nor are former participants condoning a return to horse farming or earlier technologies. At the time of its introduction, the inexpensive pull-type combine was the answer to farmers' needs.. Change was inevitable in that context, and it is unlikely that operators would have decided any differently even had they been able to predict the wider impact of their decisions.

The change from threshing ring member to combine owner becomes more significant in the context of wholesale changes in rural life, from occupational evolutions to school and church consolidation and general neighborhood disintegration. For many older midwesterners, the threshing ring serves as a reminder of a time when shared participation and local traditions were guideposts of social activity and expectations. In contrast, they perceive today's world as marked by a deteriorating quality of life due to the lack of a healthy rural climate for meeting social needs. Threshing has attained a special symbolic status in this duality, and contemporary discourse about cooperative threshing functions as a form of social criticism. According to this worldview, the rural crisis is older than the difficulties of the last decade. The present situation, however, clearly demonstrates that the disruption of long-standing occupational patterns is both a social and an economic disaster. Some families are having to give up land they have farmed for generations, but an even wider segment of the rural population is faced by the reality that occupational "progress" has led to sociocultural loss. It is not only that "neighbors don't get together like they used to," but also that "people don't have any idea anymore about traditions in their own places, they've lost so much."[8] To "talk threshing" is, then, to point to a time when occupational efforts were not isolated from the opportunity to maintain beneficial cultural and social norms. The topic is a reminder that if agriculture is "a way of life," it has at times been pursued in such a manner as to support basic local community needs. Threshing participation satisfied a requirement to complete the grain harvest, and in such a way that it also fulfilled shared perceptions of a good lifestyle. In completing the season's tasks, rural residents organized and performed their work according to central values and attitudes grounded in local traditions and expectations. Farmers view current agricultural structures and rural evolutions as the result of outside influences and decisions made with little sensitivity to or understanding of traditional rural patterns; in contrast, threshing experiences suggest things familiar, comfortable, and shared.

APPENDIX 1
John B. Miller Diary, 1842 (Miami County, Ohio)

The following excerpts are from the 1842 John B. Miller Diary at the Ohio Historical Society in Columbus. Although Miller generally wrote an entry for each day, I list here only those notations dealing with grain threshing and winnowing (which he calls "cleening"). Miller's word order and spellings are not changed; brackets ([]) are used to enclose information needed to clarify Miller's statements. At the end of his diary, Miller notes "Grain for 1842" includes 83 bushels of oats, 57 ¼ bushels of rye, and 148 ¾ bushels of oats.

January

3—thrashed[1] off C [clover] Seed in after noon   Snowed
4 and 5—thrashed off C seed   fine weather
6—thrashed off C seed finished   Rained af No [afternoon]
14—helped Wm to thrash
17—tramped Clover Stuff   a windy fine daye
19—tramped C sead   fine day
20—tramped and Cleened up Clover Sead   Cold
21—wirking at Clover Sead tramped and Cleened
24—wirked and Cleened up 6 Bush C sed
28—put in a Stack of Rye

February

2—we thrashed Rye   Cloudy did not see the Sun
3—thrashed and Cleened up Rye   Rained all da
5—We thrashed Rye   a fair day Warm
7—We thrashed Rye   warm and muddy
8 and 9—We thrashed some Rye   Verry Cold
10—thrashed Some Rye and Cleened up 22 Bush
11—put in a stack of Rye in afternoon
12—Cleened up 21 ½ Bush of Rye in Piqua
14 and 15—thrashed rye
16—Wm Moore halled a stack of [straw?]
18—thrashed Rye and finished   Snowd
26—Cleened up 23 ¼ Bushels Rye

July

18—Halled in Wh [wheat] for Wm
19—Halled in stacks   Total dozens[2] Wheat 286 Rye 40   in Stack wh 92 Rye 30
20—Halled in and finished and tramped

---

1. Like many farmers of this period, Miller uses *thrash* to refer to threshing with a flail; *tramping* implies treading with horses.
2. *Dozens* refers to the number of bundles; generally one dozen equaled the amount of sheaves in one shock.

wheat in barn 152 dozens trampt 42 dozen
thrashed 10 dozen Rye out of field
22—took in Rye and Stackd   Halled in 10 dozen Rye and fenced stacks
27—Halled 4 lods in last stack and finish   Cloudy and wind

August

2—thrashed Rye   fin day
4—halled Oats for Wm
9—thrast and Cleened flax seed
11—stacked 2 [oat] stacks   first stack 52 dozen   Second stack
   57 dozen   in Barn 10 dozen   tramped a flooring
12—tramped Oats
16—cleened up Oats
25—tramped Wheat   dull wether
26—Rained all day   Cleaned up Wheat som

September

30—tramped a flooring of oats in aft No

October

3—tramped Oats
4—Set up C seed and thrashed buckwheat
5—Cleened up Wheat
6—tramped wheat   adams sent horse [for tramping?]
14—Cleened up Wheat
21—Thrashed off Some C Seed   a fine day
22—Rained and Cleened up C Seed on floor
28—Thrashed off C Seed and finished

November

18—Tramped Clover Seed   very Cold and Windy
19—Tramped Clover seed   Cold ground   frost up
24—Cleened Clover seed
25—Tramped and Cleened C Seed
26—wirking at C seed
28—wirking at C seed and finished

APPENDIX 2
Ring Bylaws Examples

A. Bylaws of Prairie Grove Threshing Company[1]

Article 1.
Section 1. This association shall be known as the Prairie Grove Threshing Company.

Article 2.
Section 1. Its object shall be to reduce the price of threshing wheat and oats to a minimum.

Article 3.
Section 1. A day's work shall consist of 10 hours. The difference in price shall be 11 cents per hundred bushels for oats and 16 cents per hundred bushels for wheat and rye. No difference in price shall be made whether a man furnishes a team or only his own labor.

Section 2. The time of commencing work shall be 7 o'clock, A.M. and every member who is late shall be fined at the rate of 25 cents per hour which shall be paid to the treasurer, sickness excepted.

Section 3. A man refusing to pay his fine is dismissed from the ring until he pays his fine.

Article 4.
Section 1. The company shall appoint two members to solicit threshing outfits for the best terms, time and service for threshing and they shall report the same at the next meeting which report shall be confirmed or rejected and when said report or succeeding report is accepted, it shall be binding on all members of the company.

Article 5.
Section 1. Each member is to pay for his threshing within 10 days after the completion of the company's work, to the treasurer of the company who shall immediately pay the same to the owner of the threshing outfit.

Section 2. There shall be but two threshing seasons; one for oats and one for wheat. The threshing shall begin at a point selected by the company, which shall not be the same place two successive years, and each member shall thresh in regular turn determined by his location, and if any member refuses to thresh in his turn, he shall wait until the last job—the first refusing shall be the first outside the regular list and the second refusal shall be the second in the outside list and so on.

Article 6.
Section 1. The secretary shall keep an account of the number of bushels threshed by each member and his statement shall be conclusive in the settlement between members.

---

1. Charles E. Finney, Fulton County, Indiana; ca. 1920-1945.

Article 7.

Section 1. It shall be the duty of the president to take general charge of the threshing outfit and of the members and shall direct all parties in the execution of their duties and his decision when threshing is in progress is final. He shall also have the power to call meetings and all members shall respond or pay a fine of 25 cents to the treasurer of the company.

Section 2. The president shall notify all members when the first job of threshing begins.

Article 8.

Section 1. All members shall pay 10 cents per year which may be increased or decreased by a two-thirds majority at any regular meeting.

Section 2. All officers shall make a report to the company on demand of any member; but sufficient time shall be given him to make the report.

Article 9.

Section 1. All members having signed the secretary's minutes shall be considered as having signed these by-laws.

Section 2. The terms of officers shall be one year and until a successor is elected.

B. Bylaws of the Mount Vernon Threshing Union[2]

This threshing union shall be known as the Mount Vernon Threshing Union which shall consist of not less than 14 or more than 18 members. Officers to be elected as follows: President, secretary-treasurer, captain and a committee of three members.

Article 1.

Duties of Officers:

A. President shall call all meetings and preside.

B. Secretary-treasurer shall keep a record of all meetings and also keep a record of the amount of grain threshed at each job and reckon all financial settlements and also have charge of the grain bags.

C. The committee shall perform all business as instructed and directed by the Union, such as hiring a machine, etc.

D. The captain shall have charge of all threshing, each member to work under his orders. The captain to keep the grain and falling bundles cleaned up around the machine.

Article 2.

[unclear] . . . cases to be regulated by the Captain.

Article 3.

Threshing to begin at an agreed point and carried out by rotation, reversing the order each year.

Article 4.

Each member will furnish his own dinner and go home for supper (threshing machine crew to board where threshing). Teams have to furnish feed where threshing.

Article 5.

Each member will furnish 10 grain bags, plainly marked with owner's name.

---

2. Thomas Kiner, Wabash County, Indiana; ca. 1915-1935.

Article 6.

Within 30 days after threshing, a settlement shall be made and all differences shall be settled at a rate per 100 bushels. Twenty-five cents per hundred bushels for wheat and 40 cents per hundred bushels for rye and barley and 20 cents per hundred bushels for oats. Thresher to receive his pay at same settlement meeting.

Article 7.

Each member by his signature agrees to abide by these by-laws and carry them out with as much peace and harmony as possible.

Article 8.

Members shall provide for a good ice cream social or watermelon carving at the close of the season's threshing.

NOTES

Preface

1. A brief definition of terms used in this study will prevent future confusion. *Mechanization* refers to the substitution of machine processes for tasks previously involving human or animal labor. *Technology* denotes the sum total of available knowledge, tools, and devices centered around either premechanical or mechanical processes. *Technique* is used to describe the process of completing the task at hand, and can be associated with the use of any technology.
2. F. B. Mumford, "A Century of Missouri Agriculture," p. 277.
3. This assumption is central to the work of "cultural ecology," a branch of anthropology and ethnology owing a large debt to concepts first developed by Julian Steward.
4. Nils-Arvid Bringeus, *Jarnplogen som Innovation*, and Erich Klein, "Die Entwicklung des Hohenheimer Pfluges."
5. Paul W. Gates, *The Farmer's Age*, p. 373.
6. Earle D. Ross, *Iowa Agriculture*, pp. 88–90.
7. Charles H. Fuller, *Advertisers' Directory of Leading Newspapers and Magazines* (Chicago: Chas. H. Fuller's Advertising Agency, 1903), pp. 187–89 and 279–84, and *Newspaper and Magazine Directory* (Chicago: H. W. Kaster and Sons, 1923), pp. 532–39.

I. Flailing and Treading

1. *American Thresherman* 15 (1906): 12. This description resembles the Roman *Tribulum*, a heavy wooden platform mounted on rollers and then dragged by oxen over the grain. An unsupported claim of using "sleds or wheels" for threshing is Edward J. Lettermann, *Pioneer Farming in Iowa*, p 93.
2. Joseph C. G. Kennedy, "Process of Invention in Threshing Implements," pp. 95–96; Robert L. Jones, "The Introduction of Farm Machinery into Ohio Prior to 1865," p. 5; *American Farmer* 2 (1820): 109; Charles W. Dickerman, *How to Make the Farm Pay*, p. 134; John Beale Bordley, *Essays and Notes on Husbandry and Rural Affairs*, pp. 249–55; Harold B. Gill, "Wheat Culture in Colonial Virginia"; Clarence H. Danhof, *Change in Agriculture*, p. 221; Leo Rogin, *The Introduction of Farm Machinery in Its Relation to the Productivity of Labor in the Agriculture of the United States during the Nineteenth Century*, pp. 157–59 and 178–80; and Beauveau Borie IV, *Farming and Folk Society*.
3. Alexander Fenton, "Hand Threshing in Scotland"; C. O'Danachair, "The Flail and Other Threshing Methods"; idem, "The Flail in Ireland"; J. Geraint Jenkins, *Life and Tradition in Rural Wales*, pp. 47–50; and Thomas Hennell, *Changes in the Farm*, pp. 168–74.
4. John Reynolds, *My Own Times*, p. 90. French farmers in the Midwest were likely familiar with the treading process (*depiquage*), as it was the common threshing technique in the Midi and other south and southeast areas of France.
5. Interview with Rose Reusser, Elgin, Iowa, August 10, 1980; Susan Swartz,

untitled manuscript in Indiana University Folklore Archives, IUFA 68/136, 1967, p. 36; Angie Kumlien Main, "Annals of a Wisconsin Thresherman," p. 304.

6. Asbury Good-Knight, "Wheat Raising in Pioneer Missouri," p. 504.

7. Miller Diary, Appendix A; Martin Welker, *Farm Life in Central Ohio Sixty Years Ago*, p. 31; and Wiley Britton, *Pioneer Life in Southwest Missouri*, pp. 90–91.

8. Miller Diary, 1842, and Kennedy, "Process of Invention," p. 95.

9. Willis Berry Account Books, entries for fall and spring threshing of grains in 1838 and 1840.

10. The following description of the flailing process is based primarily on interviews with three men who occasionally flailed portions of grain harvests through the 1920s and 1930s. Interviews with Joseph Miller, Montgomery County, Ohio, December 1, 1979; Herbert Kleinman, Parke County, Indiana, September 21, 1980; and Ernst Schroeder, Greene County, Iowa, April 14, 1979.

11. Similar flails are described in Paul M. Shoger, *Threshing Rings of Kendall County, 1875–1955*, p. 9; Welker, *Farm Life in Central Ohio*, p. 33; Roberts S. Withers, "Threshing Time in Early Day Clay County Was Indeed a Social Event," p. 7; and John W. Hills, "Threshing Then and Now," p. 536.

12. Commercial products were widely available during the mid-nineteenth century. Factory-made flails in 1846 could be bought for 75 cents each or $7.50 per dozen. See *Cultivator* 3 (1846): 117.

13. Drury Diary, August-December, 1838.

14. Hubbard Diary, September 9–14, 1844. Hubbard notes in his diary that this yield is low because of blight.

15. Page Diary, November 3–5, 1844.

16. *Thirteenth Annual Report of the Commissioner of Labor, 1898*, pp. 25, 65–75, 84–85, 446–53, and 470–71. Also see John Woods, *Two Years' Residence on the English Prairie of Illinois*, p. 204; *Farm, Orchard, and Fireside* 39, no. 2 (July, 1868): 1; William C. Howells, *Recollections of Life in Ohio from 1813 to 1840*, p. 32; Jones, "Introduction of Farm Machinery," p. 6; John B. Conner, *Indiana Agriculture*, p. 8; Kennedy, "Process of Invention," p. 100; and Charles E. Merrifield, "The Importance of Mechanical Appliances to Successful Farming," p. 227.

17. Stewart Diary, entries between August 13, 1820, and July 9, 1821.

18. Oliver John Felton, "Pioneer Life in Jones County," p. 240; Herbert Anthony Kellar, ed., *Solon Robinson, Pioneer and Agriculturalist*, p. 368; Rodney C. Loehr, "Introduction," pp. 14–15; and Donald A. Hutslar, "The Ohio Farmstead," p. 234.

19. Good-Knight, "Wheat Raising in Pioneer Missouri," p. 504. Southern Indiana examples are preserved today at Spring Mill State Park.

20. Howells, *Recollections*, p. 22; Hutslar, "The Ohio Farmstead," p. 233; and Swartz manuscript, p. 37. For Pennsylvania German constructions, see Borie, *Farming and Folk Society*, pp. 15–36.

21. Thomas Fessenden, *The Complete Farmer and Rural Economist*, p. 74; Welker, *Farm Life in Central Ohio*, p. 32; Hutslar, "The Ohio Farmstead," p. 234; and, Nils P. Haugen, "Pioneer and Political Reminiscences," p. 134.

22. James Flint, *Flint's Letters from America, 1818–1820*, p. 84.

23. Branson Harris, *Some Recollections of My Boyhood*, p. 25. Also see Hugh H. Shepard, "Background of a Pioneer," p. 182; Welker, *Farm Life*, p. 32; Melvin D. Osband, "My Recollections of Pioneers and Pioneer Life in Nankin," p. 440; Patrick Shireff, *A Tour through North America*, p. 225.; McKee Diary, August 8, 1839; and Woods, *Two Years' Residence*, p. 204.

24. Welker, *Farm Life*, p. 31. Also see Howells, *Recollections*, pp. 154–56; Jones, "Introduction of Farm Machinery," p. 5; and David E. Schob, *Hired Hands and Plowboys*, pp. 104–105.

25. Welker, *Farm Life*, p. 31.

26. Herbert Kleinman interview; Joseph Miller interview; and interview with Charles Petersen, Decorah, Iowa, August 4, 1978.

27. Jared van Wagenen, *The Golden Age of Homespun*, p. 242; Danhof, *Change in Agriculture*, p. 221; and Walter Needham and Barrows Mussey, *A Book of Country Things*, p. 32.

28. Gates, *The Farmer's Age*, p. 116; Howells, *Recollections*, p. 62; W. A. Lloyd, J. I. Falconer, and C. E. Thorne, *The Agriculture of Ohio*, p. 52; *History of McHenry County, Illinois* p. 527; and *Farmer's Centennial History of Ohio, 1803–1903*, p. 11.

29. Jacob Stewart Ledger, November-December, 1817.

30. William Gardner Diary, April, 1832, and May and November, 1833; Anthony Stranahan Ledger, October and December, 1827; and Schob, *Hired Hands*, p. 106.

31. Enoch Jones Daybook, April 4 and July 10, 1840.

32. Stewart Ledger, 1817.

33. Lesher Diary, 1846 and 1848.

34. Hills, "Threshing Then and Now," p. 536.

35. George H. Weaver, "Autobiography of Dr. Ephraim Ingals," p. 288; Ernest L. Bogart, *Economic History of American Agriculture*, p. 27; and Benjamin H. Hibbard, *The History of Agriculture in Dane County, Wisconsin*, p. 123.

36. Osband, *My Recollections*, p. 40; Gershom Flagg, "Pioneer Letters of Gershom Flagg," p. 162; Jones, "Introduction of Farm Machinery," p. 5; Main, "Annals," pp. 303–304; Weaver, "Autobiography," p. 288.

37. Loehr Diary, May-June, 1837. For other examples of an oblong design, see Ellen Harley, "Family Memories," unpublisheed manuscript at Indiana State Historical Society Library. The author was born in 1823 and died in 1904. This "memory" is based on activities around 1840; Flagg, "Pioneer Letters," p. 162; and McKee Diary, February 22, July 23, 1838, and March 25, 1839.

38. Main, "Annals," pp. 303–304.

39. Margaret E. Archer Murray, "Memoir of the William Archer Family," pp. 363–64.

40. Hills, "Threshing Then and Now," p. 536; Henry S. K. Bartholomew, *Pioneer History of Elkhart County, Indiana*, pp. 108–109; Lloyd et al., *The Agriculture of Ohio*, p. 52; Hibbard, *Dane County*, p. 123; and John B. Parkinson, "Memories of Early Wisconsin and the Gold Mines," pp. 121–22.

41. Britton, *Pioneer Life*, p. 90, and McKee Diary, February 23, 1838.

42. Bogard (1855–65): 27–28, and Frank Egleston Robbins, "The Personal Reminiscences of General Chauncey Eggleston," p. 308; Drury Diary, 1838; and Warren Diary, 1834.

43. *American Agriculturalist* 1 (1843): 342; Weaver, "Autobiography," p. 288; Hills, "Threshing Then and Now," p. 536; and John Goodell, ed., *Diary of William Sewall, 1797–1846*, entries for October 2, 1837, and January 31, 1839.

44. Loehr Diary, periodic entries of January-May, 1838.

45. Goodell, *Diary of William Sewall*, entries for August 24–27, 1837, January 31, February 4, and May 16, 1838. Eliza W. Farnham, *Life in Prairie Land*, p. 284; Good-Knight, "Wheat Raising," p. 504; McKee Diary, February 23 and 24, 1838, and July 23 and 26, 1839; *Minnesota Farmers' Diaries*, William Brown Diary, February 19 and 20, 1846, p. 63; and Hibbard, *Dane County*, p. 123.

46. Robbins, "Personal Reminiscences," pp. 307–308.

47. An interesting account of winnowing among the French of Portage des Sioux in preterritorial Missouri notes the placement of wheat "in a hollow section of cottonwood—about five feet long. To one end was attached a handle and the operator grasped this, rested the end between his knees and rolled it from side to side, thus gradually separating the wheat from the chaff." In Evans Johnson, "Pioneer Times," p. 4.

48. Ernest Schroeder interview, April 14, 1979; Withers, "Threshing Time," p.

7; Haugen, "Pioneer and Political Reminiscences," p. 134; Weaver, "Autobiography," p. 288; and Britton, *Pioneer Life*, p. 91.
   49. Shoger, *Threshing Rings*, p. 7.
   50. Harris, *Some Recollections*, p. 25; Conner, *Indiana Agriculture*, p. 8; Jones, "Introduction of Farm Machinery," p. 5; and H. N. Beckwith, *History of Vigo and Parke Counties* [Indiana], p. 170.
   51. Howells, *Recollections*, p. 156.
   52. Schob, *Hired Hands and Plowboys*, p. 105.
   53. Wider family participation is described in Howells, *Recollections*, p. 156; for examples of neighborhood sharing, see Harris, *Some Recollections*, p. 25, and Beckwith, *Vigo and Parke Counties*, p. 170.
   54. Alexander Fenton, *Scottish Country Life*, pp. 91–93.

II. The Mechanization of Threshing: Initial Adoption and Accommodation

   1. Earle D. Ross, *Iowa Agriculture*, p. 43.
   2. Eugene H. Roseboom and Francis P. Weisenburger, *A History of Ohio*, p. 179; Leo Rogin, *The Introduction of Farm Machinery in Its Relation to the Productivity of Labor in the Agriculture of the United States during the Nineteenth Century*, p. 165; Lytle Diary, August, 1837, and Andrew Loehr Diary, September, 1837.
   3. John B. Conner, *Indiana Agriculture*, p. 8. Samuel Harden, comp., *Early Life and Times in Boone County, Indiana*, p. 62, and H. N. Beckwith, *History of Vigo and Parke Counties*, p. 170.
   4. Solon Justus Buck, *Illinois in 1818*, p. 133; John Goodell, ed., *Diary of William Sewall, 1797–1846*, p. 133; Russell H. Anderson, "Agriculture in Illinois during the Civil War Period, 1850–1870," p. 364; and Graeme Quick and Wesley Buchele, *The Grain Harvesters*, p. 58.
   5. Before 1820, most threshing machines used in the East were designed and produced in England. The devices usually cost over three hundred dollars, plus the cost of shipping. Only wealthier midwestern farmers considered purchase. A Wisconsin example is noted in Benjamin H. Hibbard, *The History of Agriculture in Dane County, Wisconsin*, p. 124.
   6. Solon J. Buck, "Making a Farm on the Frontier: Extracts from the Diaries of Mitchell Young Jackson"; Goodell, *Diary of William Sewall*, pp. 131–46; and Ephraim Warren Diary, 1862–64. Warren purchased his machine on October 10, 1863.
   7. *Farmer's Centennial History of Ohio, 1803–1903*, pp. 23–25; *Ohio Cultivator* 3, no. 7 (April, 1847): 1; and Buck, "Making a Farm," p. 92 and the diary extracts for August 3 through August 17, 1853.
   8. *Ohio Cultivator* 10 (1854): 67, ibid., 11 (1855): 240, and ibid., 12 (1856): 274. The last notice reports that "Moffit's Threshing Machine" was being produced solely by Owens, Lane, and Dyer in Hamilton, Ohio. Two men named Sylla and Hadlock manufactured over forty machines in their shop in Elgin, Illinois, in 1844 and 1845. See *Prairie Farmer* 5 (1845): 157.
   9. F. B. Lytle Ledger, October 17, 1854, and September 15, 1856.
   10. Nathan Parker, *The Iowa Handbook for 1856*, p. 158; and Alan G. Bogue, "Pioneer Farmers and Innovation," pp. 15–16.
   11. Jeremiah Kingsley Manuscript, November 17, 1842, letter, Collections of the Indiana State Library.
   12. Paul C. Johnson, *Farm Inventions in the Making of America*, p. 61; *Farmer's Centennial History of Ohio*, p. 129; and M. H. Brewer, "Report on the Cereal Pro-

duction of the United States," p. 140. Over 2,300 patents were issued by 1880, and the figure reached 4,951 by 1903.

13. Bars were especially common on machines designed specifically to thresh rye, as the valuable straw feed lengthwise into rollers would not be chewed during the threshing process.

14. Both designs have European precedents. Spike roller use is noted in Jared van Wagenen, *The Golden Age of Homespun*, pp. 240–41; *American Farmer* 2 (1820): 120; ibid. 3 (1821): 396–98; Kennedy, "Process of Invention," p. 95; Harold B. Gill, "Wheat Culture in Colonial Virginia," p. 391; Brewer, "Cereal Production," p. 140; Leonard E. Lathrop, *The Farmer's Library*, p. 262; and Robert L. Ardrey, *American Agricultural Implements*, pp. 103–104. For the multi-flail design, see *American Farmer* 1 (1819): 55; *Ohio Cultivator* 10 (1854): 10; [United States Patent Office,] *The Growth of Industrial Art*, p. 23; and Ardrey, *American Agricultural Implements*. The sole report of a multi-flail design in Ohio is Robert L. Jones, "The Introduction of Farm Machinery into Ohio Prior to 1865," p. 12.

15. Louis Bernard Schmidt, "The Westward Movement of the Wheat Growing Industry in the United States," p. 399. By 1839, Indiana and Illinois ranked, respectively, seventh and ninth.

16. Loehr Diary, August, 1837, and Lytle Diary, September, 1837.

17. W. A. Lloyd, J. I. Falconer, and C. E. Thorne, *The Agriculture of Ohio*, p. 231.

18. Clarence H. Danhof, *Change in Agriculture*, p. 224.

19. Samuel Long, *A Pioneer History of Wayne Township, Darke County, Ohio*, pp. 6–12.

20. Ibid., p. 32.

21. Cf. Hibbard, *Dane County*, p. 124; *Indiana State Agricultural Report, 1854* (Indianapolis, 1854), p. 82; *Recollections of the Pioneers of Lee County* [Illinois] p. 208; Jerome Wiley Letters, October 15 and 26, November 19, 1856; Edwin Warren Diary, August, 1863; and *History of Knox and Daviess County, Indiana*, p. 55.

22. The mechanical evolution of the threshing machine in the United States is treated comprehensively by Ardrey, *American Agricultural Implements*, pp. 103–112; Quick and Buchele, *The Grain Harvesters*, pp. 53–62; Kennedy, "Process of Invention," pp. 90–100; Phillip S. Rose, *The Thresher's Guide*, vol. 2, pp. 25–33; and Donald Paul Greene, "Prairie Agricultural Technology, 1860–1900," pp. 290–319. By the 1860s, a new type of separator design incorporated a "vibrating" principle to separate the grain from the straw and chaff. As the crop passed through the machine, "arms" lifted and dropped the straw and grain to aid the separation. The vibrator, or "agitator," process proved a successful innovation and became a common component in the design of most machines by 1875.

23. An early example is "Report of the Committee on Threshers," in *Indiana State Board of Agriculture Report for 1858–9* (Indianapolis, 1859), pp. 401–403.

24. Schmidt, "The Wheat Growing Industry," p. 401. By 1879, the only non-midwestern states among the top ten producers were California (#7) and Pennsylvania (#10).

25. Danhof, *Change in Agriculture*, p. 82.

26. *American Agriculturalist* 9, no. 1 (January, 1849): 19.

27. Paul W. Gates, *The Farmer's Age*, pp. 160–63; Conner, *Indiana Agriculture*, pp. 14–15; Charles W. Burkett, *History of Ohio Agriculture*, pp. 64–66; Anderson, "Agriculture in Illinois," pp. 43–45; and James Caird, *Prairie Farming in America*, p. 30. The growth of grain markets along the Great Lakes was phenomenal. In 1838, grain shipments from Chicago totaled 78 bushels; by 1860, the figure surpassed 10 million bushels.

28. Except for the Depression of 1857, farmers benefited from decent grain prices between 1855 and 1870. They owed their good fortune to national and international demands created by the Civil War and the Crimean War.

29. Frank King Manuscript, p. 3; Earle D. Ross, ed., *Diary of Benjamin F. Gue in Rural New York and Pioneer Iowa, 1847–1856*, p. 44; Asenath H. Gable, "Lovingly Submitted," pp. 20–21; and Benjamin H. Gavitt, *Eighty Years in Iowa*, p. 27.

30. Swedish ethnographer Sigurd Erixon coined the term *cultural fixation*. See Sigfrid Svensson, "On the Concept of Cultural Fixation."

31. Interview with Herbert Kleinman, September 21, 1980, Parke County, Indiana; Interview with W. Pelser, March 23, 1983, Gasconade County, Missouri, by Barry Bergey.

32. Kleinman interview. This discussion includes only small grain threshing. There are many people in the southern areas of the region and throughout the Upland South who can cite twentieth-century "flailing" of peas or beans. The process typically involved placing the harvested crop in a sack and "flailing" the entire sack with a stick to hull or dehusk the contents.

33. Horse sweeps commonly powered the crude grinders, mills, and spiked rollers used during the Colonial period.

34. The power inadequacies of tread powers became more evident as threshing machines were built with increasingly larger cylinders. Paul C. Johnson, *Farm Power in the Making of America*, p. 16.

35. *Cultivator* 5 (1848): 164; Rogin, *Introduction of Farm Machinery*, pp. 184–9; *Prairie Farmer* 10 (1850): 269; and ibid. 36 (1876): 12.

36. LeRoy Shutes, "Stack Threshing, Ioway—1890s," p. 4.

37. Alan G. Bogue, *From Prairie to Corn Belt*, p. 200.

38. Andrew Estrem, "An Early Norse Settlement in Iowa," p. 389.

39. O. J. Felton, "Pioneer Life in Jones County," p. 238; Shutes, "Stack Threshing," p. 5; Anonymous Diary [Fulton, Ohio], February 9, 1847; Thomas Page Diary, April 27-May 7, 1846; Benjamin Linvill Diary, August 23, 1878; and Lewis Mighell Diary, March 2–4, 1857.

40. Rare instances of treadmill use by itinerant operators are described in *Prairie Farmer* 10 (1850): 209, and *American Threshermen* 17, no 2 (June, 1924): 31–32.

41. Thomas G. Fessenden, *The Complete Farmer and Rural Economist*, p. 330, and *Valley Farmer* (St. Louis) 2 (1850): 204. Correspondents carried on a discussion on the size of operation appropriate to ownership of a treadmill in the pages of the *Ohio Farmer* in 1872. The majority recommended purchase on farms of around 200 acres.

42. Lesher Diary, 1848–49; *Prairie Farmer* 6 (1847): 707; Andrew Stranahan Ledger, April, 1845; Ringle Diary, August, 1865; and Page Diary, September, 1845. Also *Michigan Farmer* 11 (1853): 265; John W. Hills, "Threshing Then and Now"; and *Prairie Farmer* 6 (1846): 207.

43. *Cultivator* 8 (1841–42): 31.

44. R. W. Brunskill, *Illustrated Handbook of Vernacular Architecture*, pp. 142–43, and *Vernacular Architecture of the Lake Counties*, pp. 87–89; J. A. Hellen, "Agricultural Innovation and Detectable Landscape Margins"; John Fraser Hart, *The Look of the Land*, pp. 124–25; Stuart MacDonald, "The Early Threshing Machine in Northumberland," pp. 168–70; and Kenneth Hutton, "The Distribution of Wheelhouses in the British Isles."

45. Alexander Fenton, *Scottish Country Life*, pp. 86–87.

46. A rare call for construction of a permanent "horse-course" is F. W. O'Neill and H. L. Williams, *The American Farmer's Hand-Book*, pp. 526–27. The authors reveal a British orientation in their references to grain as "corn" and illustration of an overhead sweep design rarely employed in the United States.

47. *Michigan Farmer* 11 (1853): 265; *Western Farmer and Gardener* 2, no. 2 (November, 1840): 46; *Prairie Farmer* 7 (1847): 124; and Josiah T. Marshall, *The Farmer's and Emigrant's Hand Book* p. 70.

48. *Valley Farmer* 2, no. 7 (July, 1850): 204.

49. Page Diary, 1845–46; Anonymous Diary [Fulton Ohio], September, 1846, and January, 1847; and, Hubbard Diary, November, 1845.
50. Elisha King Diary, August 21, 1855.
51. King Diary, September 20, 1856.
52. Drury Diary, April, 1847; Goodell, *Sewall Diary*, p. 263; and *Recollections of Lee County Pioneers*, p. 208.
53. Drury Diary, April 24 and June 18, 1847.
54. Benjamin Linvill Diary, September 22, 1882.
55. Samuel Sewall, a pioneer thresherman near Beardstown, Illinois, in the early 1840s, also experienced problems collecting payments from farmers who delayed taking their crop to market. On December 21, 1843, he "rode up to Mr. Shipley's near Petersburg for whom I have done some threshing [four months before]. He had promised to haul me some wheat last week to market in order to pay me." In Goodell, *Sewall Diary*, p. 142.
56. Hubbard Diary, November, 1845; Anonymous Diary [Fulton, Ohio], February 10, 1847; W. A. Tunnel Diary, August, 1849; and Felton, "Pioneer Life in Jones County," p. 240.
57. The formula is not a fixed one, because sweep powers did not always need resetting every time the thresherman moved the machine to a new stack pair. If the additional distance was short enough, he simply added extra tumbling rods to carry the power over the new ground. One encounters phrases such as a "four-stack setting" in Shutes, "Stack Threshing," p. 3, and Paul Corey, *Three Miles Square*, p. 104.
58. Interview with Kenneth Tracey, June 24, 1981, Spencer, Indiana. Greene County, Indiana, farmers paid $12 for a setting in the 1920s; also Mary Stitt, "Farming in the Early 1900s," p. 12.
59. Nils P. Haugen, "Pioneer and Political Reminiscences," p. 134.
60. Midwestern Farmers do not appear to have adopted the smaller hand-cranked threshing machines favored by some eastern farmers. A hand-cranked machine reported to "get-out" five to eight bushels a day is advertised in the *Indiana Intelligencer* [Charlestown] on April 19, 1821, p. 4.
61. *American Agriculturalist* 1, no. 11 (February, 1843): 342. The emphasis is in the original.
62. *Valley Farmer* 2, no. 7 (July, 1850): 212.
63. Quoted in Walter E. Kaloupek, "Agricultural Implements and Machines," p. 56. Other early machines that did not use the cylinder principle could be even more destructive. One early device was constructed on the principle of a coffee mill "and performed more than it promised by grinding as well as threshing the grain"; in Kennedy, "Process of Invention," p. 93.
64. *Ohio Cultivator* 2 (1846): 115.
65. Kennedy, "Process of Invention," p. 95, and Hubbard Diary, November 8, 1844.
66. This point is also emphasized by Ross, *Iowa Agriculture*, p. 32, and Paul David, "The Mechanization of the Reaping in the Ante-bellum Midwest," pp. 6–7.
67. Perry Miller, "The Responsibility of the Mind in a Civilization of Machines," p. 54.
68. Leo Marx, *The Machine in the Garden*, and John Bryant, "A Usable Pastoralism."
69. The clearest use of these protagonists within a threshing context is found throughout Herbert Krause's *The Thresher*.
70. Religious scruples have long been employed in opposition to materialistic technologies. See Morrell Heald, "Technology in American Culture."
71. Technology and culture theorist Jacques Ellul calls this process *self-augmentation*. He writes, "Each new machine disturbs the equilibrium of production: the

III. Nineteenth-Century Stack Threshing

1. Early mowing accounts include *Western Agriculturalist* 1 (1830): 171 and 200; ibid. 3 (1833): 86; *Ohio Farmer* 48 (1876): 223; and Thomas G. Fessenden, *The Complete Farmer and Rural Economist*, p. 74.
2. Better written accounts of nineteenth-century stacking include LeRoy Shutes, "Stack Threshing, Ioway—1890s," pp. 2–5; *Farmer's Guide* 11 (1899): 420 and 24 (1912): 760; Isaac Tate, "Recollections of a Pioneer Farmer" [ca. 1935] (Manuscript, Joint Collection of University of Missouri Western Historical Manuscripts Collections-Columbia and State Historical Society of Missouri Manuscripts); *Ohio Farmer* 46 (1874): 1171; and Gayle Hager, "Striking It Rich in the Northeast Iowa Hills," p. 27.
3. The term *host farmer* is used throughout this study to indicate the farmer whose crop is being threshed.
4. O. J. Felton, "Pioneer Life in Jones County," p. 238; Albert Britt, *An America That Was*, p. 101; E. May Crowder, "Pioneer Life in Palo Alto County," p. 167; Shutes, "Stack Threshing," p. 5; Hager, "Striking It Rich," p. 27; Laura A. McKee Diary, September, 1851; Benjamin Thrasher Diary, 1878; and Downer Diary, 1873–81.
5. Felton, "Pioneer Life," p. 238; Willis Broughton, "Drover Days, or Pioneer Life in [Bureau County] Illinois, 1862–1876," p. 114; and *Early Life of Eric Norelius (1833–1862)*, p. 147.
6. Interview with Dave Horner, Boone County, Missouri, September 16, 1984, and Robert S. Withers, "Threshing Time in Early Day Clay County Was Indeed a Social Event," June 17, 1948, p. 7.
7. Interview with Walter Meachem, Dayton, Ohio, July 14, 1981. Also see Fred W. and Robert W. Hawthorn, *Idlewild Farm*, p. 10, and Britt, *Life on an Illinois Farm*, p. 101.
8. Interview with Dan Jones, June 5, 1980, in Oak Hill, Ohio.
9. Interview with Joe Meachem, July 14, 1981, in Dayton, Ohio; also Shutes, "Stack Threshing," p. 3, and interview (by Margot Roberson) with Oscar Summers, October 6, 1984, in Fulton, Missouri.
10. Dan Jones interview.
11. Martin E. Tew, *The Autobiography of Martin E. Tew*, p. 11; Felton, "Pioneer Life," p. 102; Britt, *An America That Was*, p. 103; and Nils P. Haugen, "Pioneer and Political Reminiscences," p. 132.
12. Shutes, "Stack Threshing," p. 3.
13. Britt, *An America That Was*, p. 104. Early threshing accidents of this sort are mentioned in *Prairie Farmer* 41 (September 24, 1870): 279; Haugen, "Pioneer Reminiscences," p. 133; Tew, *Autobiography*, p. 17; and Angie Kumlien Main, "Annals of a Wisconsin Thresherman," p. 304.
14. Main, "Annals," p. 305; Shutes, "Stack Threshing," p. 2; and John Baskin, *New Burlington*, p. 138.
15. Dan Jones interview.
16. Herman Noelker, "My Life and Times," p. 30; Henry C. Taylor, *Tarpleywick*, p. 69; Tew, *Autobiography*, p. 16; Withers, "Threshing Time," p. 7; and Logan Esarey, *The Indiana Home*, pp. 68–69.
17. Doug Hasler, "The Process and Social Experience of Threshing," p. 7; R. I.

McGinnis, ed. and comp., *The Good Old Days*, p. 177; Britt, *An America That Was*, p. 105; and interview with Peter Kohlman, August 21, 1980, Brookville, Indiana.

18. Broughton, "Drover Days," p. 114.

19. *Ohio Farmer* 51 (1877): 221 and 55 (1881): 443. A literary account that reveals close familiarity with this experience is Herbert Quick, *The Hawkeye*, p. 255.

20. Paul C. Johnson, *Farm Inventions in the Making of America*, pp. 64–67.

21. Interview with Ira Edger, December 3, 1980, Greenville, Ohio; interview with Clarence Wolber, August 12, 1981, Piqua, Ohio; and Phil Einspahr, "Golden Harvest," p. 21.

22. Interview with Albert Merkle, Jefferson Township, Dubois County, Indiana, August 14, 1979.

23. *Cultivator* 4 (1847): 353. Other local attempts in Ohio to remedy dust problems include B. Hull, Trumbull County, Ohio, *Ohio Farmer* 51 (1877): 221 and *Cultivator* 6 (1858): 224, 256, 257, 287, and 362.

24. "John Arnold Farm Record, 1860," in George Keifer, *History of Rush County, Indiana*, p. 131.

25. *Recollections of the Pioneers of Lee County* [Illinois], p. 169; also see Elaine Rusk, "Threshing Meals," p. 2.

26. Donald Paul Greene, "Prairie Agricultural Technology, 1860–1900," p. 164; *American Thresherman* 28, no. 5 (September, 1925): 1; and Hasler, "Threshing," p. 9.

27. Felton, "Pioneer Life," p. 239; Mary Stitt, "Farming in the Early 1900s," p. 11; Anonymous Diary (Fulton County, Ohio), August 1 and 3, 1846; and Haugen, "Pioneer Reminiscences," pp. 142–43.

28. Haugen, "Pioneer Reminiscences," pp. 142–43; Esarey, *Indiana Home*, p. 69; McGinnis, *The Good Old Days*, p. 150; and Benjamin H. Gavitt, *Eighty Years in Iowa*, p. 136.

29. *American Agriculturalist* 17 (1858): 33. The parentheses are in the original.

30. King Manuscript, letter to Joseph Baldwin, March 17, 1858.

31. *Prairie Farmer* 6 (1846): 207.

32. E. J. Hobsbawm and J. Rude, *Captain Swing*.

33. Peter H. Argersinger and Jo Ann Argersinger, "The Machine Breakers: Farmworkers and Social Change in the Rural Midwest," pp. 393–410.

34. *Fourteenth Annual Report of Ohio State Board of Agriculture* (Columbus, 1860), pp. 484–85.

35. In a study of six townships in Ohio, Indiana, and Illinois, for example, Rebecca Shepherd found that more than fifty percent of the young men left their home townships between 1850 and 1860. See her "Restless Americans."

36. Discussions of labor shortages as a factor in favor of agricultural mechanization in the Midwest include David Schob, *Hired Hands and Plowboys*, pp. 109–110; Paul W. Gates, *The Farmer's Age*, pp. 154–57; and Russell Anderson, "Agriculture in Illinois during the Civil War Period, 1850–1870," pp. 214–18.

37. Albert and Laura McKee Diaries, 1851.

38. George Duffield Diary, July 20–22 and 27–29, and September 2–3, 1868. Duffield's operation for the year is not as large as one might expect of a man who helped found the Iowa State Agricultural Society. Other exchange patters involving five to seven farmers and crossing into tasks other than threshing are documented in Downer Diary, 1873–81; Ringle Diary, August 23-October 10, 1865; Mighell Diary, September-October, 1873; and Thomas Page Diary, May 1846.

39. Broughton, "Drover Days," p. 114.

40. James Ellis Diary, 1866–68; Edwin Warren Diary, 1863; and Ben Linvill Diary, 1873–82.

41. According to figures in the Eighth Census of 1860, Adams County farmers averaged 16.1 acres of wheat and 19.5 acres of oats.

Notes to pages 54–60 179

42. Doringh Diary, 1852–54. For similar situations, see Ringle Diary, August-September 1865 and Downer Diary, October, 1873.

43. Lewis Lesher Diary, September 27, 1846 and January 25, February 11, and March 8, 1847.

44. Thomas Page Diary, April 27 to May 7, 1846.

45. *Minnesota Farmers' Diaries, William R. Brown, 1845–46, and Mitchell Y. Jackson, 1852–63*, Jackson Diary, December 10–21, 1855.

46. *Recollections of the Pioneers of Lee County*, p. 170; Lewis Mighell Diary, March 2–8, 1857; the 1882, 1884, and 1886 threshing seasons (August and September of each year) of the Martin Holt Diary; Solon Buck, "Making a Farm on the Frontier," pp. 113–14; and Asenath H. Gable, "Lovingly Submitted," p. 27.

47. John Goodell, ed., *Diary of William Sewall, 1797–1846*. Sewall's difficulties were considerable and included persistent lawsuits against him for nonpayment of debts. New England emigrant and son of a Revolutionary War hero, Sewall never found a peaceful existence as a midwestern farmer.

48. Sodbusting is perhaps the best-known of these custom practices. See David E. Schob, "Sodbusting on the Upper Midwestern Frontier, 1820–1860." Custom sodbusters differed from itinerant threshermen in that the prairie breakers were often not local residents or established farmers.

49. Siegfried Giedion, *Mechanization Takes Command*, p. 166; Paul David, "The Mechanization of the Reaping in the Ante-bellum Midwest," pp. 3–39; and Alan L. Olmstead, "The Mechanization of Reaping and Mowing in American Agriculture, 1833–1870."

50. Thrasher Diary, July, 1878; Alan Bogue, *From Prairie to Corn Belt*, pp. 152–54; Taylor, *Tarpleywick*, p. 16; Stranahan Leedger, July, 1844, April, 1845; Russell Diary, June-August, 1859; and ("Johnson County"), in *Report of Indiana Agriculture, 1852* (Indianapolis, 1852), p. 155. There are no instances of a farmer reaping by machine and threshing by flailing or treading.

IV. Twentieth-Century Shock Threshing and Threshing Rings

1. The best discussions of steam power designs and styles are Reynold M. Wik, *Steam Power on the American Farm*; Paul C. Johnson, *Farm Power in the Making of America*; R. B. Gray, *The Agricultural Tractor, 1855–1900*; and Jack Norbeck, *Encyclopedia of American Steam Traction Engines*.

2. Norbeck, *Encyclopedia of American Steam Traction Engines*, pp. 53–273.

3. Accounts of horse-sweep usage around the turn of the century include Henry C. Taylor, *Tarpleywick*, pp. 68–69; James E. Walsh, *Black Loam of Iowa*, pp. 105, 122–23; Martin Tew, *The Autobiography of Martin E. Tew*, p. 46; *Cultivator and Country Gentleman* 61 (1891): 293; Leo Rogin, *The Introduction of Farm Machinery in Its Relation to the Production of Labor in the Agriculture of the United States during the Nineteenth Century*, pp. 184–85; and Michael Owen Jones, "Traditions of a Kansas Farmer," p. 16.

4. There are a host of styles and designs marking the development of self-feeders over the years. One popular type was the wing feeder that utilized two angled conveyers leading to the threshing cylinder. For further descriptions of self-feeders, see Paul C. Johnson, *Farm Inventions in the Making of America*, pp. 68–72.

5. Two other important innovations of the nineteenth century, the automatic weigher/bagger and the "wind stacker," are described later in this chapter.

6. Interview with Walter Schmidt, Shelby, Iowa, August 8, 1980. One Ohio farmer claimed he sprinkled garlic among his bundles to prevent "the inroads of rats and other vermin"; see *Western Farmer and Gardener* 1, no. 12 (1848): 359.

7. *Farmer's Guide* 15 (1903): 771; also Peter Sheridan, "Grandpa' Waymon Pruitt," p. 2; Ben Logan, *The Land Remembers,* p. 129; and, O. J. Felton, "Pioneer Life in Jones County."

8. Gayle Hager, "Striking It Rich in the Northeast Iowa Hills," p. 27.

9. Interview with Raymond Lightfoot, Range, Ohio, July 16, 1979, and interview with Ira Edger, Greeneville, Ohio, March 12, 1981. Complaints representing both sides of this issue between 1877 and 1882 provide an interesting debate in *Ohio Farmer* 51 (1877): 63; ibid. 60 (1881): 407; and ibid. 62 (1882): 512.

10. Moist grain confined in bulk can heat up too quickly and produce dangerous gases, leading to the spontaneous combustion of the crop. Elevator fires of this origin continue to happen today.

11. Hager, "Striking It Rich," p. 27.

12. Ohio farmer George Petit stacked grain after most of his neighbors threshed from the shock, "and for years [we] were hindered with our stacking by having to go help thrash." In *Ohio Farmer* 100 (1901): 65.

13. In years of very poor weather, farmers at the end of the run stacked their crop to prevent further spoilage or "shock sprouting" of the grain. Interview with Ira Edger, Greenville, Ohio, December 2, 1980, and Fred Downer Diaries, 1873–91.

14. Interview with Dave Horner, Boone County, Missouri, September 22, 1984; Joseph Carlson interview; and interview with William Solomon, Stockton, Illinois, April 16, 1979.

15. Interview with Ira Edger, Greenville, Ohio, December 4, 1980.

16. Interview with Basil Copes, Brookville, Indiana, February 13, 1981; *Country Gentleman* 60 (1890): 277; interview with Lloyd Johnson, Decorah, Iowa, August 5, 1978; Angie Kumlien Main, "Annals of a Wisconsin Thresherman," p. 308; Hager, "Striking It Rich," pp. 25–28; Benjamin H. Hibbard, *The History of Agriculture in Dane County, Wisconsin,* p. 27.

17. Interview with Merwin Winer and Paul Clay, St. Mary's, Ohio, December 5, 1980; interview with Peter Moeller, Waterloo, Iowa, June 14, 1977; and Sherry Lewis, "The History and Folklore of Mulberry [Indiana]," p. 9.

18. Interview with Basil Copes, Brookville, Indiana, February 6, 1981.

19. William M. Miller, "A Threshing Ring in Southern Ohio," p. 7.

20. Interview with Harold Pointer, New Unionville, Indiana, September 15, 1980. Also see Paul M. Shoger, *Threshing Rings of Kendall County, 1875–1955,* p. 76.

21. Merwin Winer interview.

22. Miller, "A Threshing Ring," p. 7; R. J. McGinnis, ed. and comp., *The Good Old Days, An Invitation to Memory,* p. 151; Basil Copes interview; and interview with Lee Smith, New Unionville, Indiana, November 4, 1980.

23. Interview with Ed Barstow, Peoria, Illinois, April 4, 1981.

24. Interview with Dan Jones, Oak Hill, Ohio, June 5, 1980.

25. Lee Smith interview.

26. Paul Clay interview and interview with Herman Wagonner, Greenville, Ohio, December 3, 1981.

27. Emil Rauchenstein and C. A. Brown, *Successful Threshing Ring Management,* p. 385. Interview with Ira Edger, Greenville, Ohio, December 3, 1980; Kenneth Tracey interview; and interview with John Holp, Lewisburg, Ohio, December 4, 1980.

28. Interview with Noah Miller, Clark, Missouri, June 13, 1984; Merwin Winer interview; and Doug Hasler, "The Process and Social Experience of Threshing," p. 5.

29. It is likely that the use of basket racks in the Midwest increased during and after World War I because of the loss of rural men to the military service and urban areas.

30. State agricultural bulletins also used the labor-saving argument to promote change. Emil Rauchenstein and C. Bonnen noted the loss at ten bushels, or about one-third of a load formed by using field pitchers and wagon drivers; they claimed also a labor savings of "one-fourth of the man hours necessary to get the bundles of grain to the threshing machine" via the use of basket racks. In *Successful Threshing Ring Management*, p. 386.

31. Wagonner interview.

32. Miller, "A Threshing Ring," p. 5; Herman Wagonner interview; Dan Jones interview; Clay and Winer interview; and McGinnis, *The Good Old Days*, p. 151. For photographs of the finery and teams, see *History and Program of Sesquicentennial Celebration*, p. 18. The practice is still evident at many of the threshermen's reunions and other events that "recreate" threshing practices.

33. This information is based on a composite of three discussions—Paul Clay interview; inteview with Virgil Fowble, Palestine, Ohio, December 3, 1980; and Ira Edger interview, December 4, 1980.

34. Ed Barstow interview, and Dana Close Jennings, *Days of Steam and Glory*, p. 8.

35. A detailed description of the wind stacker's evolution and design is H. R. Tolley, "Threshing Machine Operation," *American Thresherman and Farm Power* 24, no. 10 (October, 1919): 10–11, 54.

36. Adoption rates in various Ohio counties are noted in *Ohio Farmer* 93 (1898): 173.

37. Ira Edger, a thresherman near Greenville, Ohio, stated that the main problem of the stacker was that "it kicked out everything so hard. There were men around here, I'll tell you, that'd claim they'd been shot after getting hit with a grain out of that stacker. It wasn't losing much, you see, but you sure knew a kernel of grain if it hit you." Interview on December 3, 1980.

38. Robert S. Withers, "Threshing Time in Early Day Clay County Was Indeed a Social Event," p. 7; Michael J. Pyle, "Threshing," p. 6; Harold Pointer interview; and Ed Barstow interview.

39. Dan Jones interview.

40. Rodney C. Loehr, "Introduction," p. 14.

41. Benjamin Holt Diary, November 24, 1886.

42. Ira Edger interview, July 11, 1981; Lee Smith interview; Lara Good, *The Way It Was*, p. 47; and Mary Stitt, "Farming in the Early 1900s," p. 10.

43. Carl Hamilton, *In No Time At All*, p. 88.

44. Hasler, "Threshing," p. 8.

45. Kenneth Tracey interview; John Holp interview; Phil Einspahr, "Golden Harvest," pp. 21–23; Hager, "Striking It Rich," p.27; McGinnis, *The Good Old Days*, p. 125; and Basil Copes interview, February 6, 1981.

46. Kenneth Tracey interview; Hasler, "Threshing," p. 8; and *Farmer's Guide* 19 (1912): 720.

47. Basil Copes interview, February 13, 1981; Charlene Galloway, "The Farm," p. 2; Virgil Fowble interview; and Herman Wagonner interview.

48. Interview with Bud Ferguson by Margot Roberson, Fulton, Missouri, October 6, 1984.

49. A comprehensive treatment of threshermen's organizations and support networks is included in Reynold M. Wik's *Steam Power on the American Farm*.

50. *Newspaper and Magazine Directory* (Chicago: H. F. Kaster and Sons, 1923), pp. 534 and 536.

51. *Yearbook, Twelfth Annual Convention of Illinois Brotherhood of Threshermen*, p. 306.

52. John T. Schlebecker, "Farmers and Bureaucrats: Reflections on Technological Innovations in Agriculture," p. 652.

53. Miller, "A Threshing Ring," p. 5.
54. The designation of such cooperative ventures as butchering and silo filling as "butchering rings" or "silo-filling rings" followed the application of the term to threshing.
55. Fred Downer Diary, 1882–93; Martin Holt Diary, 1882–89; and J. L. Ferguson, "Good Feelings and Fun Enliven and Lighten Wheat Threshing 50 Years Ago."

V. Threshing Ring Organization and Formalization

1. Sylvanus Johnson, Posey County, Indiana, in *Farmer's Guide* 15 (1913): 919.
2. Report of a conversation between Sam Crabtree and S. S. Lappin, in *Indiana Farmer's Guide* 32 (1920): 230.
3. Interview with Basil Copes, Brookville, Indiana, February 6 and 13, 1981.
4. Agricultural Statistics and Reports, 1873, Franklin County, Indiana. These reports were sponsored by the State Board of Agriculture.
5. Interview with Maze Clemens, Sharpeye, Ohio, December 2, 1980; Robert S. Withers, "Threshing Time in Clay County Was Indeed a Social Event"; and Paul M. Shoger, *Threshing Rings of Kendall County, Illinois, 1875–1955*, p. 8.
6. Basil Copes interview, February 6, 1981.
7. A more elaborate discussion of this ring is J. Sanford Rikoon, "The White Plains, Indiana, Threshing Ring, 1920–1943."
8. Based on a miscellaneous page accompanying the "Minutes of the White Plains Threshing Ring."
9. *Indiana Farmer's Guide* 31 (1919): 288.
10. Interview with Virgil Bratz, September 15, 1980, Springfield, Illinois.
11. Interviews with Ira Edger, Greenville, Ohio, December 1–4, 1980; interview with Kenneth Tracey, Seymour, Indiana, June 24, 1981; and interviews with John Holp, Lewisburg, Ohio, December 4, 1980, and July 12, 1981.
12. Ira Edger interview, December 3, 1980, and Kenneth Tracey interview.
13. In addition to threshing, silo filling is the only other rural activity in which mechanization resulted generally in cooperative labor exchanges. While the members of "silo rings" often joined together in the same threshing collective, there were some important differences between the two systems. The percentage of any area's men participating in silo rings was smaller than that in threshing, because not all farmers needed or used silos. Silo filling also required smaller labor groups. Most rings averaged five to seven farmers in membership. Finally, silo filling occurred generally in the late fall, or well after the threshing. Farmers generally agree that the two tasks were viewed as discrete and closed systems.
14. Basil Copes interview; interview with Luther Breimeyer, Portland, Indiana, March 17, 1981; and *Farmer's Guide* 18 (1906): 183.
15. *Indiana Farmer's Guide* 25 (1913): 66; interview with Henry Chapman, August 23, 1980, Portland, Indiana; Ira Edger interview, December 4, 1980; *Ohio Farmer* 93 (1898): 440; and *Farmer's Guide* 24 (1912): 725.
16. Interview with Luther Breimeyer, and interview with Ed Barstow, Peoria, Illinois, April 4, 1981.
17. Kenneth Tracey interview, and Ira Edger interview, December 3, 1981.
18. "Threshing Unions" were not linked via any formal mechanisms.
19. The earliest reference is by a Fulton County, Indiana, farmer to a "threshing club" started in 1894, in *Farmer's Guide* 13 (1901): 438. The lead of Hoosiers in this evolution is also evident in early descriptions of "company rings" in Tipton County,

documented in *Ohio Farmer* 94 (1898): 262, and Montgomery County, detailed in ibid. 93 (1897): 442.

20. J. C. Rundles, "The Thrashing Ring in the Corn Belt."
21. Ibid., p. 247.
22. Emil Rauchenstein and C. A. Brown, *Successful Threshing Ring Management*.
23. Earle D. Ross, *Iowa Agriculture*, p. 86.
24. Ibid., p. 118.
25. See Mildred Thorne, "Book Farming in Iowa, 1840–1870," pp. 125–26; William C. Latta, *Indiana Farmers' Institutes from Their Origin, in 1882, to 1904*; and *Farmer's Guide* 21 (1909): 1197. Early formalized rings known as "threshing clubs" were perhaps direct outgrowths of the local farmers' club meetings of the 1890s. *Farmer's Guide* 13 (1901): 438 and 18 (1906): 256 and 422.
26. *Indiana Farmer's Guide* 31 (March 8, 1919): 3, 42; ibid. (October 25, 1919): 34–35; ibid. 33 (July 9, 1921): 8; and *Wallace's Farmer* 43 (September 13, 1918): 309; ibid. (June 20, 1919): 1275; and ibid. 44 (November 17, 1919): 665. Other state publications printed their own versions; see *Ohio Farmer* 139 (1917): 931 and Rauchenstein and Bonnen, *Successful Threshing Ring Management*, pp. 401–403.
27. Interview with Virgil Fowble, Palestine, Ohio, December 3, 1980; interview with Merwin Winer and Paul Clay, St. Mary's, Ohio, December 5, 1980; interview with Harold Pointer, New Unionville, Indiana, September 15, 1980; Maze Clemens interview; and interview with George Osgood, Boonville, Missouri, September 8, 1984.
28. The Hickory Grove Thresher's Union in Randolph County, Indiana, is typical; see *Indiana Farmer's Guide* 19 (1912): 720.
29. Hermen Noelker, "My Life and Times," p. 34.
30. Basil Copes interview; Luther Breimeyer interview; *Farmer's Guide* 23 (1911): 567; *Indiana Farmer's Guide* 31 (1919): 42; and *Farmer's Guide* 35 (1923): 788 and 799.
31. Some rings included a vice-president's position, to which was attached little responsibility or power.
32. Basil Copes interview, February 13, 1981. Also see *Wallace's Farmer* 49 (1924): 1362, and ibid. 50 (1925): 874.
33. The ring dropped the captain's position in 1939.
34. Harold Pointer interview.
35. Rauchenstein and Bonnen, *Successful Threshing Ring Management*, pp. 292–93.
36. Report of E. P. Beaver, Huntington County, Indiana, in *Indiana Farmer's Guide* 33 (1921): 730. Other relatively simple accounting procedures in Indiana rings are documented for collectives in Wabash County, see *Ohio Farmer* 139 (1917): 931; and Clayton, Indiana, in Lara P. Good, *The Way It Was*, p. 78.
37. S. S. Lappin, *Indiana Farmer's Guide* 32 (1920): 230.
38. Published documentations of other complex mechanisms include, for Clinton County, Indiana, *Indiana Farmer's Guide* 33 (1921): 970; and for Howard County, Indiana, ibid. 23 (1911): 567.
39. Basil Copes interview, February 13, 1981; Paul Clay interview; E. Joseph Penn, "The Changing American Farm Scene," p. 74; and Michael J. Pyle, "Threshing," p. 10.
40. *Farmer's Guide* 19 (1912): 720.
41. Luther Breimeyer interview; Penn, "The Changing American Farm Scene," p. 74; and William M. Miller, "A Threshing Ring in Southern Ohio," p. 13.
42. Pyle, "Threshing," p. 10.
43. John Holp interview, July 12, 1981; Dan Jones interview, Oak Hill, Ohio, June 5, 1980; *Farmer's Guide* 18 (1906): 422; ibid. 21 (1909): 907; Charlene Galloway, "The Farm," p. 2; and Carl Hamilton, *In No Time at All*, p. 85.

44. *Farmer's Guide* 19 (1912): 9.

45. *Indiana Farmer's Guide* 32, no. 13 (May 6, 1922): 10, and *Wallace's Farmer* 45 (1920): 441.

46. Kenneth Tracey interview and Ira Edger interview, December 3, 1980. The difficulties faced by a ring with little technical expertise are illustrated in a short story by Leo Ward. A new engineer quickly breaks the belt leading from the engine to the separator and almost crashes the steamer into the threshing machine. The story was first published in a 1930 issue of *Midland* and was later reprinted in *The Best Short Stories of 1931*, ed. Edward O'Brien (New York: Harper and Brothers, 1931), pp. 123–37.

47. Interview with Everett Josephs, Indianapolis, Indiana, August 21, 1981.

48. Interview with Ira Edger, July 11, 1981, and Ed Barstow interview.

49. *Wallace's Farmer* 45 (1920): 441. Other published examples of cooperatively owned machinery usage include *Indiana Farmer's Guide* 31 (1918): 288; Shoger, "Threshing Rings in Kendall County," p. 6; Frank T. Clampitt, *Some Incidents in My Life*, p. 123; and Henry C. Taylor, *Tarpleywick*, p. 111.

50. "Annual Reports of Munday Thrashing Company, 1916–1922," manuscript. I would like to thank Elizabeth H. Bevington of Terre Haute for sharing these reports.

51. Ira Edger interview, July 11, 1981; John Holp interview; and *Indiana Farmer's Guide* 30 (1918):17.

52. *Indiana Farmer's Guide* 30 (1918): 17, and 31 (1919): 288, and Grant Heilman, ed., *Farm Town, A Memoir of the 1930s*, p. 23.

53. Charles P. Loomis and J. Allan Beegle, *Rural Sociology*, p. 12.

54. Ibid.

VI. "Threshing Was Something Social, Too": Food and Practical-Joking Traditions of the Threshing Ring

1. Interview with Gladys Pyle, by Michael Jay Pyle, "Threshing," p. 14.

2. Interview with Herman Enslinger, Indianapolis, Indiana, November 17, 1980.

3. Matti Sarmela, *Reciprocity Systems of the Rural Society in the Finnish-Karelian Culture Area*, p. 110.

4. The same factors likely contribute to the major rural celebrations of Independence Day.

5. Interviews with Leola and Ira Edger, Greenville, Ohio, December 3 and 4, 1980.

6. Interview with Gladys Bates, Jackson, Ohio, August 5, 1980.

7. For examples, see Herman Noelker, "My Life and Times," p. 31; Leroy Shutes, "Stack Threshing, Ioway—1890s," p. 4; Doc Holycross, "Threshing Whistle Sounded Big Day," p. 18; and Elaine Rusk, "Threshing Meals," p. 2.

8. Interview with Ruth Barstow, Peoria, Illinois, April 4, 1981.

9. For example, see George Ewart Evans, *The Pattern under the Plough*, p. 155.

10. William Faux, *Memorable Days in America*, pp. 295–96.

11. This subject deserves a study of its own. Some of the best descriptions are Ellen Harley [1833–1914], "Family Memories," p. 26; David Turpie, *Sketches of My Own Times*, p. 25; Willis Broughton, "Drover Days, or Pioneer Life in Illinois, 1862–1876," chap. 7; and Branson Harris, *Some Recollections of My Boyhood*, pp. 32–35.

12. William Marion Miller, "A Threshing Ring in Southern Ohio," p. 9; Broughton, "Drover Days," p. 113; and, Floyd E. Whitinger, *How a Boy Was Built*, p. 71.

13. R. J. McGinnis, ed. and comp., *The Good Old Days, An Invitation to Memory,* p. 151.

14. Interview with Edna Lester, Hamilton, Ohio, June 3, 1981.

15. Pyle, "Threshing," p. 12. Also see Miller, "A Threshing Ring," p. 9.

16. Interview with Leola Edger, December 4, 1981; *Farmer's Guide* 24 (1912): 760; Doug Hasler, "The Process and Social Experience of Threshing," p. 11; Charlene Galloway, excerpts from "The Farm," in Helen Underwood, "Indiana Extension Homemakers Association Folklore District Winners, 1979–1980," p. 2; interview with Ruth Gettys, September 23, 1983, in Moberly, Missouri; Carl Hamilton, *In No Time at All,* p. 86; and Angie Kumlien Main, "Annals of a Wisconsin Thresherman," p. 306.

17. Evans, *The Pattern under the Plough* p. 153.

18. Lena Carpenter Diary, August 7 and 8, 1883.

19. Interview with Dan Jones, Oak Hill, Ohio, June 5, 1980; Main, "Annals," p. 306; Pyle, "Threshing," p. 12; Henry C. Taylor, *Tarpleywick,* p. 70; and Miller, "A Threshing Ring," p. 9. Main notes that Wisconsin thresherman Ole Olson actually looked forward to a meal of "salt pork" as a respite from "beef three times a day for weeks and months at a time." Two women, both with good reputations among threshing crews, provided "baker's bread" with their meals. Leola Edger interview, December 3, 1980, and Galloway, "The Farm," p. 2.

20. Evelyn Woods, untitled reminiscences, Indiana Extension Homemakers Association Folklore Project, 1979–80, p. 15.

21. Paul M. Shoger, *Threshing Rings of Kendall County, 1875–1955,* p. 20; Hamilton, *In No Time at All,* p. 87; and interview with Betty Crable, Seneca County, Ohio, March 17, 1980.

22. Woods, reminiscences, p. 15.

23. Edna Lester interview. For other typical long lists of preparations, see Albert Britt, *An America That Was,* p. 105; Paul Corey, *Three Miles Square,* p. 128; and Hasler, "Threshing," p. 11.

24. Donald F. Carmony, ed., "Letter Written by Mr. Johann Wolfgang Schreyer," p. 297. A Jennings County woman suggested the following: "In setting the table, arrange it just as you would if you were planning to entertain some of your stylish city friends, and don't forget the bouquet of dahlias, sweet peas or whatever flowers are most convenient to gather," in *Farmer's Guide* 25 (1913): 756. Also see Mabel Weir Grimes, "Threshing Wheat Was a Neighborhood Affair," p. 5.

25. Joanne Bell, "Lillie Cooks for Threshers," p. 124.

26. Interview with Ira Edger, Greenville, Ohio, December 2, 1980. For a parallel story, see Hasler, "Threshing," p. 27. Almost every former thresherman and threshing ring participant has a story or two with the motif of the "bad threshing meal" or "unsanitary threshing meal conditions."

27. Dan Jones interview, and interview with Leola Edger, December 2, 1981, in Greenville, Ohio. Leola met her husband, Ira, when he was hired to thresh for her father near Dayton, Ohio, around 1924. For other examples, see Hasler, "Threshing," p. 12; E. Joseph Penn, "The Changing American Farm Scene," p. 74; and J. L. Ferguson, "Good Feelings and Fun Enliven and Lighten Wheat Threshing."

28. For examples, see Lara P. Good, *The Way It Was,* p. 17; Galloway, "The Farm," p. 2; and Bell, *The Good Old Days,* p. 125. Hamlin Garland uses the motif of matchmaking during a threshing meal as the basis for a short story, "A Branch Road, Part I." In this narrative, the young man becomes so embarrassed by the attention that what began as a simple practical joke ends in creating conflict for the two central participants. In his *Main-Travelled Roads,* pp. 13–53.

29. Leola Edger interviews; Edna Lester interview; Gladys Bates interview; and Ben Logan, *The Land Remembers,* pp. 135–36.

30. Merrill E. Jarchow, "Life on a Jones County Farm, 1873–1912," pp. 322–23.

31. Interview with Lee Smith, June 23, 1981, New Unionville, Indiana. For a similar treatment of black men at mealtimes, see the description from Logan County, Kentucky, in *Cultivator and Country Gentleman* 61 (1891): 604. This report notes, in part, "The colored men had their long table in the back kitchen, presided over by the colored girl who helps in the dairy; while the cook, donning a brand new dress for the occasion, waited on the table in the house."

32. Martin E. Tew, *The Autobiography of Martin E. Tew*, p. 11.

33. *Farmer's Guide* 28 (1916): 443.

34. Leola Edger interview, and *Farmer's Guide* 24 (1912): 708.

35. Shoger, *Threshing Rings*, p. 20; Lee Smith interview; and Ed and Mary Barstow interview.

36. George Osgood interview. Also see Dana Close Jennings, *Days of Steam and Glory*, p. 12.

37. Lena Carpenter Diary, July 29-August 6, 1898. Also see Jarchow, "Jones County," pp. 322-23.

38. Britt, *An America That Was*, p. 106.

39. *Farmer's Guide* 27 (1915): 1107. As is true for most twentieth-century changes affecting threshing ring processes, the agricultural press acted as a forum for discussion, especially on those meal trends viewed as more "efficient" and "modern."

40. *Farmer's Guide* 24 (1912): 708, and Russel B. Nye, "Changes in Twentieth-Century Rural Society," pp. 27 and 32-33.

41. For Indiana examples, see *Indiana Farmer's Guide* 30 (1918): 953 and 1187. State councils also examined such things as the fees threshermen charged and their machinery expenses.

42. Interview with William Solomon, Stockton, Illinois, April 16, 1979. With only this agreement, the crew retained the possibility of altering their work pace to influence meal locations.

43. Interview with Basil Copes, February 13, 1981, in Brookville, Indiana.

44. J. Sanford Rikoon, "The White Plains, Indiana, Threshing Ring, 1920-1943," pp. 251-52.

45. Western cookwagons are described and pictured in Kirby Brumfield, *The Wheat Album* (Seattle: Superior Publishing Co., 1974), pp. 156-59; Jennings, *Days of Steam and Glory*; and Heather Robertson, *Salt of the Earth*, pp. 100-101. A cook shack used around New Burlington, Ohio, in 1913 is pictured in John Baskin, *New Burlington*, p. 139.

46. *Indiana Farmer's Guide* 23 (1911): 1171. An earlier, unsigned short article noting the use of a wholly itinerant threshing crew of eight to twelve men with a cookwagon is *Farmer's Guide* 11 (1899): 449.

47. *Farmer's Guide* 21 (1909): 770; ibid. 27 (1915): 1122; and ibid. 27 (1915): 1137. The Indiana paper was the only midwestern publication to actively support the use of traveling food wagons, although recommendations do not appear after 1918.

48. Threshermen often charged the ring for the entire amount and then were paid for meal charges at the settlement meeting. See *Indiana Farmer's Guide* 23 (1911): 1171; *Farmer's Guide* 27 (1915): 1122. Perishable goods, including dairy products, fruit, and vegetables, were bought from the host farmers, with the purchase price deducted from the threshing bill.

49. *Farmer's Guide* 27 (1915): 1107.

50. Interview with Harold Pointer, New Unionville, Indiana, September 15, 1980.

51. Dan Jones interview.

52. Anthony F. C. Wallace, "Revitalization Movements."

53. Interview with Leola Edger, December 4, 1980; also see McGinnis, *Good Old Days*, p. 125.

Notes to pages 130–42

54. Penn, "The Changing American Farm Scene," p. 75; Alice Foster, "Farming during the Depression," p. 2; Holycross, "Threshing Whistle," p. 16; and Logan, *The Land Remembers*, p. 136.
55. Ben Hayes, *'Buzz' Clark and His Brother Joe: Ohio's Cantankerous Threshermen*, p. 3.
56. Dan Jones interview and George Osgood interview.
57. Interview with Ira Edger, Greenville, Ohio, December 2, 1980.
58. Interview with Maze Clemens, Sharpeye, Ohio, December 2, 1980.
59. Hasler, "Threshing," p. 14.
60. Interview with Luther Breimeyer, Portland, Indiana, March 17, 1981.
61. Logan, *The Land Remembers*, p. 142; Main, "Annals," p. 307; and interview with Kenneth Tracey, June 24, 1981.
62. Penn, "The Changing American Farm Scene," p. 75; Pyle, "Threshing," p. 11; and Good, *The Way It Was*, p. 224.
63. McGinnis, *The Good Old Days*, p. 150; Miller, "A Threshing Ring," p. 8; and Galloway, "The Farm," p. 2.
64. Whitinger, *How a Boy Was Built*, p. 72.
65. Pyle, "Threshing," p. 12.

VII. The Continuity and Decline of Threshing Rings

1. William M. Miller, "A Threshing Ring in Southern Ohio," p. 5.
2. Interview with Virgil Bratz, Springfield, Illinois, September 15, 1980. Also see discussion of the White Plains Threshing Ring in Chap. 5.
3. See Dana Close Jennings, *Days of Steam and Glory*; Thoman B. Keith, *The Horse Interlude*, pp. 99–118; and Thomas Isern, *Custom Combining on the Great Plains, A History*.
4. H. H. Krusekopf, "Major Soil Areas of Missouri," University of Missouri College of Agriculture Agricultural Experiment Station, Circular no. 304 (Columbia, 1945), pp. 1–2.
5. Ethel Grant Inman, "Pioneer Days in Northwest Missouri—Harrison County, 1837–1873," pp. 310–11.
6. Two surviving ring members, Oscar Bram and George Osgood, began threshing with the group around 1918. Both men indicated, however, that the families listed had, in relatively unchanged combinations, threshed together at least two generations prior to this date.
7. Based on farm locations and owner names contained in *Combined Atlases of Harrison County, Missouri* (Kansas City, 1975). See the plat maps for 1876, Pt. 1, p. 45; for 1898, pt. 2, p. 26; and for 1917, Pt. 3, p. 42.
8. Interview with Oscar Bram, Booneville, Missouri, October 27, 1983.
9. Ibid.
10. Interview with Maze Clemens, December 3, 1980.
11. Ibid. Information on the Rob Clemens Ring also came from an interview with Ira Edger, Greenville, Ohio, December 3 and 4, 1980, and personal correspondence and manuscript materials of Steve Miller, Greenville, Ohio.
12. Interview with Joseph Carlson, Troy, Ohio, June 22, 1979.
13. Oliver J. Felton, "Pioneer Life in Jones County," pp. 240–41. Also see J. L. Ferguson, "Good Feelings and Fun Enliven and Lighten Wheat Threshing."
14. Interview with Basil Copes, Brookville, Indiana, February 6, 1981.
15. Interview with Ira Edger, Greenville, Ohio, December 4, 1980; Miller, "A Threshing Ring," p. 10; and interview with Charles Peterson, Decorah, Iowa, August 4, 1978.

16. R. B. Gray, *The Agricultural Tractor, 1855–1950*, pp. 21 and 58.

17. Stationary gasoline engines for farm use were available around the turn of the century. These devices seldom delivered enough power to run a separator efficiently and were rarely used for threshing. For one example, see *Farmer's Guide* 18 (1906): 128.

18. Interview with John Holp, Lewisburg, Ohio, July 12, 1981; interview with Harold Pointer, New Unionville, Indiana, September 15, 1980; Dan Jones interview; Floyd Whitinger, *How a Boy Was Built*, p. 69; and E. Joseph Penn, "The Changing American Farm Scene," p. 74.

19. Farmers rarely used tractors to pull bundle wagons. It was easier to remain in the shock row, and direct a team to move slowly forward, than to constantly move a tractor between shocks.

20. *Wallace's Farmer* 49 (1924): 988.

21. Joseph Carlson interview; John Holp interview; Joseph Meachem interview; interview with Herman Enslinger, Indianapolis, Indiana, October 17, 1980; and interview with Jerome Pepsen, Troy, Ohio, July 17, 1980.

22. For combine histories, see Allan Thompson, "The Origins of a Harvesting Revolution: The Development of the Combine Harvester in Australia, Canada, and U. S. A.," and Graeme Quick and Wesley Buchele, *The Grain Harvesters*, pp. 85–182.

23. Robert S. Withers, "Threshing Time in Early Day Clay County Was Indeed a Social Event"; interview with Paul Clay and Merwin Winer, St. Mary's, Ohio, December 5, 1980; and interview with Kenneth Tracey, Seymour, Indiana, June 24, 1981. The western patterns are described in Mary Wilma Hargreaves, *Dry Farming in the Northern Great Plains, 1900–1925*, pp. 508–509 and 518–19, and H. Grimes, "The Effect of the Combined Harvester-Thresher on Farming in a Wheat-Growing Region."

24. Harold Pointer interview; Paul Clay interview; Grant Heilman, ed., *Farm Town, A Memoir of the 1930s*, p. 25; and Quick and Buchele, *The Grain Harvesters*, p. 172. Machines harvesting only a forty-two inch path were also used, as well as eight-foot cutters that farmers typically regarded as the combines of the "big landowner."

25. Noted in *American Thresherman and Farm Power* 33, no. 8 (August, 1928): 44. Also see E. W. Lehmann and I. P. Blauser, *Combines in Illinois*.

26. In 1939, for example, the price of the Model 40 combine was $345. Between 1935 and 1958, Allis-Chalmers alone sold more than 320,000 small combines. See Quick and Buchele, *The Grain Harvesters*, pp. 172–73; Earle D. Ross, *Iowa Agriculture*, p. 279, and John A. Hopkins, *Changing Technology and Employment in Agriculture*, p. 73. Hopkins reports the sale of 42,000 units in 1938, 26,000 of which cut a swath six feet or smaller.

27. Interview with Roscoe Deller, Fremont, Indiana, May 23, 1980. Interviewed by Thomas King, Indiana University Oral History Project.

28. Interview with Raymond Hollinger, Palestine, Ohio, March 3, 1981; Basil Copes interview; Charles Peterson interview; George Keifer, *History of Rush County, Indiana*, p. 78; and Miller, "A Threshing Ring," p. 12.

29. Isern, *Custom Combining*.

30. Raymond Hollinger interview. Also see Withers, "Threshing Time," p. 7.

31. Ross, *Iowa Agriculture*, p. 279.

32. Joseph Carlson interview; interview with Merwin Winer and Paul Clay, St. Mary's, Ohio, December 5, 1980; and Harold Pointer interview.

33. Ross, *Iowa Agriculture*, pp. 180–81; Albert Mighell, *Soybeans in Iowa Farming*; Ira Edger interview; interview with Ed Bartstow, Peoria, Illinois, April 1, 1981; and J. C. Hackelman, O. H. Sears, and W. L. Burlison, *Soybean Production in Illinois*.

Older farmers have admitted that they first avoided feeding soybeans because of fears that the rich protein levels could kill a hog.

34. Roscoe Deller interview.

35. John Holp interview; E. Hill, "Correspondence," *Soybean Digest* (1949): 154; Ira Edger interview, July 11, 1981; and *American Thresherman and Farm Power* 33, no. 8 (August, 1928): 44.

36. Ira Edger interview. Manufacturers and machinery "experts" occasionally detailed their suggestions for modifying separator designs in the agricultural press or supplied special supplements to machinery catalogues and manuals.

37. John Holp interview; Roscoe Deller interview; Kenneth Tracey interview; and Quick and Buchele, *The Grain Harvesters*, p. 138. To the points raised in these paragraphs on supports for the combine must be added the dramatic growth in average farm size beginning around World War II. With larger farms came an emphasis on one or two market crops and the need to gather in a large harvest (in approximately the same amount of time).

38. *Indiana Farmer's Guide* 94 (1938): 197.

39. For example, see Morrell Heald, "Technology in American Culture," pp. 106–108, and Donald W. Shriver, "Man and His Machines," pp. 530–31.

40. Basil Copes interview, February 6, 1981, and John Holp interview.

Conclusion

1. Reynold M. Wik, "Some Interpretations of the Mechanization of Agriculture in the Far West": Thomas Isern, *Custom Combining on the Great Plains, A History*; and Dana Close Jennings, *Days of Steam and Glory*.

2. George Foster, *Traditional Societies and Technological Change*, pp. 2–3.

3. An interesting quantitative analysis of the personality traits of this shift among Danish farmers is Bruno Benvenuti's *Farming in Cultural Change*.

4. The history of this movement is best summarized in Joseph Knapp's *The Rise of American Cooperative Enterprise, 1620–1920*, and *The Advance of American Cooperative Enterprise*.

5. Linda Kravitz, *Who's Minding the Co-op?*

6. See Harold F. Breimyer, *Individual Freedom and the Economic Organization of Agriculture*.

7. For examples, see Walter Goldschmidt, *As You Sow*; Patrick Madden, *Economies of Size in Farming*; and Richard D. Rodfield, *The Direct and Indirect Effects of Mechanizing U.S. Agriculture*.

8. Interviews with Luther Breimeyer, Portland, Indiana, March 17, 1981, and with Oscar Bram, Boonville, Missouri, October 27, 1983.

BIBLIOGRAPHY

A. Published Sources, Theses, and Dissertations

Abel, Helen C. "The Social Consequences of the Modernization of Agriculture." In *Rural Canada in Transition: A Multidimensional Study of the Impact of Technology and Urbanization on Traditional Society*, edited by Marc Adelard and Walton J. Anderson, pp. 178–218. Publications of the Agricultural Economics Research Council, vol. 6. Ottawa: Mutual Press Ltd., 1966.
Allardt, Erik. "Reflections on the Rural Nature of Past and Future." *Sociologia Ruralis* 22 (1982): 99–107.
Allen, R. L. *New American Farm Book*. New York: Orange Judd and Co., 1869.
Anderson, Russell H. "Agriculture in Illinois during the Civil War Period, 1850–1870." Ph.D. dissertation, University of Illinois, 1929.
Ardrey, R. L. "The Harvesting Machine Industry." *Scientific American Supplement* 1407, no. 54 (1902): 22544–47.
———. *American Agricultural Implements*. 1894. Reprint. Wilmington, Del.: Scholarly Resources, 1973.
Arensberg, Conrad M., and Kimball, Solon T. *Culture and Community*. New York: Harcourt, Brace and World, 1965.
Argersinger, Peter H., and Argersinger, Jo Ann. "The Machine Breakers: Farmworkers and Social Change in the Rural Midwest of the 1870's." *Agricultural History* 58 (1984) : 393–410.
Arthur, Eric, and Witney, Dudley. *The Barn: A Vanishing Landmark in North America*. Boston: New York Graphic Society, 1972.
Ashby, Jacqueline A. "Technology and Ecology: Implications for Innovation Research in Peasant Agriculture." *Rural Sociology* 47 (1982) : 234–50.
Bailey, Robert C. *Farm Tools and Implements before 1850*. Spring City, Tenn.: Hillcrest Books, 1973.
Ball, C. R.; Leighty, C. E; Stine, O. C; and Baker, O. E. "Wheat Production and Marketing." In *1921 Yearbook of Agriculture*, pp. 77–160. Washington, D.C.: United States Department of Agriculture, 1921.
Ball, T. H. *Northwestern Indiana from 1800 to 1900*. Chicago: Donohue and Henneberry, 1900.
Bardolph, Richard. *Agricultural Literature and the Early Illinois Farmer*. Urbana: University of Illinois Press, 1948.
Bartholomew, Henry S. K. *Pioneer History of Elkhart County, Indiana*. Goshen: Goshen Printery, 1930.
Baskin, John. *New Burlington, The Life and Death of an American Village*. New York: New American Library, 1977.
Bates, H. E. *A Threshing Day*. London: W. and G. Foyle, 1931.
Bauman, Richard, and Abrahams, Roger, with Kalcik, Susan. "American Folklore and American Studies." *American Quarterly* 28 (1976): 360–77.
Baugarten, Karl. "Deile und Dreschen im Mecklenburgischen Hallenhaus." *Zeitschrift fur Agrargeschichte und Agrarsoziologie* 13 (1965): 28–34.
Beckwith, H. N. *History of Vigo and Parke Counties*. Chicago: H. H. Hill and N. Iddings, 1880.

[Beers]. *The History of Darke County, Ohio.* Chicago: W. H. Beers and Co., 1880.
Beinhauer, Myrtle. "The County, District, and State Agricultural Societies of Iowa." *Annnals of Iowa,* 3d ser. 20 (1935): 65–77.
Bell, Joanne. "Lillie Cooks for Threshers." In *The Good Old Days, An Invitation to Memory,* edited by R. J. McGinnis, pp. 123–26. New York: Harper and Brothers, 1960.
Benvenuti, Bruno. *Farming in Cultural Change.* Assen: Royal VanGorcum and Co., 1962.
Berardi, G. M. "Socio-economic Consequences of Agricultural Mechanization in the United States: Needed Redirections for Mechanical Research." *Rural Sociology* 46 (1981): 483–504.
Berg, Gosta. "The Introduction of the Winnowing Machine in Europe in the 18th Century." *Tools and Tillage* 3, no. 1 (1976) : 25–46.
Bernard, H. Russell, and Pelto, Pertti J. *Technology and Social Change.* New York: Macmillan Co., 1972.
Berry, Wendell. *The Unsettling of America: Culture and Agriculture.* New York: Avon Books, 1977.
Bertrand, Alvin L. *Agricultural Mechanization and Social Change in Rural Louisiana.* Louisiana State University and Agricultural and Mechanical College Bulletin no. 458. Baton Rouge: Louisiana State University, 1951.
Binnie-Clark, Georgina. *Wheat and Women,* introduction by Susan Jackel. 1914. Reprint. Toronto: University of Toronto Press, 1979.
Blandford, Percy W. *Old Farm Tools and Machinery: An Illustrated History.* Fort Lauderdale: Gale Research Co., 1971.
Blauser, I. P. *Reducing Grain Losses in Threshing.* University of Illinois Agricultural College and Experiment Station, Circular No. 311. Urbana, 1926.
Bloch, Marc. *French Rural History: An Essay on Its Basic Characteristics,* translated by Janet Sondheimer. 1931. Reprint. Berkeley: University of California Press, 1966.
Bloxsome, John Leland. "The Development of Agriculture in Indiana during the Pioneer Period." Master's thesis, University of Chicago, 1935.
Bogart, Ernest Ludlow. *Economic History of American Agriculture.* New York: Longmans, Green and Co., 1923.
Bogue, Allan G. *From Prairie to Corn Belt: Farming on the Illinois and Iowa Prairies in the Nineteenth Century.* Chicago: University of Chicago Press, 1953.
———. "Pioneer Farmers and Innovation." *Iowa Journal of History and Politics* 56, no. 1 (January, 1958): 1–36.
Bogue, Margaret Beattie. *Patterns from the Sod: Land Use and Tenure in the Grand Prairie, 1850–1900.* 1959. Reprint. New York: Arno Press, 1979.
Bordley, John Beale. *Essays and Notes on Husbandry and Rural Affairs.* Philadelphia: Budd and Bartram, 1799.
Borie IV, Beauveau. *Farming and Folk Society: Threshing among the Pennsylvania Germans.* Ann Arbor: UMI Research Press, 1986.
Boss, William. *Instructions for Traction and Stationary Engineers.* 3d ed. St. Anthony Park, Minn.: Minnesota School of Agricultural Engineering, 1906.
Boyle, Victor M., ed. "Reminiscences of a Hill-Billy." [Contributed by Paul Pritchard Van Riper]. *Indiana Magazine of History* 62, no. 1 (March, 1966): 5–50.
Breimyer, Harold F. *Individual Freedom and the Economic Organization of Agriculture.* Urbana: University of Illinois Press, 1965.
Breneman, Mary Worthy. *The Land They Possessed.* New York: Macmillan Co., 1956.
Brewer, M. H. "Report on the Cereal Production of the United States." In *Tenth Census Report on the Products of Agriculture,* pp. 1–173. Washington, D.C.: Government Printing Office, 1883.

Briggs, L. J. "A Hand Grain Thrasher." In United States Department of Agriculture Bureau of Plant Industry, Circular no. 119, pp. 23–24. Washington, D.C., 1913.
Bringeus, Nils-Arvid. *Jarnplogen som Innovation*. Lund, 1962.
Britt, Albert. *An America That Was: What Life Was Like on an Illinois Farm Seventy Years Ago*. Barre, Mass.: Barre Publishers, 1964.
Britton, Wiley. *Pioneer Life in Southwest Missouri*. Kansas City: Smith-Grieves Co., 1929.
Brown, Waldo F. *Success in Farming: A Series of Practical Talks*. Springfield, Ohio: R. S. Thompson, 1881.
Brumfield, Kirby. *The Wheat Album: A Picture and Story Scrapbook of Wheat Harvests in Years Gone By*. Seattle: Superior Publishing Co., 1974.
———. *This Was Wheat Farming: A Pictorial History of the Farms and Farmers of the Northwest Who Grew the Nation's Bread*. Seattle: Superior Publishing Co., 1968.
Brunskill, R. W. *Illustrated Handbook of Vernacular Architecture*. New York: Universe Books, 1970.
———. *Vernacular Architecture of the Lake Counties*. London: Faber and Faber, 1974.
Bryant, John. "A Usable Pastoralism: Leo Marx's Method in *The Machine in the Garden*." *American Studies* 16 (1973): 63–72.
Buck, Solon Justus. *Illinois in 1818*. 2d rev. ed. Chicago: A. C. McClurg, 1918.
———. "Making a Farm on the Frontier: Extracts from the Diaries of Mitchell Young Jackson." *Agricultural History* 4 (1930): 92–120.
———, ed. "Pioneer Letters of Gersham Flagg." In *Transactions of the Illinois State Historical Society for the Year 1910*, pp. 139–83. Springfield, Ill.: Illinois State Journal Co., 1912.
Burkett, Charles W. *History of Ohio Agriculture*. Concord, N.H.: Rumford Press, 1900.
Caird, James. *Prairie Farming in America*. New York: Appleton and Co., 1859.
Cancian, Frank. *The Innovator's Situation: Upper Middle-Class Conservatism in Agricultural Communities*. Stanford: Stanford University Press, 1979.
Carmony, Donald, ed. "Letter Written by Mr. Johann Wolfgang Schreyer." *Indiana Magazine of History* 40 (1944): 283–306.
Carrier, Lyman. *The Beginnings of Agriculture in America*. New York: McGraw-Hill Book Co., 1923.
Cheape, Hugh. "Questionnaires and the Grain Harvest in Scotland." *Folk Life* 16 (1978): 27–41.
Church, Lillian. *Partial History of the Development of Grain Threshing Implements and Machines*. United States Department of Agriculture Information Series, no. 73. Washington, D.C., 1939.
Clampitt, Frank T. *Some Incidents in My Life: A Saga of the "Unknown" Citizen*. Ann Arbor: Edwards Brothers, 1936.
Clark, Neil M. *John Deere: He Gave to the World the Steel Plow*. Moline: Desaulniers and Co., 1937.
Collins, E. J. T. *Sickle to Combine: A Review of Harvest Techniques from 1800 to the Present Day*. Berkshire, England: Museum of English Rural Life, 1972.
———. "The Diffusion of the Threshing Machine in Britain, 1790–1880." *Tools and Tillage* 2, no.1 (1972): 16–33.
Collins, Phyllis B. "Steam Engines—Threshing." In *Growing Up in Indiana*, compiled and edited by Chester L. Larkins, pp. 80–82. Leawood, Kans.: Bicentennial Publishing Co., 1980.
Colman, Gould P. "Innovation and Diffusion in Agriculture." *Agricultural History* 42, no. 3 (July, 1968): 173–87.
Conner, John B. *Indiana Agriculture: Agricultural Resources and Development of the State*. Indianapolis: William Burford, 1893.

Copp, James H. *Our Changing Rural Society: Perspectives and Trends.* Ames: Iowa State University Press, 1964.
Corey, Paul. *Three Miles Square.* Indianapolis: Bobbs-Merrill Co., 1939.
———. *The Road Returns.* Indianapolis: Bobbs-Merrill Co., 1940.
Cousins, Peter H. *Hog Plow and Sith: Cultural Aspects of Early Agricultural Technology.* Dearborn, Mich.: Greenfield Village and Henry Ford Museum, 1973.
Cregen, Eric. "Flailing in Argyll." *Folklife* 3 (1965): 90.
Crowder, E. May Lacey. "Pioneer Life in Palo Alto County." *Iowa Journal of History and Politics* 46 (1948): 156–98.
Danhof, Clarence H. *Change in Agriculture: The Northern United States, 1820–1870.* Cambridge: Harvard University Press, 1969.
———. "The Tools and Implements of Agriculture." In *Farming in the New Nation: Interpreting American Agriculture, 1790–1840,* edited by Darwin P. Kelsey, pp. 81–90. Washington, D.C.: Agricultural History Society, 1972.
David, Paul. "The Mechanization of the Reaping in the Ante-bellum Midwest." In *Industrialization in Two Systems: Essays in Honor of Alexander Gerschenkron,* edited by Henry Rosovsky, pp. 3–39. New York: John Wiley and Sons, 1966.
Demaree, Albert L. *The American Agricultural Press, 1819–1860.* New York, 1941.
———. "The Farm Journals, Their Editors, and Their Public, 1830–1860." *Agricultural History* 15, no. 3 (1941): 182–88.
Dickerman, Charles W. *How to Make the Farm Pay.* Philadelphia: Zeigler, McCurdy and Co., 1869.
Dingee, Albert. *Science of Successful Threshing.* 5th ed., rev. Racine, Wis.: J. I. Case Threshing Machine Co., 1907.
Early Life of Eric Norelius (1833–1862): Journal of a Swedish Immigrant in the Middle West, trans. Emeroy Johnson. Rock Island, Ill.: Augustana Historical Society Publications, 1934.
Einspahr, Phil. "Golden Harvest." In *Conversations with the Recent Past,* edited by Luis Torres, pp. 20–23. Decorah, Iowa: Luther College, 1975.
Ek, Sven B. "Economic Booms, Innovations, and the Popular Culture." *Economy and History* 3 (1960): 3–37.
Ellul, Jacques. *The Technological Society.* New York: Continuum Publishing Co., 1964.
———. *The Technological System.* New York: Continuum Publishing Co., 1980.
Emerson, Governeur. *The American Farmer's Encyclopedia, and Dictionary of Rural Affairs.* 3d ed. Philadelphia: Carey and Hart, 1844.
Erixon, Sigurd. "Ethnological Investigation of the Present." In *The Possibilities of Charting Modern Life: A Symposium for Ethnological Research about Modern Time,* edited by Erixon, pp. 1–22. Oxford: Pergamon Press, 1970.
———, ed. *The Possibilities of Charting Modern Life: A Symposium for Ethnological Research about Modern Time.* Oxford: Pergamon Press, 1970.
Esarey, Logan. *The Indiana Home.* Crawfordsville, Ind.: R. E. Banta, 1943.
Estrem, Andrew. "An Early Norse Settlement in Iowa." *Iowa Journal of History and Politics* 39 (1941): 387–402.
Evans, E. Estyn. *Irish Folk Ways.* London: Routledge and Kegan Paul, 1957.
———. *Mourne Country: Landscape and Life in South Down.* Dundalk, Northern Ireland: Dundalgan Press, 1967.
Evans, George Ewart. *The Pattern under the Plough: Aspects of the Folk-Life of East Anglia.* London: Faber and Faber, 1966.
———. *Tools of Their Trade: An Oral History of Men at Work, circa 1900.* New York: Taplinger Publishing Co., 1971.
Farmer's Centennial History of Ohio, 1803–1903. Springfield, Ohio: Springfield Publishing Co., 1904.
Farnham, Eliza W. *Life in Prairie Land.* New York: Harper and Brothers, 1847.

Farrell, Richard T. "Advice to Farmers: The Content of Agricultural Newspapers, 1860–1910." *Agricultural History* 51 (1977): 209–217.
Faux, William. *Memorable Days in America; Being a Journal of a Tour to the Western United States*. Reprinted in *Indiana as Seen by Early Travelers*, edited by Harold Lindley, pp. 291–326. Indianapolis: Indiana Historical Society, 1916.
Felton, Oliver John. "Pioneer Life in Jones County." *Iowa Journal of History and Politics* 29 (1931): 233–81.
Fenton, Alexander. *Scottish Country Life*. Edinburgh: John Donald Publishers, 1976.
———. "Hand Threshing in Scotland." *Acta Ethnographica* 29 (1980): 349–89.
Ferguson, Eugene S. "Technology and Its Impact on Society." In *Technology and Its Impact on Society*, edited by Sigvard Strandh, pp. 273–80. Tekniska Museet Symposia, no. 1. Stockholm: Tekniska Museet, 1979.
Ferguson, J. L. "Good Feelings and Fun Enliven and Lighten Wheat Threshing Fifty Years Ago." *Star-Journal*, Warrensburg, Missouri, July 31, 1939, p. 7.
Fessenden, Thomas G. *The Complete Farmer and Rural Economist*. Boston: Lilly, Wait, and Co., 1834.
Fife, E. D. "The Agricultural Development of the West during the Civil War." *Quarterly Journal of Economics* 20 (1906): 143–72.
Fitchen, John. *The New World Dutch Barn*. Syracuse: Syracuse University Press, 1968.
Fite, Gilbert C. *The Farmer's Frontier: 1865–1900*. New York, 1966.
Fitzherbert, Master. *The Book of Husbandry*. 1534. Reprint. London: English Dialect Society, 1882.
Flagg, Gershom. "Pioneer Letters of Gershom Flagg," ed. Solon J. Buck. In *Transactions of the Illinois State Historical Society for the Year 1910*, pp. 139–83. Springfield: Illinois State Journal Co., 1912.
Fliegel, Frederick C., and van Es, J. C. "The Diffusion-Adoption Process in Agriculture: Changes in Technology and Changing Paradigms." In *Technology and Social Change, A Festschrift for Eugene A. Wilkening*, edited by Gene F. Summers, pp. 13–28. Boulder: Westview Press, 1983.
Flint, James. *Flint's Letters from America, 1818–1820*. 1822. Reprint. Cleveland: A. H. Clark, 1904.
Foster, F. Elliott. *Types of Farming in the United States*. Washington, D.C.: Bureau of the Census, 1933.
Foster, George M. *Traditional Societies and Technological Change*. 2d ed. New York: Harper and Row Publishers, 1973.
Fox, N. E. "The Spread of the Threshing Machine in Central South England." *Agricultural History Review* 26 (1978): 26–28.
Frimannslund, Rigmor. "Farm Community and Neighborhood Community." *Scandinavian Economic History Review* 4 (1956): 62–81.
Gable, Asenath Hampton. "Lovingly Submitted. . . ." In *Pure Nostalgia*, edited by Carl Hamilton, pp. 3–44. Ames: Iowa State University Press, 1979.
Gardner, D. P. *The Farmer's Dictionary*. New York: Harper and Brothers, 1846.
Garland, Hamlin. "A Branch Road." In his *Main-Travelled Roads*, pp. 13–53. 1891. Reprint. New York: New American Library, 1962.
Garola, C. V. *Cereales*. Paris: J. B. Bailliere, 1909.
Gates, Paul W. *The Farmer's Age: Agriculture, 1815–1860*. New York: Holt, Rinehart and Winston, 1960.
———. "Problems in Agricultural History, 1790–1840." In *Farming in the New Nation: Interpreting American Agriculture, 1790–1840*, edited by Darwin P. Kelsey, pp. 33–58. Washington, D.C.: Agricultural History Society, 1972.
Gavitt, Benjamin H. *Eighty Years in Iowa*, ed. Benjamin H. Gavitt and A. T. DeGroot. Private printing, 1948.
Giedion, Sigfried. *Mechanization Takes Command: A Contribution to Anonymous History*. New York: Oxford University Press, 1948.

Gilfillan, S. *The Sociology of Invention.* Chicago: Follett Publishing Co., 1935.
Gill, Harold B. "Wheat Culture in Colonial Virginia." *Agricultural History* 52 (1978): 380–93.
Goldschmidt, Walter. *As You Sow: Three Studies of the Social Consequences of Agribusiness.* Montclair, N. J.: Allanheld, Osmun, and Co., 1978.
Good, Lara P. *The Way It Was; Autobiography, Part I: In the Begining.* Private printing, 1967.
Good-Knight, Asbury. "Wheat Raising in Pioneer Missouri." *Missouri Historical Review* 16 (1921): 592–95.
Goodell, John, ed. *Diary of William Sewall, 1797–1846.* Beardstown, Ill., 1930.
Gordon, Leon M. "Effects of the Michigan Road on Northern Indiana, 1830–1860." *Indiana Magazine of History* 46 (1950): 377–402.
Grant, H. Roger, and Purcell, L. Edward, eds. *Years of Struggle: The Farm Diary of Elmer G. Powers, 1931–1936.* Ames: Iowa State University Press, 1976.
Gray, R. B. *The Agricultural Tractor, 1855–1950.* Saint Joseph, Mich.: American Society of Agricultural Engineers, 1975.
Greene, Donald Paul. "Prairie Agricultural Technology, 1860–1900." Ph.D. dissertation, Indiana University, 1957.
Griffiths, D. *Two Years' Residence in the New Settlements of Ohio.* 1835. Reprint. Ann Arbor: University Microfims, 1966.
Grimes, H. "The Effect of the Combined Harvester-Thresher on Farming in a Wheat-Growing Region." *Scientific Agriculture* 9 (1929): 773–82.
Grimes, Mabel Weir. "Threshing Wheat Was a Neighborhood Affair." *Montgomery* [Ohio], *Your County Magazine* 7 (1977): 4–5.
Growth of Industrial Art, The. Washington, D.C.: United States Patent Office, 1888.
Hackelman, J. C.; Sears, O. H.; and Burlison, W. L. *Soybean Production in Illinois.* University of Illinois Agricultural Experiment Station Bulletin no. 310. Urbana, 1928.
Hager, Gayle. "Striking It Rich in the Northeast Iowa Hills." In *Conversations with the Recent Past*, edited by Luis Torres, pp. 24–32. Decorah, Iowa: Luther College Press, 1975.
Hall, A. Rupert. "On Knowing, and Knowing How to. . . ." *History of Technology* (1978): 91–104.
Halsted, Byron D. *Barns, Sheds, and Outbuildings.* 1881. Reprint. Brattleboro: Stephen Greene Press, 1977.
Hamilton, Carl. *In No Time at All.* Ames: Iowa State University Press, 1974.
Hamilton County Agricultural Club, comp. *The Western Agriculturalist and Practical Farmer's Guide.* Cincinnati: Robinson and Fairbank, 1830.
Harden, Samuel. *Early Life and Times in Boone County, Indiana.* Indianapolis: Carlton and Hollenbeck, 1887.
Hargreaves, Mary Wilma. *Dry Farming in the Northern Great Plains, 1900–1925.* Cambridge: Harvard University Press, 1957.
Harlan, Edgar R., ed. "William Savage: Iowa Pioneer, Diarist, and Painter of Birds." *Annals of Iowa* 19, no. 2 (October, 1933): 83–114.
Harris, Branson. *Some Recollections of My Boyhood.* Indianapolis: Hollenbeck Press, 1908.
Hart, John Fraser. *The Look of the Land.* Englewood Cliffs, N.J.: Prentice-Hall, 1975.
Haugen, Nils P. "Pioneer and Political Reminiscences." *Wisconsin Magazine of History* 11, no. 2 (December, 1927): 121–52.
Hawthorn, Fred W., and Hawthorn, Robert W. *Idlewild Farm: A Century of Progress.* Lake Mills, Iowa: Graphic Publishing Co. 1976.
Hayes, Ben. *"Buzz" Clark and His Brother Joe: Ohio's Cantankerous Threshermen.* Ohio Valley Folk Publications, 61. Chillicothe: Ross County Historical Society, 1961.

Hayter, Earl W. *The Troubled Farmer, 1850–1900: Rural Adjustment to Industrialism.* Dekalb: Northern Illinois University Press, 1968.

Heald, Morrell. "Technology in American Culture." In *American Character and Culture: Some Twentieth Century Perspectives*, edited by John A. Hague, pp. 103–117. Deland, Fla.: Everett Edwards Press, 1964.

Heilman, Grant. "Threshing Season." *American West* 11 (1974): 20–29.

———, ed. *Farm Town, A Memoir to the 1930s.* Brattleboro: Stephen Greene Press, 1974.

Hellen, J. A. "Agricultural Innovation and Detectable Landscape Margins: The Case of the Wheelhouse in Northumberland." *Agricultural History Review* 20 (1972): 140–54.

Hennell, Thomas. *Changes in the Farm.* Cambridge: Cambridge University Press, 1936.

Herskovitz, Melville J. "Motivation and Culture-Pattern in Technological Change." *International Social Science Bulletin* 6, no. 3 (1954): 388–400.

Hibbard, Benjamin H. *The History of Agriculture in Dane County, Wisconsin.* Bulletin of the University of Wisconsin, 101, Economic and Political Science Series, vol. 1, no. 2. Madison: University of Wisconsin, 1904.

Hildreth, Samuel Prescott. *Pioneer History, Being an Account of the First Examinations of the Ohio Valley.* Cincinnati: H. W. Derby and Co. 1848.

Hill, Leonard H. "Gleanings from a Farmer's Diary, 1836–43." *Piqua Daily Call,* April 6, 1968, p. 8.

Hills, John W. "Threshing Then and Now." *American Livestock Journal* 70 (September 28, 1916): 536.

Hiner, James. "On Distinguishing 'A Machine' from Its System." *American Quarterly* 14 (Winter, 1962): 612–17.

History and Program of Sesquicentennial Celebration [Lewisburg, Ohio]. Private printing, 1966.

History of Knox and Daviess County, Indiana. Chicago: Goodspeed Publishing Co., 1886.

History of McHenry County, Illinois. Chicago, 1885.

History of Wayne, Fayette, Union, and Franklin Counties, Indiana. Chicago: Goodspeed Publishing Co., 1894.

Hobsbawm, E. J., and Rude, J. *Captain Swing.* London: Routledge and Kegan Paul, 1969.

Holbrook, Stewart H. *Machines of Plenty: Pioneering in American Agriculture.* New York: Macmillan Co., 1955.

Holycross, Doc. "Threshing Whistle Sounded Big Day." *Whitley County Historical Society Bulletin* [Columbia City, Indiana] (1978): 16–19.

Hopkins, John A. *Changing Technology and Employment in Agriculture.* 1941. Reprint. New York: Da Capo Press, 1973.

Howells, William Cooper. *Recollections of Life in Ohio from 1813 to 1840.* Cincinnati, 1895.

Hurst, W. M., and Church, L. M. *Power and Machinery in Agriculture.* United States Department of Agriculture, Miscellaneous Publication no. 157. Washington, D.C.: Government Printing Office, 1933.

Hutslar, Donald A. "The Ohio Farmstead: Farm Buildings as Cultural Artifacts." *Ohio History* 90, no. 3 (Summer, 1981): 221–37.

Hutton, Kenneth. "The Distribution of Wheelhouses in the British Isles." *Agricultural History Review* 24, no. 1 (1976): 27–41.

Indiana State Board of Agriculture Report for 1899–1900. Indianapolis: State Printers, 1900.

Inman, Ethel Grant. "Pioneer Days in Northwest Missouri—Harrison County, 1837–1873." *Missouri Historical Review* 22, no. 3 (April, 1928): 307–330.

Bibliography

Iowa State Agricultural Society Report, 1857. Des Moines, 1858.
Isern, Thomas. *Custom Combining on the Great Plains, A History.* Norman: University of Oklahoma Press, 1980.
Jarchow, Merrill E. "Life on a Jones County Farm, 1873–1912." *Iowa Journal of History and Politics* 49, no. 4 (October, 1951): 311–38.
Jenkins, David. "The Community and Land in South Cardiganshire at the Close of the Nineteenth Century." *Folk Life* 8 (1970): 5–12.
Jenkins, J. Geraint. *Life and Tradition in Rural Wales.* London: J. M. Dent and Sons, 1976.
Jennings, Dana Close. *Days of Steam and Glory.* Aberdeen, S.D.: North Plains Press, 1968.
Johnson, Elmer. *Care and Repair of Farm Implements, Number 5: Grain Separators.* United States Department of Agriculture Farmers Bulletin, no. 1036. Washington, D.C.: Government Printing Office, 1919.
Johnson, Evans. "Pioneer Times." (Boonville) *Missouri Democrat*, February 23, 1894, p. 7.
Johnson, Paul C. *Farm Inventions in the Making of America.* Des Moines: Wallace-Homestead Book Co., 1976.
———. *Farm Power in the Making of America.* Des Moines: Wallace-Homestead Book Co. 1978.
Johnstone, Paul H. "Turnips and Romanticism." *Agricultural History* (1938): 244–55.
Jones, L. J. "The Early History of Mechanical Harvesting." *History of Technology* (1979): 101–148.
Jones, Michael Owen. "Traditions of a Kansas Farmer." Master's thesis, Indiana University, 1966.
Jones, Robert L. "The Introduction of Farm Machinery into Ohio Prior to 1865." *Ohio History* 58 (1949): 1–20.
———. *Ohio Agriculture during the Civil War.* Publications of the Ohio Civil War Centennial Commission, no. 7. Columbus: Ohio State University Press, 1962.
Kaloupek, Walter E. "Agricultural Implements and Machines." Master's thesis, Iowa State University, 1936.
Keifer, George. *History of Rush County, Indiana.* Rushville, 1959.
Keith, Thomas B. *The Horse Interlude: A Pictorial History of Horse and Man in the Inland Northwest.* Moscow: University Press of Idaho, 1976.
Kellar, Herbert Anthony, ed. *Solon Robinson, Pioneer and Agriculturalist: Selected Writings, Volume 1, 1825–1945.* Indianapolis: Indiana Historical Society, 1936.
Kelsey, Darwin P., ed. *Farming in the New Nation: Interpreting American Agriculture, 1790–1840.* Washington, D.C.: Agricultural History Society, 1972.
Kennedy, Joseph C. G. "Process of Invention in Threshing Instruments." In *Preliminary Report on the Eighth Census, 1860,* pp. 90–100. Washington, D.C.: Government Printing Office, 1862.
Kimbal, Solon T. "Rural Social Organization and Co-operative Labor." *American Journal of Sociology* 55 (1949–50): 38–49.
Klein, Erich. "Die Entwicklung des Hohenheimer Pfluges." *Zeitschrift fur Agrargeschichte und Agrarsoziologie* 10 (1962): 45–56.
Klingaman, O. E. "The Heavy Breaking Plow." *Annals of Iowa* 21 (1938): 143–49.
Knapp, Joseph G. *The Rise of American Cooperative Enterprise, 1620–1920.* Danville, Ill.: Interstate Printers and Publishers, 1969.
———. *The Advance of American Cooperative Enterprise, 1920–1945.* Danville, Ill.: Interstate Printers and Publishers, 1973.
"Knure Steernson's Recollections: The Story of a Pioneer." *Minnesota History* 4 (1921): 135–36.
Kovacs, L. "Die Ungarischen Dreschflegel und Dreschmethoden." *Acta Ethnographica* 1 (1950): 41–95.

Krause, Herbert. *The Thresher*. Indianapolis: Bobbs-Merrill Co., 1946.
Kravitz, Linda. *Who's Minding the Co-op?* Washington, D.C.: Agribusiness Accountability Project, 1974.
Kuuse, Jan. *Interaction between Agriculture and Industry*. Goteberg: Publications of the Institute of Economic History of Gottenberg University, 1974.
Larkins, Chester L. *Growing Up in Indiana, Volume Four*. Leawood, Kans.: Bicentennial Publishing Co., 1980.
Lathrop, Leonard E. *The Farmer's Library*. Windsor, Vt.: Wyman Spooner, 1826.
Latta, William C. *Indiana Farmers' Institutes from Their Origin, in 1882, to 1904*. Lafayette: Purdue University Press, 1904.
———. *Outline History of Indiana Agriculture*. Lafayette: Lafayette Printing Co., 1938.
Lehmann, E. W., and Blauser, I. P. *Combines in Illinois*. University of Illinois Agricultural Experiment Station Bulletin no. 316. Urbana, 1927.
Lettermann, Edward J. *Pioneer Farming in Iowa*. Des Moines: Living History Farms, 1972.
"Lewisburg [Ohio] History and Program of Sesquicentennial Celebration." Private printing, 1968.
Lindley, Harold, ed. *Indiana as Seen by Early Travelers*. Indianapolis: Indiana Historical Commission, 1916.
Lionberger, Herbert F. *Adoption of New Ideas and Practices*. Ames: Iowa State University Press, 1960.
Lloyd, W. A.; Falconer, J. I.; and Thorne, C. E. *The Agriculture of Ohio*. Ohio Agriculture Experiment Station Bulletin no. 326. Wooster: Ohio Agricultural Experiment Station, 1918.
Loehr, Rodney C. "Introduction." In *Minnesota Farmers' Diaries, William R. Brown, 1845–46, and Mitchell Young Jackson, 1852–63*, pp. 1–33. Publications of the Minnesota Historical Society, Narratives and Documents, vol. 3. St. Cloud: Minnesota Historical Society, 1939.
Lofgren, Orvar. "Family and Household among Scandinavian Peasants: An Exploratory Essay." *Ethnologia Scandinavica* (1974): 17–52.
Logan, Ben. *The Land Remembers: The Story of a Farm and Its People*. New York: Viking Press, 1975.
Long, Samuel. *A Pioneer History of Wayne Township, Darke County, Ohio*. 1901. Reprint. Versailles, Ohio, 1978.
Loomis, Charles P. *Social Systems: Essays on Their Persistence and Change*. Princeton: D. Van Nostrand Co., 1960.
Loomis, Charles P., and Beegle, J. Allan. *Rural Sociology: The Strategy of Change*. Englewood Cliffs, N.J.: Prentice-Hall, 1957.
Loomis, Ormond. "The Tradition-Oriented Farmer." Ph.D. dissertation, Indiana University, 1980.
McCutcheon, W. A. "The Stationary Steam Engine in Ulster." In *Folk and Farm: Essays in Honor of A. T. Lucas*, edited by Caoimhin O'Danachair, pp. 127–50. Dublin: Royal Society of Antiquaries of Ireland, 1976.
MacDonald, Stuart. "The Early Threshing Machine in Northumberland." *Tools and Tillage* 3, no 3 (1978): 168–84.
———. "Furthur Progress with the Early Threshing Machine: A Rejoiner." *Agricultural History Review* 26 (1978): 29–32.
McGinnis, R. J., ed. and comp. *The Good Old Days, An Invitation to Memory*. New York: Harper and Brothers, 1960.
McManigal, J. W., and Heilman, Grant. *Farm Town: A Memoir of the 1930's*. Brattleboro: Stephen Greene Press, 1974.
McMillen, Wheeler. *Ohio Farm*. Columbus: Ohio State University Press, 1974.
Madden, Patrick. *Economies of Size in Farming: Theory, Analytic Procedures, and a Review of Selected Studies*. United States Department of Agriculture Agricultural Eco-

nomics Report no. 107. Washington, D.C.: Economics, Cooperatives, and Statistical Services, 1976.
Main, Angie Kumlien. "Annals of a Wisconsin Thresherman." *Wisconsin Magazine of History* 11 (1927–28): 301–308.
Marshall, Josiah T. *The Farmer's and Emigrant's Hand Book*. Boston: H. Wentworth, 1852.
Martin, George A. *Farm Equipment and Hand Tools: A Practical Manual*. New York: O. Judd Co., 1887.
Marx, Leo. *The Machine in the Garden: Technology and the Pastoral Ideal in America*. New York: Oxford University Press, 1964.
Mead, Margaret. *Cultural Patterns and Technological Change*. New York: Mentor Books, 1975.
Merrifield, Charles E. "The Importance of Mechanical Appliances to Successful Farming." In *Indiana Board of Agriculture Annual Report, 1883*, pp. 226–28. Indianapolis, 1883.
Mighell, Albert. *Soybeans in Iowa Farming*. Iowa State Agricultural Experiment Station Bulletin no. 309. Ames: Iowa State College, 1934.
Miller, Perry. "The Responsibility of the Mind in a Civilization of Machines." *American Scholar* 31, no. 1 (Winter, 1961–62): 51–69.
Miller, William Marion. "A Threshing Ring in Southern Ohio." *Hoosier Folklore* 5, no. 1 (March, 1946): 3–13.
Miner, Horace. *Culture and Agriculture: An Anthropological Study of a Corn Belt County*. Occasional Contributions from the Museum of Anthropology, University of Michigan, no. 14. Ann Arbor: University of Michigan Press, 1949.
Minnesota Farmers' Diaries, William R. Brown, 1845–46, and Mitchell Young Jackson, 1852–63. Publications of the Minnesota Historical Society, Narratives and Documents, vol. 3. St. Cloud: Minnesota Historical Society, 1939.
Mitchell, Roger. "From Fathers to Sons: A Wisconsin Family Farm." *Midwest Journal of Language and Folklore* 10, no. 1–2 (Spring/Fall, 1984): 1–167.
Mumford, F. B. "A Century of Missouri Agriculture." *Missouri Historical Review* 15, no. 2 (1921): 277–97.
Mumford, Lewis. *Technics and Civilization*. New York: Harcourt, Brace, and World, 1934.
Murray, Margaret E. Archer. "Memoir of the William Archer Family." *Annals of Iowa*, 3d ser. 39, no. 5 (Summer, 1968): 359–77.
Needham, Walter, and Mussey, Barrows. *A Book of Country Things*. Brattleboro: Stephen Greene Press, 1965.
Neeley, Wayne Caldwell. *The Agricultural Fair*. New York: Harper and Brothers, 1935.
Nelson, Lowry. "The American Rural Heritage." *American Quarterly* 1, no. 3 (1949): 225–34.
Norbeck, Jack. *Encyclopedia of American Steam Traction Engines*. Sarasota: Crestline Publishing Co., 1976.
Nourse, E. G. "Some Economic and Social Accompaniments of the Mechanization of Agriculture." *American Economic Review*, Supplement, 20 (1930): 114–32.
Nutting, William Porter. "Starting Life in Warren County." *Iowa Journal of History and Politics* 39 (1941): 180–99.
Nye, Russel B. "Changes in Twentieth-Century Rural Society." *Midcontinent American Studies Journal* 10 (1969): 25–40.
O'Danachair, Caoimhin. "The Flail and Other Threshing Methods." *Journal of the Cork Historical and Archaeological Society* 60 (1955): 6–14.
―――. "The Flail in Ireland." *Ethnologia Europaea* 4 (1970): 51–55.
Olmstead, Alan L. "The Mechanization of Reaping and Mowing in American Agriculture, 1833–1870." *Journal of Economic History* 35 (1975): 211–42.

O'Neill, F. W., and Williams, H. L. *The American Farmer's Hand-Book*. New York: R. Worthington, 1880.
Orchard, Hugh. "Threshing Time." In *Old Orchard Farm*, edited by Hugh Orchard, pp. 79–87. Ames: Iowa State College press, 1952.
Osband, Melvin D. "My Recollections of Pioneers and Pioneer Life in Nankin." *Michigan Pioneer and Historical Society Historical Collections* 14 (1889): 431–83.
Parker, Nathan H. *The Iowa Handbook for 1856*. Boston: John P. Jewett and Co., 1856.
Parker, William N. "A Note on Regional Culture in the Corn Harvest." In *Farming in the New Nation: Interpreting American Agriculture, 1790–1840*, edited by Darwin P. Kelsey, pp. 181–89. Washington, D.C.: Agricultural History Society, 1972.
Parkinson, John B. "Memories of Early Wisconsin and the Gold Mines." *Wisconsin Magazine of History* 5 (1921–22): 119–41.
Partridge, Michael. *Early Agricultural Machinery*. New York: Frederick A. Praeger, 1969.
Peate, Iowerth C. *Tradition and Folk Life: A Welsh View*. London: Faber and Faber, 1972.
Penn, E. Joseph. "The Changing American Farm Scene." In *Growing Up in Indiana*, Volume Four, edited by Chester Larkins, pp. 73–75. Leawood, Kans.: Bicentennial Publishing Co., 1980.
Perkins, J. A. "Harvest Technology and Labour Supply in Lincolnshire and the East Riding of Yorkshire." *Tools and Tillage* 3, no. 1 (1976): 47–58.
Pleasant, Hazen Hayes. *A History of Crawford County, Indiana*. Private printing, 1926.
Power, Richard L. *Planting Corn Belt Culture: The Impress of the Upland Southerner and Yankee in the Old Northwest*. Indianapolis: Indiana State Historical Society, 1953.
Preliminary Report on the Eighth Census, 1860. Washington, D.C.: Government Printing Office, 1862.
Quick, Graeme R., and Buchele, Wesley F. *The Grain Harvesters*. St. Joseph, Mich.: American Society of Agricultural Engineers, 1978.
Quick, Herbert. *The Hawkeye*. Indianapolis: Bobbs-Merrill Co., 1923.
Rasmussen, Wayne D. "The Impact of Technological Change on American Agriculture." *Journal of Economic History* 20 (1962): 578–91.
Rauchenstein, Emil, and Brown, C. A. *Successful Threshing Ring Management*. University of Illinois Agricultural Experiment Station Bulletin no. 267. Urbana: University of Illinois, 1925.
Recollections of the Pioneers of Lee County [Illinois]. Dixon, Ill.: A. Kennedy, 1893.
Redfield, Robert, and Warner, W. Lloyd. "Cultural Anthropology and Modern Agriculture." In *1940 Yearbook of Agriculture: Farmers in a Changing World*, pp. 983–93. Washington, D.C.: United States Department of Agriculture, 1940.
Reifel, August J. *History of Franklin County, Indiana*. Indianapolis: B. F. Bowen, 1915.
Reynolds, John. *My Own Times*. Private printing, 1855.
Richards, William T. *The Era of Steam in Licking County, Ohio: The Agricultural Aspect*. Granville, Ohio: Granville Letter Shop, 1976.
Rikoon, J. Sanford. "The White Plains, Indiana, Threshing Ring, 1920–1943." *Indiana Magazine of History* 80, no. 3 (September, 1984): 227–63.
Robbins, Frank Egleston. "The Personal Reminiscences of General Chauncey Eggleston." *Ohio Archaeological and Historical Publications* 41 (1932): 284–320.
Robertson, Heather. *Salt of the Earth*. Toronto: James Lorimer and Co., 1974.
Robinson, Solon. *Facts for Farmers; Also for the Family Circle*. New York: A. J. Johnson, 1869.

Rodfield, Richard D. *The Direct and Indirect Effects of Mechanizing U.S. Agriculture.* Montclair, N.J.: Allenheld, Osmun, and Co., 1980.

Rogers, Everett M., with Floyd Shoemaker. *Communication of Innovations: A Cross-Cultural Approach.* New York: Free Press, 1971.

Rogin, Leo. *The Introduction of Farm Machinery in Its Relation to the Productivity of Labor in the Agriculture of the United States during the Nineteenth Century.* Berkeley: University of California, 1931.

Rome, Adam Ward. "American Farmers as Entrepreneurs, 1870–1900." *Agricultural History* 56, no. 1 (January, 1982): 37–49.

Rose, Phillip S. *The Thresher's Guide.* 2 vols. Madison: American Thresherman, 1910, 1913.

Roseboom, Eugene H., and Weisenburger, Francis P. *A History of Ohio.* New York, 1945.

Ross, Earle D. "The Evolution of the Agricultural Fair in the Northwest." *Iowa Journal of History and Politics* 24 (July, 1926): 277–302.

———. *Iowa Agriculture: An Historical Survey.* Iowa City: State Historical Society of Iowa, 1951.

———, ed. *Diary of Benjamin F. Gue in Rural New York and Pioneer Iowa, 1847–1856.* Ames: Iowa State University Press, 1962.

Rundles, J. C. "The Thrashing Ring in the Corn Belt." In *1918 Yearbook of Agriculture*, pp. 247–68. Washington, D.C.: Government Printing Office, 1919.

Russell, Howard S. *A Long Deep Furrow: Three Centuries of Farming in New England.* Hanover: University Press of New England, 1976.

Sandklef, Albert. *Singing Flails: A Study in Threshing-Floor Constructions, Flail-Threshing Traditions, and the Magic Guarding of the House.* Folklore Fellows Communication no. 136. Helsinki: Somalainen Tiedeakatemia, 1949.

Sarmela, Matti. *Reciprocity Systems of the Rural Society in the Finnish-Karelian Culture Area (with Special Reference to the Social Intercourse of Youth).* Folklore Fellows Communication no. 207. Helsinki: Somalainen Tiedeakatemia, 1969.

Schafer, Joseph. *The Social History of American Agriculture.* New York: Macmillan Co., 1936.

Scheiber, Harry N. *Ohio Canal Era: A Case Study of Government and the Economy, 1820–1861.* Athens: Ohio University Press, 1969.

Schlebecker, John T. *Whereby We Thrive: A History of American Farming, 1607–1972.* Ames: Iowa State University Press, 1975.

———. "Farmers and Bureaucrats: Reflections on Technological Innovation in Agriculture." *Agricultural History* 51 (1977): 641–55.

Schmidt, Hubert. "Farming in Illinois a Century Ago as Illustrated in Bond County." *Journal of Illinois State Historical Society* 31 (1938): 138–60.

Schmidt, Louis B. "The Westward Movement of the Wheat Growing Industry in the United States." *Iowa Journal of History and Politics* 18 (1920): 396–412.

———. "The Internal Grain Trade of the United States, 1860–1890." *Iowa Journal of History and Politics* 19 (1921): 196–245.

Schob, David E. "Sodbusting on the Upper Midwestern Frontier, 1820–1860." *Agricultural History* 47 (1973): 47–56.

———. *Hired Hands and Plowboys: Farm Labor in the Midwest, 1815–1860.* Urbana: University of Illinois Press, 1975.

Schultz, Theodore W. *Transforming Traditional Agriculture.* Studies in Comparative Economics, vol. 13. New Haven: Yale University Press, 1964.

Seashore, Carl E. "Pioneering in Iowa." *Palimpsest* 22 (1941): 178–83.

Shepard, Hugh H. "Background of a Pioneer." *Palimpsest* 27 (1946): 176–88.

Shepherd, Rebecca A. "Restless Americans: The Geographic Mobility of Farm Laborers in the Old Midwest, 1850–1870." *Ohio History* 89, no 1 (Winter, 1980): 25–45.

Shireff, Patrick. *A Tour through North America.* Edinburgh, 1835.
Shoemaker, Alfred L. *The Pennsylvania Barn.* Lancaster: Franklin Dutch Folklore Center, 1955.
Shoger, Paul M. *Threshing Rings of Kendall County, 1875–1955.* Kendall County Bicentennial Commission Monograph Series, no. 5. Yorkville, Ill.: Kendall County Record, 1976.
Shover, John. "On the State of Agricultural History." *American Quarterly* 28 (1976): 504–511.
Shriver, Donald W. "Man and His Machines: Four Angles of Vision." *Technology and Culture* 13, no. 4 (October, 1972): 531–55.
Smith, T. Lynn, and Post, Lauren C. "The County Butchery: A Cooperative Institution." *Rural Sociology* 2 (September, 1937): 335–37.
Spicer, Edward H., ed. *Human Problems in Technological Change.* New York: John Wiley and Sons, 1952.
Stadtfield, Curtis. *From the Land and Back.* New York: Scribners Publishers, 1972.
Stephens, Henry. *The Book of Farm Implements and Machines.* Edinburgh and London: William Blackwood and Sons, 1858.
Stephenson, James H. *Traction Farming and Traction Engineering.* Chicago: Frederick J. Drake, 1913.
Steward, Julian H. *Theory of Culture Change: The Methodology of Multilinear Evolution.* Urbana: University of Illinois Press, 1955.
Strandh, Sigvard. *Technology and Its Impact on Society.* Tekniska Museet Symposia, no. 1. Stockholm: Tekniska Museet, 1979.
Summers, Gene F., ed. *Technology and Social Change in Rural Areas: A Festschrift for Eugene A. Wilkening.* Boulder: Westview Press, 1983.
Svensson, Sigfrid. "On the Concept of Cultural Fixation." *Ethnologia Europaea* 6 (1972): 129–56.
Swierenga, Robert P. "Towards the 'New Rural History': A Review Essay." *Historical Methods Newsletter* 6 (June, 1973): 111–21.
Taylor, Carl C. "The Contribution of Sociology to Agriculture." In *1940 Yearbook of Agriculture: Farmers in a Changing World,* pp. 1042–55. Washington, D.C.: United States Department of Agriculture 1940.
Taylor, Henry C. *Tarpleywick: A Century of Iowa Farming.* Ames: Iowa State University Press, 1970.
Tew, Martin E. *The Autobiography of Martin E. Tew.* Clarkfield, Minn.: Clarkfield Advocate, 1940.
Thaer, Albert D. *The Principles of Practical Agriculture,* translated by William Shaw and Cuthbert W. Johnson. New York: C. M. Saxton and Co., 1856.
Thirteenth Annual Report of the Commissioner of Labor, 1898: Hand and Machine Labor. Washington, D.C.: Government Printing Office, 1899.
Thompson, Allan. "The Origins of a Harvesting Revolution: The Development of the Combine Harvester in Australia, Canada, and U.S.A." *Tools and Tillage* 3, no. 2 (1977): 67–77.
Thompson, Dave O., Sr., and Madigan, William L. *One Hundred and Fifty Years of Indiana Farming.* Indianapolis: Indiana Historical Bureau, 1969.
Thorne, Mildred. "A History of Agriculture in Southern Iowa, 1833–1900." Ph.D. dissertation, Iowa State University, 1946.
———. "Book Farming in Iowa, 1840–1870." *Iowa Journal of History* 49, no. 2 (April, 1951): 117–42.
Todd, S. Edwards. *The American Wheat Culturalist: A Practical Treatise on the Culture of Wheat.* New York: Taintor Brothers and Co., 1868.
Tolley, H. R. *The Efficient Operation of Thrashing Machines.* United States Department of Agriculture Farmers Bulletin no. 991. Washington, D.C.: June, 1918.

Torres, Luis, ed. *Conversations with the Recent Past.* Decorah, Iowa: Luther College Press, 1975.
Turpie, David. *Sketches of My Own Times.* Indianapolis: Bobbs-Merrill Co., 1903.
Van Wagenen, Jared. *The Golden Age of Homespun.* Ithaca: Cornell University Press, 1953.
Vilppula, H. *Das Dreschen in Finland.* Kansatieteellinen Arkisto 10. Helsinki, 1955.
Wallace, Anthony F. C. "Revitalization Movements." *American Anthropologist* 58 (1956): 264–81.
——. *Rockdale: The Growth of an American Village in the Early Industrial Revolution.* New York: W. W. Norton and Co., 1980.
Walsh, James E. *Black Loam of Iowa.* Lake Mills, Iowa: Graphic Publishing Co., 1963.
Ward, Leo. "The Threshing Ring." 1930. Reprinted in *The Best Short Stories of 1931,* ed. Edward O'Brian, pp. 123–37. New York, 1931.
Weaver, George H. "Autobiography of Dr. Ephraim Ingals." *Journal of the Illinois Historical Society* 28, no. 4 (January, 1936): 279–308.
Weintraub, Dov. "Traditions and Development: Another Look at Some Unsolved Problems." *Rural Sociology* 37, no. 4 (December, 1972): 578–90.
Welker, H. Clare. "Our First Year on a Nebraska Farm." *Nebraska History* 37, no. 1 (March, 1956): 51–58.
Welker, Martin. *Farm Life in Central Ohio Sixty Years Ago.* Tract no. 86, vol. 4, Western Reserve Historical Society. Cleveland: Western Reserve Historical Society, 1925.
Wendel, C. H. *Encyclopedia of American Farm Tractors.* Sarasota: Crestline Publishing Co., 1979.
Weston, Nathan. *The Cost of Production of Corn and Oats in Illinois in 1876.* Illinois Agricultural Experiment Station Bulletin no. 50. Urbana: University of Illinois, 1898.
Whitaker, James W., ed. *Farming in the Midwest, 1840–1900: A Symposium.* Washington, D.C.: Agricultural History Society, 1974.
Whitinger, Floyd E. *How a Boy Was Built: On the Road through New Hope Church.* Frankfort, Ind.: Private printing, 1976.
Wiegelmann, Gunther. "Innovations in Food and Meals." *Folk Life* 12 (1974): 20–30.
Wik, Reynold M. *Steam Power on the American Farm.* Philadelphia: University of Pennsylvania Press, 1955.
——. "Some Interpretations of the Mechanization of Agriculture in the Far West." *Agricultural History* 49 (1975): 73–83.
Wilkening, Eugene A. "Some Perspectives on Change in Rural Societies." *Rural Sociology* 29 (1964): 1–17.
Withers, Robert S. "Threshing Time in Early Day Clay County Was Indeed a Social Event." *Liberty* [Missouri] *Tribune,* June 17, 1948, p. 7, and June 24, 1948, p. 7.
Wolfe, George Wood. *A Pictorial Outline History of Darke County, Ohio.* Newark, Ohio: Lyon and Ickles, 1890.
Woods, John. *Two Years' Residence on the English Prairie of Illinois.* 1822. Reprint. Chicago: R. R. Donnelley and Sons, 1968.
Yearbook, Twelfth Annual Convention of Illinois Brotherhood of Threshermen, February 28, March 1 and 2, 1922. Danville, Ill.: Illinois Printing Co., 1922.
Yearbook, Twenty-first Annual Convention of Illinois Brotherhood of Threshermen, March 3, 4, 5, 1931. N.p., 1931.
Yerkes, Arnold P. and Church, L. M. *Cost of Harvesting Wheat by Different Methods.* United States Department of Agriculture Bulletin no. 627. Washington, D.C.: GPO, 1918.
——. *An Economic Study of the Farm Tractor in the Corn Belt.* United States De-

partment of Agriculture Farmer's Bulletin no. 719. Washington, D.C.: GPO, 1916.

Young, James N., and Coleman, A. Lee. "Neighborhood Norms and the Adoption of Farm Practices." *Rural Sociology* 24 (1959): 372–80.

B. Oral Interview Sources

NOTE: Unless otherwise specified, the following interviews were conducted by J. Sanford Rikoon, and all tapes and transcripts are in the possession of the author. The locations given are those for the interviews and are not necessarily descriptive of the specific communities in which the interviewees lived or worked.

Barstow, Edward; Peoria, Illinois; April 4, 1981.
Barstow, Ruth; Peoria, Illinois; April 4, 1981.
Bates, Gladys; Jackson, Ohio; August 5, 1980.
Bollinger, Robert; Washington Court House, Ohio; August 9, 1980.
Bram, Oscar; Boonville, Missouri; October 27, 1983.
Brandston, William; Piqua, Ohio; December 4, 1980.
Bratz, Virgil; Springfield, Illinois; September 15, 1980.
Breimeyer, Luther; Portland, Indiana; March 17, 1981.
Brewer, Ray; Greene County, Indiana; October 26, 1977; interviewed by Doug Hasler, Indiana University Folklore Archives.
Carlson, Joseph; Troy, Ohio; June 22, 1979.
Chapman, Henry; Portland, Indiana; August 23, 1980.
Clay, Paul; St. Mary's, Ohio December 5, 1980.
Clemens, Maze; Sharpeye, Ohio December 2, 1980.
Copes, Basil; Brookville, Indiana; February 6 and 13, 1981.
Copes, Mary; Brookville, Indiana; February 6, 1981.
Cravens, William; Springfield, Illinois; May 6, 1981.
Deller, Roscoe; Fremont, Indiana; May 23, 1980; interviewed by Tom King, Indiana University Oral History Project.
Edger, Ira; Greenville, Ohio; December 1–5, 1980, and July 11–12, 1981.
Edger, Leola; Greenville, Ohio; December 1–5, 1980, and July 11–12, 1981.
Enslinger, Herman; Indianapolis, Indiana; October 17, 1980.
Ferguson, Bud; Fulton, Missouri; October 6, 1984; interview by Margot Roberson.
Fowble, Virgil; Palestine, Ohio December 3, 1980.
Gregg, Earl; West Jefferson, Ohio; July 16 and 23, 1979.
Horner, Dave; Boone County, Missouri; September 22, 1984.
Hollinger, Raymond; Palestine, Ohio; March 3, 1981.
Holp, John; Lewisburg, Ohio; December 4, 1980, and July 12, 1981.
Huntley, Clarence; July 15, 1981.
Johnson, Lloyd; Decorah, Iowa; August 5, 1978.
Jones, Dan; Oak Hill, Ohio; June 5, 1980.
Josephs, Everett; Indianapolis, Indiana; August 21, 1981.
Kleinman, Herbert; Rockville, Indiana; September 21, 1980.
Kleinman, Joseph; Rockville, Indiana; September 21, 1980.
Kohlman, Peter; Rockville, Indiana; September 21, 1980.
Kotter, Jake; New Bremen, Ohio; July 23, 1979.
Kuhn, Herbert; Minster, Ohio; March 24, 1981.
L., W.; Washington County, Illinois; February 14, 1981.
Lester, Edna; Hamilton, Ohio; June 3, 1981.
Lightfoot, Raymond; Range, Ohio; July 23, 1979.

Bibliography

Meachem, Joseph; Dayton, Ohio; July 14, 1981.
Meachem, Walter; Dayton, Ohio; July 14, 1981.
Merkle, Albert; Dubois County, Indiana; August 14, 1979.
Miller, Joseph; Montgomery County, Ohio; December 1, 1979.
Miller, Noah; Clark, Missouri; June 4 and 13 and July 17, 1984.
Moeller, Peter; Waterloo, Iowa; June 14, 1977.
Osgood, George; Boonville, Missouri; September 8, 1984.
Pepsen, Jerome; Troy, Ohio; July 17, 1980.
Petersen, Charles; Decorah, Iowa; August 4, 1978.
Pointer, Harold; New Unionville, Indiana; September 15, 1980.
Reusser, Rose; Elgin, Iowa; October 9, 1977.
Sacquitne, Ida; Decorah, Iowa; February 16, 1981.
Schmidt, Walter; Shelby, Iowa; August 8, 1980.
Schroeder, Ernst; Cedar Rapids, Iowa; April 14, 1979.
Smith, Carrie; New Unionville, Indiana; June 26, 1981.
Smith, Lee; New Unionville, Indiana; November 4 and 11, 1980.
Solomon, William; Stockton, Illinois; April 16, 1979.
Summers, Oscar; Fulton, Missouri; October 6, 1984; interview by Margot Roberson.
Tracey, Kenneth; Seymour, Indiana; June 24, 1981.
Wagonner, Herman; Greenville, Ohio; December 3, 1981.
Winer, Merwin; St. Mary's, Ohio; December 5, 1980.
Winkler, Fred; Dayton, Ohio; July 14, 1981.
Wolber, Clarence; Piqua, Ohio; August 12, 1981.

C. Unpublished and Manuscript Sources

NOTE: The following abbreviations are used to cite manuscript depositories: IHS (Illinois Historical Society; Springfield); ISHDMC (Iowa State Historical Department Manuscript Collection; Des Moines); ISHSL (Indiana State Historical Society Library; Indianapolis); IUFA (Indiana University Folklore Archieves; Bloomington); MJC (Joint Collection, University of Missouri Western Historical Manuscript Collection, and State Historical Society of Missouri Manuscripts; Columbia); OHS (Ohio Historical Society; Columbus); and WSHL (Wisconsin State Historical Library).

1. Diaries, Journals, Letters, Daybooks

Angel, Jasper; Diary; Kosciusko County, Indiana; ISHSL.
Anonymous Account Book; Daviess County, Indiana; ISHSL.
Anonymous Diary; [Bowman family?] Knox County, Ohio; OHS.
Anonymous Diary; Franklin County, Ohio; OHS.
Anonymous Diary; Fulton County, Ohio; OHS.
Arnold, John; Diary; Rush County, Indiana; ISHSL.
Buttle, Anson; Diary; Eastern Wisconsin; WSHL.
Campbell, Lewis; Diary; Washington County, Iowa; ISHDMC.
Carpenter, Lena; Diary; De Kalb County, Illinois; IHS.
Dague, Harry; Diary; Raymond, Ohio; OHS.
Doringh Diary; Walnut Grove Farm; Adams County, Ohio; IHS.
Downer, Fred; Diary; DeKalb County, Illinois; IHS.
Drury, John; Diary; Mercer County, Illinois; IHS.
Duffield, George; Diary; Van Buren County, Iowa; ISHDMC.
Forder, Albert; Letters; Washington County, Indiana; ISHSL.

Gardner, William; Ledger; Freedom, Ohio; OHS.
Hamilton, Mary; Letters; Fort Wayne County, Indiana; ISHSL.
Holt, Martin; Diary; Oneida, Illinois; IHS.
Hubbard, Charles; Diary; Lee County, Illinois; IHS.
Humphries, Thomas; Diary; Saline County, Missouri; MJC.
Hunt, Thomas; Letters; ISHSL.
Jones, Enoch; Daybook; West Liberty, Ohio; OHS.
King, Elisha; Letters and Diary; Milroy, Indiana; ISHSL.
Legg, John Miller; Diary; Rush County, Indiana; ISHSL.
Lesher, Lewis; Ledger; New Carlisle, Ohio; OHS.
Linvill, Benjamin; Diary; Cabel, Ohio, and Marion, Indiana; OHS.
Loehr, John Jacob; Diary; Stark County, Ohio; OHS.
Lytle, F. B.; Ledger; South Lebanon, Ohio; OHS.
McKee, Laura; Diary; Adams County, Illinois; IHS.
Mighell, Lewis James; Diary; DeKalb County, Illinois; IHS.
Miller, John; Diary; Miami County, Ohio; OHS.
Page, Thomas; Journal; Lee County, Illinois; ISH.
Ringle, Martin; Diary; Lorain County, Ohio; OHS.
Russell, Charles; Log Books; Portage County, Ohio; OHS.
Shirk, Samuel; Diary; Franklin County, Indiana; ISHSL.
Stewart, Jacob; Ledgers and Minute Books; Fairfield County, Ohio; OHS.
Stranahan, Andrew; Ledger; Dublin and Plainfield, Ohio; OHS.
Thrasher, Benjamin; Diary; Adair County; MJC.
Tunnel, William; Journal; Greene County, Illinois; ISH.
Warren, Edwin and Ephraim; Diaries; Rock Island County; ISH.
Wiley, Jerome; Letters; Metamora, Indiana; ISHSL.
Young, John H.; Daybook; Fairfield County, Ohio; OHS.

2. Manuscripts, Autobiographies and Reminiscences

"Annual Reports of Munday Thrashing Company, 1916–1922," private collection.
Barstow, Ed. Threshing Records. Peoria County, Illinois; possession of Ed Barstow.
Broughton, Willis. "Drover Days, or Pioneer Life in Illinois, 1862–1876." Bureau County, Illinois; IHS.
Edger, Ira. Threshing Records. Darke County, Ohio; possession of Ira Edger.
Foster, Alice. "Farming during the Depression." Indiana Homemakers Extension Folklore Project, 1979–80; ISHSL.
Galloway, Charlene. "The Farm." Indiana Homemakers Extension Folklore Project, 1979–80; ISHSL.
Goodrich, Beverly. "Butchering, Haymaking, and Threshing." 1972; IUFA.
Harley, Ellen. "Family Memories." Ca. 1900–1910; ISHSL.
Hasler, Doug. "The Process and Social Experience of Threshing." 1977; IUFA.
Holp, Homer. Threshing Records. Lewisburg, Ohio; possession of John Holp.
Johnson, Howard. "Autobiography." Ca. 1950, Marion County, Indiana; ISHSL.
King, Frank. ["Reminiscences."] Huntington County, Indiana; ISHSL.
Lewis, Sherry. "The History and Folklore of Mulberry [Indiana]." 1973; IUFA.
Litvin, Martin. "Journal of a Prairie Farmer, Volume 1, 1882–1885: The Daily Writings of Martin S. Holt." N.d.; IHS.
Miller, Grace. "Cooking for Threshers." Indiana Homemakers Extension Folklore Project, 1979–80; ISHSL.
Minutes of the White Plains Threshing Ring; ISHSL.
Noelker, Herman. "My Life and Times." Gasconade County, ca. 1960–1965; MJC.
Pyle, Michael Jay. "Threshing: A Process and Experience." Marshall, Indiana, 1974; IUFA.

Rusk, Elaine, "Threshing Meals." Indiana Homemakers Extension Folklore Project, 1979–80; ISHSL.
Sheridan, Peter. "Grandpa' Wayman Pruitt." 1976; IUFA.
Shutes LeRoy. "Stack Threshing, Ioway—1890's." Carroll County, Iowa, 1968; ISHSL.
Stitt, Mary. "Farming in the Early 1900s." 1979; IUFA.
Swartz, Susan. [Untitled.] 1967; IUFA.
Tracey, Kenneth. Threshing Records. Jackson County, Indiana; possession of Kenneth Tracey.
Underwood, Helen. "Indiana Homemakers Extension Association Folklore District Winners, 1979–1980." ISHSL.
Von Sycke, John. Threshing Records. Marion County, Indiana; ISHSL.
Wilke, William. "Remembrances of a Franklin County Farmer." 1935; MJC.
Woods, Evelyn. [Untitled reminiscences.] Indiana Homemakers Extension Folklore Project, 1979–80; ISHSL.

INDEX

Accidents: in stack threshing, 42–43, 44; with self-feeding separators, 60; with stored grain, 180
Adams County, Illinois, 54
Adoption: of threshing machines in Midwest, 20–38 *passim*; by progressive farmers, 21; by craftsmen, 21–22; by young farmers, 54; a. of steam engines, 58–59; process of, 109–110; a. of combines, 147–48; a. of soybeans, 150, 151
Agricultural press: threshing studies, 61–62, 70; impact on threshing style, 96–97, 102, 111, 186; support of tractor adoption, 146
Agriculture: grain in Midwest, 1, 25–26, 35, 114; societies, 21; cycles, 32–33, 36, 54–56, 62, 63, 86, 94–95; innovation in, 37; structural aspects, 154–55
Agriculture, United States Department of, 97, 154
Albany, New York, 21
Allen, A. B. (company), 21
Allis-Chalmers Company, 143, 148, 188
Alton, Illinois, 47
American Agriculturalist, 49
American Farm Equipment: The Magazine of Power Farming, 82
American Thresherman, 80, 82
Ames, Ben, 23
Anglo-Americans, 64, 137, 140
Arnold, James, 22
Arnold, John, 46–47
Ashton, Illinois, 47
Aultman-Taylor Company, 25, 45
Aydolette, Otis, 96

Barley: Midwest crops, 1, 25; threshing, 3, 7, 27; stacks, 65
Barn: design and threshing, 10–11, 31–32, 39; threshing floors, 10–11; for storing grain, 39; for storing straw, 76–78
Barstow, Ed, 69
Basket wagons, 70, 72
Beardstown, Illinois, 56
Beef, as status food, 117–18
Berry, Willis, 4
Black Americans: segregated at threshing meals, 123; as threshing ring members, 139–40; as threshermen, 139–40
Boone County, Indiana, 20
Boston, Massachusetts, 21
Bram, Oscar, 138, 139

Bratz, Virgil, 92
British Isles: impact on U.S. threshing, 1–2, 3; flails, 4; women and harvest work, 18; stacking grain, 39
Britt, Albert, 125
Brookville, Indiana, 66, 90
Broughton, James, 54
Buchanan, James, 73
Bucking straw, 44–45
Buckwheat, 1, 11
Buffalo County, Nebraska, 49
Bundle drivers: labor skills, 68–70, 72–73; labor relationships, 70–72
Bundle haulers, 66. *See also* Bundle drivers
Bureau County, Illinois, 44, 54
Butler County, Ohio, 6–7, 46, 67, 135, 136–37

Cabel, Ohio, 34
Canals, 23, 25
Canton, Ohio, 25
Capper-Volstead Act, 161
Captain Swing, 51
Carlisle, Ohio, 13, 55
Carpenter, Lena, 118, 124–25
Case, J. I. (company), 24–25, 31, 45, 57, 58, 80, 143
Charles City, Iowa, 143
Charles M. Russell and Company, 25
Chesapeake Bay, 1
Chicago, Illinois, 25, 82, 174
Children, 115, 132
Cincinnati, Ohio, 25
Clay County, Missouri, 4
Clemens, "Uncle" Rob, 139–40
Clements, Maze, 140
Cleveland, Ohio, 16
Clover seed, 3, 165–66
Columbus, Ohio, 108
Combine (combined harvester-thresher): adoption, 146, 147–48; impact on threshing process, 147–48; impact on labor, 148; custom work, 148–49; resistance to, 149–50; and individuality, 152
"Company" Ring, 141. *See also* Threshing ring, formal structures
"Concord Plan," 103–104
Conesville, Iowa, 95
Conner, John, 20
Cookwagons, 126–28, 156
Cooperative work: during mechanization, 20,

Index

Cooperative work:—*continued*
  23; in stack threshing, 48; in larger threshing groups, 54, 160–61; with other implements, 57; as social norm, 86, 113, 140–41; patterns and mechanization, 87; decline in farm cycles, 94–95; social functions of, 113–14, 133–34; among women, 116–17; and wider social networks, 136–37, 142; continuity, 157–58; in silo-filling, 182. *See also* Threshing machines, cooperative ownership; Reciprocal labor
Cooperatives, agricultural, 98–99, 161
Crabtree, N. B. and S. W., 103
Cultural ecology, 170
Cultural fixation, 27
Cultural style: of threshing rings, 86, 87, 135–36, 139, 157; as innovation process, 110–11; of meal patterns, 127
Custom threshing, 24, 108. *See also* Threshermen
"Cyclone Stacker," 73. *See also* Straw, automatic stackers

Dane County, Wisconsin, 14
Darke County, Ohio, 4, 23, 27, 62, 64, 76, 92, 93, 96, 139, 151
Daviess County, Indiana, 116
Dayton, Ohio, 54
Dearborn County, Indiana, 92, 127
Decorah, Iowa, 3
DeKalb County, Illinois, 85, 118
Deller, Roscoe, 150–51
"Dinner for Threshers," 120–21
Doringh, Charles, 54
Downer, Fred, 85
Drivers, sweep power, 28, 43
Drury, Albert, 6, 33, 34
Dubois County, Indiana, 46
Duffield, George, 52

East Anglia, England, 118
East Coast, U.S., 1–2
East Moline, Illinois, 54
Eden Valley, England, 31
Edger, Ira, 64, 92, 93, 151
Eggleston, General Chauncey, 16
Elgin, Illinois, 173
Ellis, James, 54
Ellul, Jacques, 176
Emery Company, 21
Emery Railroad Treadmill, 31
England: threshing patterns, 2, 11, 14, 31; opposition to mechanization, 50–51; harvest meals, 116, 118
English, William, 23–24
Enslinger, Herman, 113, 134
Estrem, Andrew, 29
Ethnic influences, 2–3, 27, 90, 123. *See also* German-Americans; Norwegian-Americans

Europe, Central: immigrants and threshing, 2–3, 64; mowing grain, 39
Evansville, Indiana, 25

Fairfield County, Ohio, 3, 9
Family farms: and self-sufficiency, 152–53; in the 1980s, 154, 161–62
Fanning grain. *See* Winnowing
Fanning mills, 19, 24
Farm Clubs, 21, 98
"Farmer's Friend," 73. *See also* Straw, automatic stackers
Farmer's Guide (Indiana), 96, 99, 124
Farmers: initial adopters, 21, 23–24; evaluations of change, 63–64, 159; measures of occupational ability, 68–69, 70–72, 79; attitudes towards threshing ring style, 87–88, 140–41; organized movements, 98; evaluations of threshing meals, 116–18, 127–28; attitudes toward collective work, 133–34; choices of new technologies, 151–53, 157; and efficiency, 162. *See also* Host farmer
Farmers' Institutes, 98, 103
Faux, William, 116
Flail: designs and styles, 1, 4–9; couplings, 4–7; factory-made, 171
Flailing: Colonial patterns, 1–2; Midwest patterns, 2–14 *passim*; compared to treading, 2–4, 11, 14–15; techniques, 4–6, 9–13; outputs, 6–9; labor needs, 8, 11, 145; sessions, 9–10; in barns, 10–11; outdoor contexts, 11–12; in groups, 11–13; end of period, 20, 23, 27; persistence after mechanization, 27, 35–36, 175; costs compared to machine threshing, 49–50; social dimensions of work, 79–80, 87
Flint, James, 11
Folk process: defined, 109; innovation in, 109–10; demise of, 110–11; mentioned, 108
Folk speech, 129
Fordson tractor, 143, 144
Foster, George, 156–57
Frankfort, Indiana, 132
Franklin County, Indiana, 76, 142, 148
Freedom, Ohio, 13
French immigrants, 2, 170, 172
Frok, P. C., 81
Fulton County, Indiana, 167–68

Gaar-Scott Company, 25, 45, 58
Gardner, William, 13
Garland, Hamlin, 185
Gasconade County, Missouri, 27
German-Americans: manual threshing, 3, 4, 9, 15, 27; threshing systems, 64–65; mentioned, 64, 90, 91
Giedion, Siegfried, 57
Grain: as Midwest cash crop, 1–2, 23, 25, 26, 35, 174; storage, 10; stacks, 39–40

Granaries, 10, 47
Grand Blanc, Michigan, 31
Great Plains: threshing patterns, 70, 108, 135, 156; meals, 127; combine patterns, 147, 149
Greene County, Indiana, 72, 77
Growth of Industrial Art, 12, 16

Hamilton, Carl, 77
Hamilton, Ohio, 173
Hamilton County, Ohio, 20
Hancock County, Illinois, 3–4
Harris, Isiah, 11, 18
Harrison County, Missouri, 137–38
Hart-Paar Company, 143
Heck, Oliver, 127–28
Henry County, Iowa, 22
Hired labor: in flailing and treading, 2, 8, 11, 13–14, 16; for mechanical threshing, 47–48, 54, 68, 79; costs, 49–50; opposition to mechanization, 50–51; scarcity of, 51
Holp, Homer, 92, 93
Horse powers. *See* Sweep powers; Tread powers
Horses: used in treading, 1, 3, 14–15; on threshing machine powers, 27–31; accidents, 29; on bundle wagons, 72
Hortonville, Indiana, 107
Hortonville Farmers Bank, 108
Host farmer: stack threshing roles, 53–54, labor positions, 47, 74; delegation of crew, 53; social status, 79, 114–16, 141; organization of crews, 90; aesthetics, 115–16; meal responsibilities, 126
Howells, William, 18
Hubbard, William, 7
Huber Manufacturing Company, 81
Huntington, Indiana, 81
Huntington County, Indiana, 103

Illinois: crops, 1, 25–26; threshing mechanization, 20–23; threshing practices, 30, 55, 69, 73, 82, 137; meals, 126; combines in, 148
Indiana: threshing mechanization, 20, 22–23; crops, 25–26; threshing practices, 35, 36, 42, 67, 73, 74, 81, 96–97; meals, 116, 122, 124, 127; practical jokes, 131–32; combines in, 148
Indiana County Councils of Defense, 125–26
Individualization: development of, 94–95, 110; and combine adoption, 147–48, 152
Innovation: as cultural process, 109–11, 159–60; in meal patterns, 123–24, 126–29; economic and domestic, 128; impact on social organization, 135–36
Internal combustion engines, 143
Iowa: grain crops, 1, 26; threshing practices, 15, 29, 53, 59, 65, 89

Iowa State Agricultural Society, 178
Isern, Thomas, 149

Jackson, Mitchell Young, 55
Jackson County, Indiana, 34, 92, 93
Jackson County, Ohio, 43, 76
Jefferson, Thomas, 152
Jefferson County, Ohio, 36
Johnson County, Indiana, 119
Jokes, practical: social functions of, 113, 129–30, 131, 132; contexts, 130; between crew members, 130; with threshermen, 131–32; with children, 132
Jones, Dan, 43
Jones, Enoch, 13
Jones County, Iowa, 15, 122
Joseph Pope (company), 21

Kaskaskia, Illinois, 2
Kendall, Wisconsin, 1
King, Elisha, 33
King, George, 49
Kleinman, Herbert, 5, 11
Kriegbaum brothers, 81

Labor: for flailing and treading, 9–10, 14, 16; in winnowing, 18–19; on sweep power and treadmill, 30; by families, 33; exchanges, 33, 39–40; positions and skills, 40–48, 65–78 *passim*; hierarchies, 42–43, 78–80, 82–83; costs in rings, 51, 107–108; divisions, 66, 139, 140; crew sizes compared, 83–84, 143–45; problems in larger cooperatives, 89–90, 95–96; schedules, 102–104; specialization, 160–61
Labor, United States Commission of, 8
Lake counties, England, 31
Lake County, Illinois, 7
Lakeland, Minnesota, 55
Largesse-spending, 118
Lee County, Illinois, 7, 32, 47, 55
Legends, 142
Lesher, Andrew, 13, 30, 55
Linvill, Benjamin, 33
Loehr, Frederick, 15–16
Logan County, Illinois, 92
Loomis, Charles, 109
Lowry, H. N., 46
Lyons, Indiana, 131
Lytle, Frank, 22

McCormick-Deering, 152
Machine crew, 47–48, 84
Machine in the Garden, 37
McKee, Laura and Albert, 52
Madison County, Iowa, 107
Marco, Indiana, 131
Marion, Ohio, 81
Marshall, Indiana, 133–34

Index

Marshall County, Illinois, 135
Marx, Leo, 37
Maryland, 1
Massilon, Ohio, 81
Meachem, Joe, 42–43
Meals, threshing: charges for, 104, 124, 126; at ring meetings, 105–106; status foods, 105, 117–19; traditions, 116; aesthetics, 117–18, 119–21; quantities and contexts, 119–21; social components, 119–21; changes in traditional patterns, 123–29; problems, 124–26; carrying dinners, 125–26, 128, 158; proverbs, 129; mentioned, 49, 95. *See also* Cookwagons; Women
Mechanization: of threshing, 23–27, 45; obstacles to threshing, 32–38; of farm tasks compared, 57, 114; impact on thresherman's status, 79–80; impact on rural role models, 82–83; impact on cooperative patterns, 87, 160–61; and social determinism, 156; and social norms, 159; and labor specialization, 160–61
Mercer County, Illinois, 6, 33, 58
Merkle, Albert, 46
Miami County, Ohio, 3, 7, 21, 141, 165–66
Miller, John, 3, 165–66
Miller, William, 67, 135
Milroy, Indiana, 33
Minnesota, 82, 123
Missouri: threshing patterns, 3, 6, 8, 49, 73; granaries, 10; crops, 65
Missouri River, 80, 156
Moffit, James, 21–22, 173
Montgomery County, Ohio, 43, 54
Mount Vernon Threshing Union, 168–69
Mowing grain, 39, 55
Munday, James and Zeno Earl, 107
Munday Threshing Company, 107–108
Murphey, Ohio, 52
Murray, Margaret Archer, 15

Nashua, Iowa, 122
National Association of Brotherhoods of Threshermen, 82
National Farmers' Alliance, 98
New Carlisle, Ohio, 15, 30
New England, 1–2, 13
New York, 2, 21, 22
Northumberland, England, 31
Norwegian-Americans, 1, 14, 29, 35, 63, 65

Oakville, Iowa, 77
Oats: as Midwest crop, 1, 2, 25, 34; threshing of, 3, 4, 6–8, 69, 76–77, 161; combining of, 149–51
Occupational cycles, 32–33. *See also* Agriculture, cycles
Ohio: crops, 25–26; threshing practices, 11, 36, 40, 41, 44, 49, 55, 67, 82, 86, 96, 137; threshing mechanization, 20, 33; meals, 115, 124; practical jokes, 130–31; combines in, 150
Ohio Cultivator, 36, 46
Ohio State Agricultural Report (1859), 51
Old Northwest, 2, 22
Olson, Ole, 14
Order of Patrons of Industry, 98
Orkney, Scotland, 31
Ormson, O. K., 1
Osage County, Missouri, 80
Osage River, Missouri, 80
Owens, Lane, and Dyer (company), 173
Oxen: in animal threshing, 1, 3, 14; in mechanical threshing, 29–30

Pacific Northwest, 108, 147
Page, James, 7, 32, 55
Paris, Ohio, 15, 23
Parke County, Indiana, 5, 6–7, 11, 20, 27, 106
Parsons-Hawkeye self-feeder, 61
Patent Office, United States, 22
Pennsylvania, 1–2
Peoria County, Illinois, 69, 76
Perry County, Illinois, 138
Piqua, Ohio, 21
Pitts, Hiram, 24, 25
Pitts Brothers (company), 21
Portage des Sioux, Missouri, 173
Power Farming, 82
Prairie Grove Threshing Company, 167–68
Preble County, Ohio, 92, 93, 95
Princeton, Illinois, 54
Proverbial sayings, 129
Publications. *See* Agricultural press
Pyle, Clarence, 105–106
Pyle, Gladys, 113, 134

Racine, Wisconsin, 24, 80
Railway powers. *See* Tread powers
Randolph County, Indiana, 96, 105
Rational culture change, 108, 109–11, 128
Reapers, 57, 91
Reciprocal labor: in stack threshing, 51–54; continuities, 52–53; networks, 54, 95–96; and change, 64, 87–88. *See also* Cooperative work
Reel, Joe, 77
Reynolds, John, 2
Richmond, Indiana, 25, 45
Rob Clemens Ring, 140
Robinson, Solon, 25
Robinson and Company, 58
Rock Creek Threshing Ring, 137–39
Rock County, Minnesota, 34–35
Rock Island, Illinois, 54
Romanticism, 151–52

Ross, Earle, 20, 98
Rundles, J. C., 97
Rush County, Indiana, 46
Rye: as Midwest crop, 1, 2, 25, 34; threshing of, 3, 6–7, 27, 165–66

Sac County, Iowa, 46
St. John's Creek, Missouri, 100
St. Joseph, Michigan, 80
St. Louis, Missouri, 25, 65
Sarmerla, Matti, 113–14
Scandinavians (in Midwest), 3, 11
Schlebecker, John, 82
Schmidt, Louis, 26
Schmidt, Walter, 60
Scotland, 2, 31
Seed grain, 3, 4, 27, 35–36
Self-sufficiency, 152–53
Separators. *See* Threshing machines
Setting charges, 34–35
Sewall, Samuel, 56, 176
Shahn, Ben, 133
Sharpeye, Ohio, 139
Sheffield, Illinois, 54
Shelby, Iowa, 60
Shutes, LeRoy, 28, 43
Silo-filling, 182
Social functions: of labor relationships, 70; of ring meetings, 105–106; of cooperative labor, 113–14, 133–34; of meals, 121–23, 127; of practical jokes, 129–32
Social status: feeder, 43; field pitcher, shock threshing participants, 78–80; threshermen, 78–80, 82–83; host farmer, 115–16
Sociotechnical development: defined, 156–57
South Lebanon, Ohio, 22
Soybeans, 150–51, 189
Spencer County, Indiana, 123
Spike pitchers, 66. *See also* Threshing: shock, field pitchers
Stacking grain: techniques, 39, 61–62; master builders, 56–57, 62
Stateline Threshing Ring (Ohio), 136–37
Steam engines: adoption, 58–59; impact on threshing, 59–60; cost, 59; impact on labor hierarchy, 79–80
Steuben County, Indiana, 150–51
Steward, Julian, 170
Stewart, Jacob, 9, 13
Stille, August, 122
Straw: impact on threshing process, 3, 6, 9; domestic and farm uses, 3, 9–10, 15–16, 30–31, 35, 46–47, 76–77, 147; crews, 44–46, 73–78; stacks, 44, 45–47, 73, 75; carriers, 45; storage shortage, 47, 61; automatic stackers, 73–75, 135; shelters, 75–76; and combines, 150
Stump, Umphrey, 62

"Successful Threshing Ring Management," 97
Sweep powers: designs and styles, 27–29; manufacturers, 27, 28; capacity, 28; crew, 28; drivers, 28, 43; impact on barn use, 31–32; in stack threshing, 39, 49; replaced by steam power, 58–59; late uses of, 59
Swiss-Germans, 3
Systematization, 100–101, 108

Tazwell County, Illinois, 103
Technological change: opposition to, 32–38; as specialized change, 37; and occupational aesthetics, 75–76; and occupational status, 79–80; and social organization of work, 135–36, 151–52; and family farms, 152–53; social consequences of, 153, 155–57, 159; and cultural norms, 154; and regional patterns, 156
Tennessee, 2
Tew, Martin, 123
Thrashing. *See* Threshing
"Thrashing Ring in the Cornbelt," 97
Thresher World and Farmers' Magazine, 61
Thresherman's Review, 80, 82
Threshermen: early period, 22, 24; use of horse powers, 30; seasonal work schedules, 32–33, 56, 62–63, 93–94, 124; charges to farmers for work, 33–35, 46–47, 176; relations with local farmers, 33–34, 63, 141–42; machinery and schedule problems, 55–56; as custom operators, 55–57; compared to other custom operators, 56–57, 179; as professional class, 59, 80, 82; social status, 79–80, 82–83; periodicals, 80, 82; associations, 82; arrangements with threshing rings, 96, 100–101, 107; relations with machine crew, 131–33; social joking forms, 131–32; as threshing ring members, 138–40; Black American, 139–40; impact of tractors on, 146; shift to custom combining, 148–49
Threshing: sleds, 1; floors, 10–11; season length, 33, 48, 52–55, 114; delays, 56, 62–63
—barn: nineteenth century, 39; revitalized by strawstackers, 75, 76–78; crew composition, 84
—stack t.: work roles, 39–48; band-cutters, 40–43, 65; stackmen, 40–41; feeders, 40–44; tools, 41–42; social prestige of labor positions, 43, 65; straw crew, 44–46; grain crew, 47; neighborhood organization for, 51–54, 87; compared to shock threshing, 60–65, 96, 145; motivations for continuity, 63–65, 158; crew composition, 83–84
—shock t.: compared to stack threshing, 60–65, 96; benefits, 60–61; work roles, 65–78; field pitchers, 66–68; bundle drivers, 66–

Index

—shock t.:—*continued*
73; labor relationships, 70–72; straw crew, 73–78; blowerman, 74–75; grain crew, 78; crew social hierarchies, 78–80, 82–83; crew composition, 83–84, 145; impact on work organization, 85–86; mentioned, 39, 60, 140

Threshing machines: early adoption, 20–27; manufacturers, 21, 22, 24–25, 80; early designs, 22–23, 173, 174; sales patterns, 25, 27; powers to run early devices, 27–31; grain weighers on, 33, 135; complaints about performance, 35–36; conservative criticism of, 36–37; impact on landscape, 37; crews for itinerant runs, 47–48, 84; breakdowns, 55–56; designed for steam engine power, 60–61; self-feeding, 60, 72–73, 179; windstackers, 73–74; cooperative ownership of, 106–108; social impact of, 156–57; hand-cranked, 176

Threshing ring: defined, 83; core characteristics, 83; etymology, 84–85; as a folk group, 87–88, 158; decline of, 142–43; impact of tractor adoption, 144–46; as community activity, 158–59; as contemporary symbol, 162–63

—organizational aspects: gradual formation, 85; continuity with older patterns, 85–86; variations in, 87, 92–94, 158; core members, 90–91, 101–102, 137; shift to larger groups, 90–94; impact of farm press, 97–98; meal schedules, 124–25; reasons for continuity, 136–41; work order, 140; conflicts between members, 141–42; comparisons between regions, 156–57; informal base, 158

—formal structures: by-laws, 99–100, 107, 167–69; officers and roles, 101–102, 160, 183; impact on individuals, 99–101, 160; "difference" systems, 101, 102–104; timekeepers, 102–103; meetings, 104–106; altering meal patterns, 125–27

—formalization movement: geographic characteristics, 96–97; period of change, 94–95, 97–98; motivations for, 97–99; and local norms, 111–12, 160–61; resistance to, 137–42 *passim*

Threshing union. *See* Threshing ring, formal
Tiffin, Ohio, 3
Tipp City, Ohio, 141
Togrim, Willard, 63
Toledo, Ohio, 23
Tracey, Kenneth, 34, 92, 93
Tractors: cost, 143; Midwest adoption, 143, 147; impact on threshing technology, 143–44; impact on threshing labor, 143–46
Traditions: persistence in farming, 27, 109–10, 140–41, 158; in Midwest, 36; of grain storage, 39; of mutual aid, 51–52; defining reciprocal work, 53, 110; and innovation, 63–64, 109–11, 157–58, 159–60; sanctions change, 158
Transportation: impact on mechanization, 21, 23, 25, 27, 37
Tread powers: general designs, 27–28, 30–31; cost, 30, 50; multi-purpose use, 30; favored by large farmers, 30; use in barns, 31–32, 39
Treading patterns: descriptions, 1, 14–16; Colonial patterns, 1–2; compared to flailing, 2–4, 11, 12, 14–15; labor crews, 14, 145; work contexts, 14–15; outputs, 15–16; end of use, 20, 27; persistent use during mechanization era, 27, 32, 35–36; social dimensions, 14–15, 87
Treadmills, 30–31, 38. *See also* Tread powers
Tribulum, 170
Tromping grain. *See* Treading patterns
Turkey Run High School, 134

Union Center Threshing Ring, 103
University of Illinois Agricultural Experiment Station, 97
Upland South, 175

Valley Farmer (St. Louis), 35
Van Buren County, Iowa, 52
Vandalia, Illinois, 25
Virginia, 1

Wabash County, Indiana, 168–69
Wages: flailing and treading, 13–14; other farm tasks, 13–14; paid threshing crews, 148–49
Wagons, 68, 70, 78, 146, 180, 188
Wallace, Anthony, 128
Wallace's Farmer, 61, 96, 99
Walls brothers, 95
Walnut Grove Farm, 54
Ward, Leo, 184
Warren, Edwin, 54
Warren County, Illinois, 125
Washington, Indiana, 116
Washington County, Indiana, 127
Wayne County, Indiana, 11, 18
Wayne Township (Darke County), Ohio, 23
Welker, Martin, 11
West Cumberland, England, 31
West Liberty, Ohio, 13
Wheat: as Midwest crop, 1–2, 25, 34; threshing of, 3, 6–9, 18, 165–66; combine threshing, 149–50
Wheeler Company, 21
White Plains Threshing Ring, 90–92, 102, 138, 148–49
Whitinger, Floyd, 132
Williams, Nathan, 103–104
Winneshiek County, Iowa, 63

Winnowing: descriptions, 1, 16–19; techniques, 17–18, 172; tools, 17–18; blankets, 17; machines, 19
Winthrop, Maine, 21
Wisconsin, 25, 57, 65
Women: as harvest laborers, 14; aiding in winnowing, 18; at ring meetings, 105–106; social status, 116–17; reputations as cooks, 119–20; socializing at meals, 121–22; dissatisfaction with meals, 125; attitudes towards change in meal patterns, 128–29
Wood, Grant, 77, 120
Work codes, 66–67